ECONOMICS
The Essentials

second edition

ECONOMICS
The Essentials
second edition

WILLIAM M. SCARTH

McMaster University

Harcourt Canada

Toronto Montreal Fort Worth New York Orlando
Philadelphia San Diego London Sydney Tokyo

Canadian Cataloguing in Publication Data

Scarth, William M., 1946–
   Economics : the essentials

2nd ed.
Includes index.
ISBN 0-7747-3683-6

1. Economics   I. Title.

HB171.5.S28 2000   330   C99-931542-0

Acquisitions Editor: Megan Mueller
Developmental Editor: Rebecca Conolly
Production Editor: Stephanie Fysh
Production Co-ordinator: Cheryl Tiongson
Copy Editor: Dallas Harrison
Cover Design: Rivet Art + Design
Interior Design: Sonya V. Thursby, Opus House Incorporated
Typesetting and Assembly: Carolyn Hutchings Sebestyen
Printing and Binding: Transcontinental Printing Inc.

Cover art: *The Ozone Connection/Trou Bleu* by Joseph Muscat © 1992, CARfac© Collective. All rights reserved. Acrylic on canvas. 54" x 36".

Harcourt Canada
55 Horner Avenue, Toronto, ON, Canada M8Z 4X6
Customer Service
Toll-Free Tel.: 1-800-387-7278
Toll-Free Fax: 1-800-665-7307

This book was printed in Canada.

1 2 3 4 5   04 03 02 01 00

To Kathy

PREFACE

Free trade, social policy reform, debt reduction ... One cannot take an active part in public policy debate without running up against economic analysis on a daily basis. Increasingly, individuals feel that they are at the mercy of specialists (interviewed in the news media) in their attempts to form independent opinions on these issues. But while economic analysis is central to modern life, it is not easy to learn in bits and pieces. It is not surprising, then, that introductory economics is among the three courses taken most often at most universities.

But a principles course at university is often geared to preparing students for specialist training in the discipline. As a result, the typical text is an encyclopedia on the subject. While policy applications are included, the reader must find these discussions within the larger block of material that stresses formal definitions and theorems. Many students become discouraged since the principles course and text cover more formal material than was really wanted.

Of course, instructors and textbook writers have been aware of this common reaction for many years. Inevitably, the response seems to be that this state of affairs is essentially unavoidable because economics is a difficult and technical subject. There is no point in pretending otherwise by teaching a series of partial truths that will need to be "unlearned" later by students who go on in the subject. More important, students who do not go on will never realize how "dangerous" a little learning may be.

This book is based on my belief that there *is* a way out of this dilemma. This belief is based on the principle that the topics to be covered in an introductory treatment must be carefully selected. Only those that are absolutely required for learning how economists think and how the central policy issues can be understood are included. These topics are then treated rigorously and thoroughly. The idea is for readers to learn a limited number of topics well. I am convinced that this goal is preferable to having people know just a little bit about a large set of topics or having people lose interest when forced to try to master a lot about many less central topics.

Thus, it is through a bold selection of topics, not dropping the level of rigour, that this book imparts an in-depth understanding of economic analysis without ever departing from a focus on policy issues for more than a page or two. Central topics such as positive versus normative statements, incentives, supply and demand, producer and consumer surplus, competition, monopoly, game theory, asymmetric information, externalities, marginal productivity, the determination of GDP, productivity growth, inflation, unemployment, interest rates, and exchange rates are covered in detail. But other subjects, such as detailed elasticity calculations, extended multiplier derivations, indifference curves, monopolistic competition, monopsony, and IS-LM are left out completely. Also, the book is thin on factual (both historical and institutional) material. The rationale is that this material can be picked up elsewhere (as is noted in each chapter's suggestions for further reading and Web activities), and it is the general understanding of the economist's approach to policy questions that is in short supply.

Obviously, some very valuable insights have had to be dropped; while some economists will cringe at these exclusions, the non-specialist's time constraint must be respected. In any case, the central policy questions can all be appreciated without any more formal modelling than what is included.

A Summary of What Is to Come

The focus of the book is on what a market system does well and what it does poorly. On each question, there is a consistent focus on both efficiency (the concept economists often emphasize) and equity (the issue on which the general public often most focuses). Here is a whirlwind tour of the book.

There are ten chapters each on microeconomics and macroeconomics. Microeconomics, from the Greek *micro* (meaning "small"), focuses on questions of detail such as the allocation of resources across particular industries and the distribution of income across individuals. Macroeconomics, from the Greek *macro* (meaning "large"), focuses on the entire economy as a unit and considers questions such as what determines the overall level of output in the economy, the general level of interest rates faced by all borrowers, the rate of inflation, the exchange rate, and so on.

The first two chapters discuss the role of theory, opportunity cost, supply and demand, and the invisible hand. They show how the invisible hand fights back when legal restrictions that attempt to overrule the forces of supply and demand are imposed. Also, basic analysis is used to explain how, and in what circumstances, the burden of taxes can be shifted to others.

The next two chapters take a look "behind the scenes" to see why demand and supply curves make sense in terms of underlying behaviour. The fundamental principle — that any activity should be expanded up to the point that additional benefits are just pushed down to the level of the additional costs — is discussed. It is applied to the household decision concerning which goods to buy and to the decisions of firms concerning which inputs to hire and how much output to produce. A central insight carried into later chapters is that the area under the demand curve indicates the benefit to society of any activity, while the area under the supply curve indicates the value to society of the resources used to produce that item.

Chapters 5 and 10 extol the virtues of free markets by documenting in detail why a market system dominates central planning (so it is not surprising that so many countries have given up on planning in recent years) and by measuring the benefits of embracing free trade.

The remaining chapters in the microeconomics section of the book (Chapters 6 through 9) provide balance by considering some of the reasons why unfettered markets do not do everything well. Market failure can result from market power, incomplete information, and spillover effects, and many are concerned that income is distributed in an undesirable way by free markets. In Chapter 6, we consider monopoly, regulation, and competition policy. In Chapter 7, we use game theory to explain how firms interact with one another when there are just a few firms in an industry. We also consider how incomplete information and incentive problems create unemployment. In Chapter 8, we see why government financing, though not government provision, of public goods is needed. Also in Chapter 8, we evaluate the rationale behind subsidizing activities that generate beneficial externalities and why emission taxes (or tradeable emission permits) represent a mechanism whereby market forces can be harnessed to alleviate one of the market's fundamental limitations.

Paying factors of production according to their productivity is efficient since doing so ensures that scarce (and therefore expensive) factors are used carefully. But payment according to productivity leads to equity problems since many individuals own only one abundant factor: unskilled labour. Most attempts to redistribute income generate inefficient outcomes, such as the poverty trap that is an integral part of traditional welfare programs. Chapter 9 explains how incomes are determined by marginal productivity, how the international mobility of capital makes it difficult to avoid shifting some taxes to those receiving lower incomes, and how a negative income tax may help to accomplish society's redistribution objectives more effectively.

The study of macroeconomics begins in Chapter 11, where the basic measures (GDP, the unemployment rate, and the consumer price index) are discussed. The tools of aggregate supply and demand are introduced, as is the macro version of the invisible hand. The economy has a self-correction mechanism: wages and prices rise whenever the economy is trying to produce more than it can on a sustainable basis, and wages and prices fall whenever unemployment is high. Debate about the effectiveness of this self-correction mechanism is what lies behind the dispute concerning whether the government should have a stabilization policy (to iron out the fluctuations in economic activity) or whether the attempt to stabilize the economy just adds more unpredictability to its course.

The government can either adjust its spending and taxes (its fiscal policy) or the level of interest rates and the exchange rate (its monetary policy) if it wants to try to stabilize economic activity. Chapters 12 and 13 consider fiscal policy by evaluating the multiplier process that follows government initiatives in the short run and the accumulating debt problem that can develop in the longer run if a balanced fiscal policy is not pursued.

Chapters 14 and 15 discuss the development of banking so that the details of Bank of Canada policy can be understood. It is stressed that, for a country such as Canada (which represents just a tiny fraction of the world financial markets), there is only a limited ability to affect the level of Canadian interest rates. Thus, monetary policy is treated as the same thing as exchange rate policy.

An integration of fiscal and monetary policy is provided in Chapters 16 and 17. A supply and demand analysis of the economy's markets for both goods and money is used to show that fiscal and monetary policies can sometimes be very ineffective. For example, a "crowding-out effect" operates through exchange rates. An increase in government spending (intended to create jobs) can so bid up the value of the Canadian dollar that just as many jobs are destroyed in the export- and import-competing sectors. Another important result of the analysis is that Canada must have a flexible exchange rate to have an inflation rate that is different from that prevailing in the United States. Finally, it is explained why there is a temporary — not permanent — trade-off between unemployment and inflation.

The final three chapters focus on the drive for increased prosperity over the longer term instead of short-run stabilization policy. Chapter 18 discusses the history of international monetary arrangements, explaining why the system changed when it did and why there have been so many financial crises in recent years. The connection between the more integrated world economy and growing income inequality is investigated. Chapter 19 explains that the increase in material living standards that we have enjoyed stems from rising productivity. Productivity growth has slowed down since the mid-1970s, however, so policies that might increase the rate of growth are considered. The experience of both the formerly planned and the developing economies is explored, and, at the analytical level, both standard growth theory and the debates about trickle-down and percolate-up economics are examined in detail. Chapter 20 considers three alternatives for raising living standards: investing in free trade, education, and debt reduction. All three initiatives involve short-term pain for long-term gain, so a formal benefit–cost analysis — complete with representative numerical calculations — is presented for each policy.

The book ends with a reminder of its central theme: by relying on our knowledge of private incentives when considering social and economic policy, we can minimize the trade-off between our equity and efficiency objectives. Institutional arrangements that allow us to harness the force of private interest in the pursuit of public policy objectives will prove to be durable and effective.

Learning Aids

Beyond the book's brevity and user-friendly exposition, three features are designed to facilitate learning. First, the book contains an appendix with 100 **Questions and Answers** that allow you to deepen your understanding of the analysis. You can practise answering both multiple-choice and critical-thinking questions. Because economics is a technical subject, there is no substitute for simply trying questions to see whether you have actually mastered the material. Since the practice questions are listed by chapter, it is easy for you to determine which pages you might need to review if the questions identify gaps in your understanding.

The second pedagogic aid is the **Suggestions for Further Reading** list at the end of each chapter. These lists provide brief annotations, so you can tell which items will be more interesting for you. The readings have been carefully selected to make it straightforward for you to link economics to current policy debates, history, religion, experiences in other countries, and everyday life. Suggested **Web Activities** are also listed at the end of each chapter. These varied Web sites provide convenient access to factual data, institutional detail, and debate — all of which will increase your appreciation of the analytical reasoning that is the focus of the book. Advice about what to expect at each site is included in the references given here.

The third learning aid is the road map provided by each chapter's **Learning Objectives** and **Summary** of key concepts. Each chapter begins with a checklist of the three most important concepts that you are expected to understand after reading it. The final paragraphs in the chapter summary reiterate the key points. Important terms are boldfaced, as they are in the core of each chapter, so it is easy to spot that part of the chapter you should reread if you do not feel confident at the chapter's end.

Since the book identifies three learning objectives on the first page of each of the twenty chapters, it emphasizes 60 key insights that you will gain by studying this book. By skimming this list in advance, you will appreciate how different topics relate to one another, and this should avoid your "not seeing the forest for the trees." If you review this list again — after reading the book — it becomes a convenient checklist for identifying any gaps in your learning.

New in This Edition

This brief section of the Preface is useful for instructors who may be familiar with the first edition of this book. It was gratifying that many users appreciated the brevity and clarity of the first edition. The suggestions for revision are easily summarized: "Don't let the book creep up to encyclopedic length, but do add a few key topics that simply must be there." My response has been to add three chapters and numerous inserts throughout the original material. With ten chapters each on microeconomics and macroeconomics, the book now fits the standard length of a teaching term much better. Following are some of the key features of the revision.

- Important microtopics — such as oligopoly, game theory, asymmetric information, moral hazard, adverse selection, second-best issues, and government failure — are treated in the new chapter "Co-ordination Failure and Incomplete Information."
- An efficiency–wage model of unemployment is used to evaluate both calls for tax cuts (from those on the right) and proposals for addressing poverty among the less skilled (from those on the left).
- Benefit–cost analysis — with appropriate discussion concerning hypothetical compensation — is used extensively to link core theory and applied questions.
- Long-run questions of growth and productivity get equal billing with stabilization policy. Growth theory, bubbles in asset markets, and commitment in macro–policy-making are among the topics now emphasized.
- A host of topical items is now included: discriminating monopoly, insurance, statistical discrimination, tax reform, the constraints imposed by a more integrated world economy, the dynamics of government debt and deficits, the monetary conditions index, exchange rate volatility, and the currency-union controversy.

The point of this book is to outline the ways in which economists think — within the context of the major issues of the day. I could not have maintained this claim without these extensions. Some of the new material has raised the analytical demands on the reader a little, but this is a small price to pay for a true integration of economic theory and applied analysis.

Acknowledgements

A number of individuals have helped to produce this book. First, there are the several thousand McMaster University students who have allowed me to experiment while teaching. In addition to letting me have so much fun, they have taught me the key traits of a successful text: brevity, clarity, and enthusiastic concern that every reader develops the confidence that stems from an independent understanding of the issues. Second, I have received a number of helpful comments from individuals who reviewed the entire manuscript: Ake Blomqvist, Cathy Boak, Avi Cohen, Fazal Dar, Tony Myatt, Susan Murgatroyd, Keith MacKinnon, David Robinson, and Andy Muller. Third, I have benefited from the tireless efforts of the editors and production staff at Harcourt Canada. For this second edition, Rebecca Conolly, Larry Gillevet, Megan Mueller,

Ken Nauss, Stephanie Fysh, Liz Radojkovic, and Dallas Harrison in particular have been patient and effective. I am also grateful to Harcourt Canada for allowing me to adapt several questions from a study guide (published earlier with Craig Swan) for inclusion in this book.

In addition to these many debts, I must acknowledge the understanding and flexibility of the people with whom I live. My sons, Brian and David, have patiently endured my letting the project intrude on our time together. My wife, Kathy, has been a constant support and effective adviser. This book is dedicated to Kathy — the one who makes everything work.

A Note from the Publisher

Thank you for selecting *Economics: The Essentials*, Second Edition, by William M. Scarth. The author and the publisher have devoted considerable time to the careful development of this book. We appreciate your recognition of this effort and accomplishment.

We want to hear what you think of *Economics: The Essentials*, Second Edition. Please take a few minutes to fill in the stamped reader reply card at the back of the book. Your comments and suggestions will be valuable to us as we prepare new editions and other books. You may also contact the author directly at scarth@mcmaster.ca.

CONTENTS

Macroeconomics

Appendix

Index

CHAPTER ONE

The Issues and Methods of Economics

LEARNING OBJECTIVES

After reading this chapter, you should understand
- why limited resources force society to make choices and why economists distinguish efficiency, equity, and opportunity cost when considering these choices;

- how economists use theory and why they emphasize positive, not normative, questions; and
- what supply and demand curves represent and how they help us to understand things such as why minimum wage laws create unemployment.

INTRODUCTION

This book will introduce you to the tools economists use to understand how the economy functions, and it will give you insights into the policy decisions governments make. Economics studies the choices that are available to society. For instance, which social programs are most conducive to raising income standards? What are the costs and benefits of free trade? What are the most effective ways to reduce unemployment?

THE PROBLEM OF CHOICE

Every society faces a problem of choice because its resources — its labour, raw materials, machines, and factories — are limited. Economists emphasize this fact of life with a graph. Most readers will be familiar with the use of graphs to show important *facts* but the use of graphs to show *ideas* may be less familiar. Since the study of economics involves an extensive use of graphs in this way, we must master the approach immediately.

We begin our study of society's choices by focusing on just two possible goods that an economy could produce: food and manufactured items. Figure 1.1 indicates at a glance that society faces a trade-off concerning how it can allocate its scarce resources between these two uses. We measure physical units of food out from the origin (the point denoting zero quantities) along the horizontal axis and physical units of manufactured goods out from the origin along the vertical axis. There are no recorded numbers along the axes since what is important is that bigger quantities are denoted by points farther out from the origin along each axis.

Resources are scarce, and we cannot have everything. One option for society is to put absolutely every resource into the farming sector and to produce as much food as we can. The dot on the food axis in Figure 1.1 marks

FIGURE 1.1
*Production Possibilities
Curve*

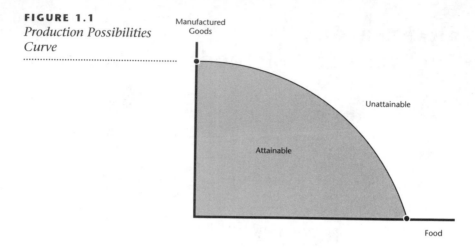

off a distance that denotes this maximum amount of food that it is possible to produce. But all food and no manufactured goods is an extreme allocation of resources. The other extreme is to put all our labour, machines, and other resources into the manufacturing sector and to produce as much as we can in that area. The dot on the vertical axis in Figure 1.1 indicates that other extreme resource allocation — getting all manufactured goods and no food. Society can choose a number of outcomes between these extremes, and the curved line in Figure 1.1 illustrates the results of all these intermediate possibilities.

Economists draw this line bowed out because resources are specialized. Since most resources are more productive when used in particular industries, we lose progressively more of one good (say, manufactured goods) as we transfer resources over to the farming sector. We first transfer those workers who are least suitable to manufacturing activities, and only then do we start transferring those who are least suitable for the agricultural sector.

Economists call the line in Figure 1.1 the nation's **production possibilities curve** since it marks the boundary of all choices that are *feasible*. All points on or below the production possibilities curve are feasible or attainable, given society's limited resources, but only the outcomes shown by the points right on the curve itself are consistent with society using all its available resources in an efficient manner.

The negative slope of the curve shows at a glance that society faces a choice or trade-off. If we want more of one item, we have to move more resources into that industry, and that means moving resources out of the other industry so that we have to give up some of the other item. This trade-off is illustrated in Figure 1.2.

Initially, society obtains the combination of food and manufactured goods denoted by point A. Then people decide that they want more food —

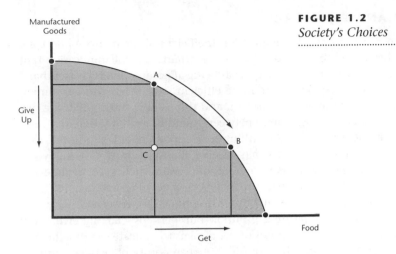

FIGURE 1.2
Society's Choices

say, the amount given by the distance that point B is to the right of the origin. Figure 1.2 indicates how many manufactured goods society has to give up (represented by distance AC) to satisfy its bigger appetite (the extra food represented by distance CB).

INEFFICIENCY

Society could produce a combination of goods like that denoted by point C in Figure 1.2, a point that is not even on the boundary of our feasible set. There is something unfortunate in being at some interior point such as C, since it is physically possible to move to many points along the production possibilities curve (between points A and B) that involve more of everything. Because these possibilities exist, economists call an allocation of resources that yields outcome C **inefficient**.

How can the economy get stuck at an inefficient point? One reason is a general reduction in economic activity. When we have a prolonged recession, there are unemployed men and women and unused machines and factories. One job of economic analysis is to help us understand why recessions develop, and this problem is investigated in the second half of the book.

There is another reason for getting stuck at an inefficient point. Even if we have no unemployed resources, we can use those resources badly. For instance, suppose we had all the people who were particularly good farmers employed in the manufacturing sector and all the people who were good at manufacturing employed at growing crops. Such a misallocation of resources prevents us from using each resource to its best advantage, and the result is that less of everything is produced. In later chapters, it is explained in detail how misallocations develop and how policy can be used to help avoid them.

EQUITY AND EFFICIENCY

We have seen that point C in Figure 1.2 is inefficient, while points A and B are not since they are on the boundary of what is attainable. One implication that might seem to follow from this fact is that being at point A or B is "better than" being at point C. These points are more efficient, but there's another dimension to what makes things good or bad, and that is how those goods are distributed. At all points on the curve between A and B, we have more of everything, but at these points the distribution of goods might be skewed to a particular rich group, and others may receive almost nothing. Often government policies intended to redistribute income toward the less fortunate force the economy to move from a point such as A or B down to one such as C.

Throughout this book, we encounter this trade-off between policies that are good on **equity** or fairness grounds but perhaps bad on **efficiency** grounds. One of the main purposes of the book is to indicate some of the better policies for minimizing this conflict between equity objectives and efficiency objectives.

OPPORTUNITY COSTS

We have been using the production possibilities curve to illustrate how economists measure costs. As noted, the choice of increasing our food consumption entails that we must incur the cost of giving up some manufactured goods. You will notice that there are no dollar costs mentioned in this discussion. Economists simply say that the cost of food is the *forgone alternative*: manufactured goods.

As an everyday example of this approach, suppose you decide to go to university. In calculating the costs, you add up expenses such as tuition and books for a total of something like $5000 per year. But one of the major costs of your attending university (even though no actual payment is involved) is the earnings you forgo by not taking a job, let's say $25 000 per year — much more than the actual costs paid out to go to university. Economists call this concept of cost **opportunity cost**, and it must be understood to avoid confused decision making in everyday life.

The opportunity cost of any action is the value of the best forgone alternative — that is, the value of what you have to give up to take that action.

SPECIALIZATION, INVESTMENT, AND GROWTH

Thus far, I have emphasized that at each point in time an efficient society faces a trade-off. More of one good requires the sacrifice of another. But many societies have shown over the years that they have more of everything. This simple observation must mean that societies can somehow move their production possibilities curve farther out from the origin through time. How is this expansion possible?

There are two main ways we can achieve an expansion of our production possibilities. One is to move to production methods involving increased *specialization*. The more workers do precise tasks, and get particularly good at them, the more productive they become. This is one way that nations get wealthy.

Investment is another way in which we can move our production possibilities curve out from the origin. By withholding some of our resources from producing either food or manufactured consumer goods today, we can use the leftover resources to invest in more machines and factories and research. By doing so, we have fewer consumer goods today, but in subsequent years our workers will have more machines to work with. This increase leads to higher productivity, which means an expanded position for our production possibilities curve in those future years. This is why some people are in favour of government policies that stimulate investment in new machines, technical knowledge, and education. If labour becomes more productive, then workers will have higher standards of living.

The increase in future productivity is not free — the opportunity cost is a reduced standard of living today. One way to see this is to divide the goods that society produces into two categories: investment goods (e.g., machines) and consumption goods (e.g., CDs and sandwiches). At any point in time, our limited resources force us to choose among the outcomes indicated by a production possibilities curve like that shown in Figure 1.3. As long as we choose to be at any point other than A (e.g., B), we are consuming less than we could now; however, with more machines available next year, the production possibilities curve will be expanded then. If we choose a point such as C (and sacrifice a lot of consumption now), we will be rewarded with an even bigger increase in our standard of living in the future (as shown in the right-hand panel of Figure 1.3). Investment is a policy that involves "short-term pain for long-term gain."

FIGURE 1.3
Investment and Growth

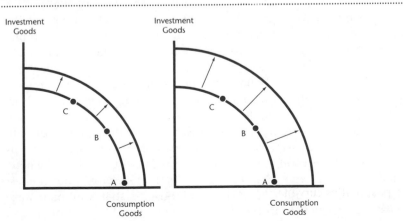

Investment
Goods

Consumption
Goods

Investment
Goods

Consumption
Goods

THE ROLE OF THEORY IN ECONOMICS

The production possibilities curve is a simple model that illustrates the concept of opportunity cost used in economic theory. All theories involve simplifying assumptions, so it is appropriate at this stage to consider whether a theory requires "realistic" simplifying assumptions to be useful. An analogy is instructive. Think of using a map to find your way in a strange city. A map with too much detail is confusing. You want one that just shows the main streets so that you can find your way around more easily. Such a map is like a scientific theory or model — it deliberately leaves out some of the detail so that the essential elements of a problem stand out more clearly. Of course, it is possible to strip away too much detail. A map that shows just the major highways around and through a city is of no use for locating even major points of interest within the city.

Just as there is no "right" or "wrong" level of detail for maps (it depends on what the map is to be used for), there is no "right" level of abstraction in science. All theories have somewhat unrealistic assumptions. Indeed, the purpose of theory is to help understanding by deliberately leaving out some detail. The test of whether this abstraction process is helpful or not is whether a theory's predictions are borne out in fact, not whether its assumptions are unrealistic. Throughout this book, you will see that, like all scientists, economists use theory in this way.

POSITIVE AND NORMATIVE ISSUES

Another key point that must be appreciated before we go any further in using economic theory is the distinction between positive and normative statements. **Positive** statements are propositions that can be settled by an appeal to the facts. They are either true or false. An example might be "Lower taxes lead people to give more money to charity." Statements like this are what economics can examine and test.

Normative statements involve words such as "should" or "ought": "We ought to give money to charity." People cannot settle such a claim on the basis of logic and appeal to fact. The only thing we can say about a normative statement is that it is or is not consistent with a certain set of values. Economists have no right to tell the rest of society what its values ought to be. Thus, economics can clarify positive, not normative, issues. Suppose you were asked to evaluate this statement: "Minimum wage laws are good because they redistribute income from the rich to the poor." What can economics do to shed some light on this proposition? The first thing to do is to separate the normative part from the positive part of the statement. The normative part is that it is good to redistribute income from the rich to the poor. Economics cannot tell you whether doing so is right or wrong. But the rest of the statement, the positive part, is the proposition that minimum wage laws redistribute income from the rich to the poor. On that, economics can offer you something. I devote the remainder of this introductory chapter to explaining what basic economics can say on this question.

It turns out that we must learn the tools of **supply and demand** to pursue this question. Why? Because for us to guess at what minimum wage laws do, we need a model of what economists call the *unskilled labour market*. The term *market* does not refer to a specific physical location. It is simply the entire set of transactions between buyers and sellers of an item — in this case, hours of work by unskilled individuals. If we have a model that highlights how this set of transactions takes place, then we can explain the essentials of how wages and employment levels are determined, both with and without a minimum wage law.

SUPPLY AND DEMAND

We build our model with diagrams. We divide up the task by considering (in turn) the two groups that take part in the exchange of labour. First, there are the firms that are the demanders of labour — they want to use people's time to produce goods. Second, there are the suppliers of labour — the households who have the hours available to work and are trying to get jobs.

To start off, let us assume that we are the managers of a firm and that an interviewer is asking us how much labour we would hire at various wages. Of course, many things affect how much labour we would like to hire (e.g., business taxes and the prices of other inputs — such as machines — to the production process), but the interviewer asks us to assume that there are no changes in these other influences. Our answers to the questions are summarized in Figure 1.4.

The interviewer starts by asking how much labour we would hire at some high wage rate. Suppose we answer the small number of hours indicated by the short distance along the quantity of labour axis in Figure 1.4. The interviewer

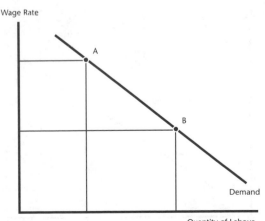

FIGURE 1.4
Labour Demand

records our answer by plotting the dot marked point A in Figure 1.4. This dot represents the wage–employment combination that we said was our choice. The interviewer then asks us to consider another possible wage rate, say, the much lower one indicated by the height of point B in Figure 1.4. We answer that, with labour much cheaper, we would find it profitable to hire more workers. Again, the interviewer records our answer, along with the quoted wage, as another wage–employment combination that we would accept (point B).

We can think of the interviewer doing this for many wage rates and for all firms, and then adding up all the answers and recording them as a whole series of dots in the graph. When the observations are all connected together in a line, it looks like what is labelled "demand" in Figure 1.4. The negative slope of this line, down from left to right, reflects the simple fact that firm managers (like anyone else) buy more of something when it becomes cheaper and less of something when it becomes more expensive. In applied work, of course, economists must carefully estimate this relationship (which may be curved). But since we are interested only in the underlying logic here, the negative slope is what is important. For simplicity, we use a straight line. Economists call this line the *labour demand curve*; it shows firms' hiring intentions for all possible wage rates.

Now we derive a similar response for the suppliers of labour — the households in our economy. Again, we can think of an interviewer asking us to assume no changes in all those other things that affect our decisions to work more or less (e.g., level of safety at the workplace, availability of unemployment insurance) and to focus on how many hours we would be willing to work at various wage rates. Figure 1.5 records the answers that our interviewer would obtain.

Think of the interviewer saying "If the wage rate is low, how much would you work?" Your answer would probably be a small number of hours

FIGURE 1.5
Labour Supply

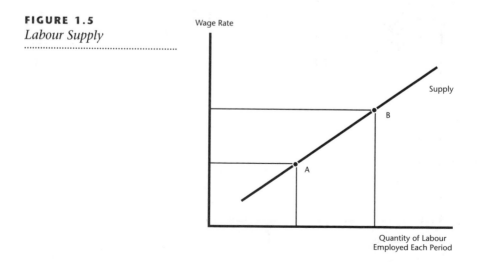

— at a very low wage, you do not find the job very appealing. The interviewer records your answer as the low-wage–low-employment combination shown by point A in Figure 1.5 (and records a similar observation for everyone else). Then the interviewer asks you to consider a much higher wage rate and asks, "If the wage rate is twice as high, how much would you want to work?" You (and others) would answer with some larger quantity. Again, the interviewer would record your answer as a dot in the graph — point B in Figure 1.5. As before, the interviewer could join all the responses. This time the result is a positively sloped line, up from left to right. This line is the graphical version of an if–then statement that says how much people would work at alternative wages. Economists call this line the *labour supply curve*.

Although some people react to a higher wage by working less (on the ground that they can achieve their target level of earnings by working fewer hours), evidence shows that this reaction is outweighed by the many people prepared to give up more of their time to work only if rewarded by higher pay. The positive slope of the labour supply curve reflects this fact. Everyone is aware that overtime wage rates are higher than normal wage rates. This simple observation illustrates the positive slope of the labour supply curve.

PUTTING SUPPLY AND DEMAND TOGETHER

We have derived both the supply and the demand curves individually. Each represents just half of the complete story. The level of employment and the level of wages get determined by the interaction between these two curves. In Figure 1.6, we see buyer and seller reactions in the same graph. Suppose history gave us some particular wage rate, say, the low wage indicated by the height of the horizontal line in Figure 1.6. What would happen if we just start our labour market off at that wage?

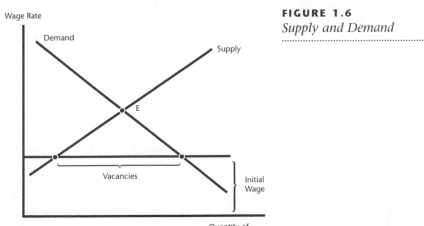

FIGURE 1.6
Supply and Demand

We would find that, at this low wage rate, households do not want to work very much. They want to work only the number of hours indicated by the dot determined by the intersection of the current-wage line and the households' supply curve for labour. Furthermore, at this low wage rate, firms find labour a bargain, and they want many men and women working — a number of hours given by the intersection of the given-wage line with the labour demand curve.

There is excess demand for labour in Figure 1.6. Excess demand means unfilled job vacancies, so firms are not satisfied with the outcome. Given this frustration, what is likely to happen? Firms will try to take labour from each other by offering a higher wage rate to get workers to move. So the current-wage line will drift up over time as the firms compete for workers. When will this process end? As the wage rate rises, more people supply labour (because the return to work is higher), and the firms cut back their demands for labour (because labour is getting more and more expensive). Eventually, this process ends when there is no excess demand — that is, when we get to point E in Figure 1.6.

We choose the letter E to stand for **equilibrium**. E is the equilibrium outcome since it is the point at which both buyers' and sellers' curves intersect, so that everyone on both sides of the market is satisfied. With no unemployment or unfilled vacancies, there is no frustration and therefore no reason for any labour market participant to alter his or her behaviour. Thus, all adjustments in wage and employment levels come to an end at point E.

We have just described how a competitive bidding process works in a free market, in this case the market for unskilled labour. Economists assume that point E in Figure 1.6 is the market outcome if we did not have a minimum wage law.

A MINIMUM WAGE LAW

Now suppose the government decrees that the equilibrium wage in Figure 1.6 is just too low a wage rate for unskilled people. Suppose the government passes a law saying that it is unlawful for firms to pay any wage rate less than the height of the horizontal line that has been added in Figure 1.7. What would happen?

At such a high price for labour, firms want to hire a smaller number of workers. Firms slide up their demand curves from point E to point B, and some workers are laid off (and this is shown by the leftward arrow along the employment axis). But households want to work more; in terms of work wanted, households slide up their labour supply curves (again, see the arrow along the quantity of labour axis in Figure 1.7). The result is excess supply of labour, and the more widely known word for this excess supply is *"unemployment."* Thus, the minimum wage law makes the market outcome move from point E to point B, and unemployment results. We get what the government wanted on the vertical axis — the higher wage rate. But we obtain an unintended effect along the horizontal axis — unemployment.

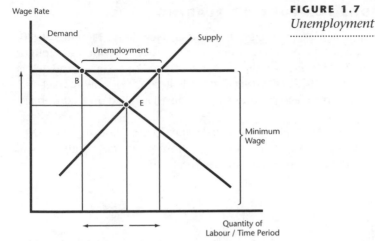

FIGURE 1.7
Unemployment

So minimum wage laws do not necessarily provide more income for the poor at all. The people who are lucky enough to keep their jobs get higher income, but quite a few people lose their jobs, so their income goes from a perhaps discouraging low level to no income whatsoever — and that is not a transfer toward the less fortunate. Provincial data clearly show that the provinces with the highest minimum wage rates have the highest proportion of their unemployed in the unskilled category. Thus, our simple theory accurately reflects the data. One major result of minimum wage rate legislation is unemployment among a large number of the people whom the policy was designed to help.

SUMMARY

This analysis of minimum wage legislation is an example of what economics can do. It can question the positive elements of a policy without having to get into the thorny issue of whether individuals have the same values. Logically, settling positive issues comes before arguing about values. In the next chapter, the supply and demand model will be developed more extensively so that we can begin in earnest our study of what a market system does well and what it does poorly.

Here is a review of some of the key concepts covered in this chapter. We have seen that economics is the **study of choices**. Society must trade off one objective for another since our resources are limited. We illustrated this **trade-off** by discussing the concept of **opportunity cost** and by considering the **production possibilities curve**. We saw that there can also be a trade-off between **efficiency and equity** objectives.

We distinguished **positive** and **normative** statements. Economics can make its biggest contribution by focusing on positive issues. Finally, we introduced the tools that will be used throughout the remainder of the book — the tools of **supply and demand**.

SUGGESTIONS FOR FURTHER READING

T.G. Buchholz, *New Ideas from Dead Economists* (New York: Penguin, 1990), Chapters 1, 2 — an amusing account of the history of economic thought.

R.L. Heilbroner, *The Making of Economic Society* (New York: Simon and Schuster, 1953, revised 1972) — a brief and lively account of how market societies developed from early economic systems that relied on tradition and command.

S.E. Landsburg, *The Armchair Economist: Economics and Everyday Life* (New York: Free Press, 1993), Chapters 1–5 — a humorous and insightful book guaranteed to change the way you interpret everyday life.

WEB ACTIVITIES

www.irpp.org

The Web site of the Institute for Research on Public Policy in Montreal, the Institute's *Policy Options* (available in both libraries and on the World Wide Web) has many informative short articles — for example, in the September 1997 issue, "Is Economics Relevant?"

CHAPTER TWO
Supply and Demand

LEARNING OBJECTIVES

After reading this chapter, you should understand

- how supply and demand analysis can be extended to illuminate many issues, such as low incomes in agriculture and the pattern of taxation by government;

- how selfish behaviour in a market system acts like the invisible hand of a social planner to allocate society's resources efficiently; and

- how the invisible hand fights back when governments try to overrule market forces with price controls.

INTRODUCTION

In the previous chapter, I introduced the tools of supply and demand. But we must dig deeper to fully appreciate how these tools can be used to analyze a number of questions. Which goods are available to you? What prices, rents, and taxes do you have to pay? What determines how steeply we should draw the supply and demand curves? What determines the positions of these curves? This chapter is devoted to exploring these issues. First, we consider the question of slope, which leads us to what economists call elasticity.

THE ELASTICITY OF SUPPLY AND DEMAND

It is helpful to review briefly our minimum wage analysis. From Figure 1.7 (p. 11), you will recall that, without the policy, equilibrium exists at point E, where both demand and supply are satisfied. But with the minimum wage, the outcome moves from point E to point B, and the diagram shows the key result of the policy: higher wages for those who keep their jobs, but a decreased quantity of labour demanded leads to layoffs and unemployment. Intended and unintended effects of the policy are very much affected by the slope of the demand curve for unskilled labour, and this is illustrated by the two alternative graphs in Figure 2.1. Clearly, the minimum wage policy is much less appealing in the right-hand panel of Figure 2.1 since the problem of unemployment is dramatically bigger there. What has caused this larger effect? The fact that the demand curve is flatter.

To understand this effect more clearly, we need some measure of how much the quantity demanded responds to price changes that is independent of the units we choose to measure prices and quantities. We call this measure of responsiveness **elasticity**. It is defined as the percentage change in quantity demanded that comes about when there is a given percentage change in

FIGURE 2.1

Unemployment and Labour–Demand Elasticity

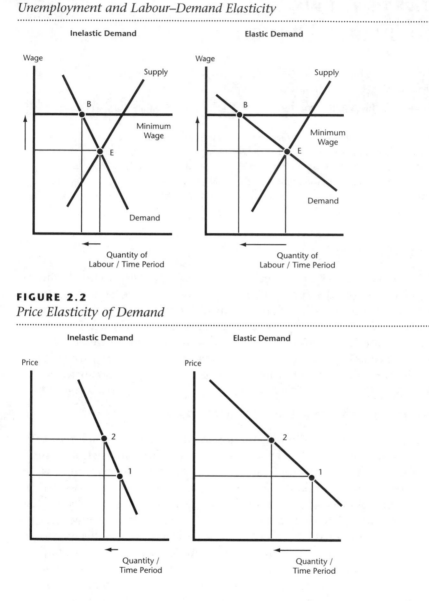

FIGURE 2.2

Price Elasticity of Demand

price. In calculating this formula, it is customary to ignore the minus sign in-volved since the demand curve is a negatively sloped relationship.

Consider the two demand curves in Figure 2.2 that could represent household buying intentions for any commodity. Economists say that the demand curve on the right is *elastic*, since there is quite a large percentage change in quantity demanded, and that the demand curve on the left is *in-elastic*, since there is a much smaller percentage response in quantity de-manded for the same change in price.

Letting P, Q, and Δ stand for price, quantity, and "the change in" each variable, we can calculate the price elasticity of demand as follows:

Elasticity $= -$ (% change in Q)/(% change in P)

$\qquad = -$ (ΔQ/average Q)/(ΔP/average P)

$\qquad = - [(Q_2 - Q_1)/(Q_2 + Q_1)]/[(P_2 - P_1)/(P_2 + P_1)]$

where the subscripts 1 and 2 stand for the two points on the demand curve (like the two dots on each curve in Figure 2.2) that define the range over which the responsiveness of demand is being measured. Notice that, when a minus sign is inserted in the formal definition of elasticity, the price elasticity of demand always turns out to be a positive number.

Demand is said to be elastic if quantity responds proportionately more than price (i.e., if the elasticity coefficient exceeds one) and inelastic if quantity responds proportionately less than price (i.e., if the elasticity coefficient is less than one).

The most important thing that determines the elasticity of demand is whether there are any close substitutes available for the item. For an absolute necessity, demand is completely inelastic. It is drawn as a vertical line to reflect the fact that it must be purchased no matter what the price. An example is the demand for insulin by diabetics. It does not matter how much the price rises; diabetics do not demand less insulin. The opposite extreme case is an item for which buyers have perfect substitutes available. In this case, demand is infinitely elastic, and it is shown as a horizontal line. An example might be a particular brand of soap that is virtually indistinguishable from other brands. If the price of that particular soap rises much, most buyers switch to another brand.

Elasticity of supply is defined in a similar manner, although no negative sign is added to the definition since supply already represents a positive relationship between price and quantity.

Now that we have clarified how economists measure the responsiveness of demands and supplies, we are ready to return to the minimum wage analysis. Unfortunately for unskilled workers, it is easy for firms to find substitutes for them (by simply moving to more automated production methods). The demand curve for unskilled labour is therefore quite **elastic**, so the right-hand panel in Figure 2.1 is the realistic one. Thus, the unwanted result of minimum wage legislation, the layoffs that result from the policy, is substantial.

We have been focusing on the elasticity of the demand for labour; however, as the references to insulin and soap indicate, the same method of analysis is applicable to consumer goods. We will now consider the wheat market as an application of supply and demand in this field. Food is a necessity, so the demand curve for grain is rather inelastic. This fact has forced farm revenues to fall over the years, as we will see.

A SUPPLY AND DEMAND ANALYSIS OF FARM INCOMES

Figure 2.3 shows supply and demand curves for grain. One supply curve is labelled "years ago" because we wish to examine the implications of the vast

FIGURE 2.3
Farm Incomes
....

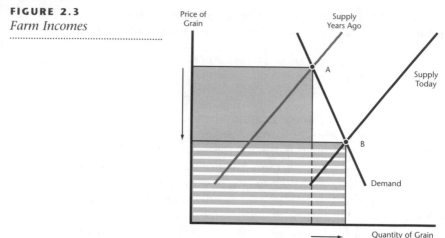

technological changes that have occurred in farming methods over many decades. These changes have dramatically increased productivity in agriculture, with the result that today's supply curve is much farther to the right. We can think of the outcome in the grain markets as moving from an initial equilibrium at point A many years ago to a new equilibrium at point B. What has happened to the total sales revenue of farms during this period?

Farmers used to receive a high price per unit (indicated by the height of point A) on each of the units they sold (and that total quantity is indicated by the amount by which point A is to the right of the origin in Figure 2.3). Total sales revenue (i.e., price times quantity sold) was equal to the area of the shaded rectangle with point A at its corner (the base [quantity] times the height [price]).

After the technological improvements lower farm costs, farmers receive a lower price per unit (indicated by the height of point B) on an increased number of units sold (again indicated by point B), so sales revenue is now the shaded rectangle involving horizontal white lines with point B at its corner. Because the demand for grain is inelastic, the percentage increase in quantity sold is much smaller than the percentage decrease in price per unit, so farmers' sales revenues have been shrinking rather dramatically. This is the main reason why governments throughout the world have operated major subsidy programs for their agricultural industries. The ultimate cause of this government activity is the combination of three things: a concern for maintaining income standards for farmers, the technological improvements in agriculture, and the price inelasticity of the demand curve for food.

SHIFTS IN THE SUPPLY AND DEMAND CURVES

The analysis of farm income trends has underlined two general points: knowledge of elasticity is fundamental to understanding many developments in our economy, and we must become familiar with those things that cause supply and demand curves to change position. In the previous chapter, we supposed that we were the managers of a firm, and we considered only one determinant of the amount of labour demanded — its price, which is the wage rate. The fact that the demand curve is negatively sloped is the geometric way of showing an inverse dependence — that is, the quantity of labour demanded is inversely related to the wage rate. (The higher the wage rate, the less labour demanded; the lower the wage rate, the more labour demanded).

But the wage is only one of the influences on the quantity of labour demanded. There are other important determinants, such as the price of the product that the firm sells. If the price of the product doubled, it would be a great time to sell more commodities, so the firm would try to acquire more labour to produce the extra output. Similarly, if there were a large increase in the price of labour-saving machines, the firm would likely increase its demand for labour to minimize its costs of production. Thus, the higher the price of a substitute input, such as labour-saving machines, the greater the firm's demand for this particular input — labour.

So there are many things that affect the amount of labour demanded (and we have just mentioned three: the wage rate, the price of the product, and the prices of other inputs). There is a fourth item in our discussion as well, the quantity of employment itself. The problem is that even with this partial list we have four things, and we are trying to draw a graph in which there are only two dimensions. The solution is to choose two of the four variables to put on the axes: the wage rate and the quantity of employment. We call this partial relationship the *demand curve*. The effect of wage changes on the quantity demanded is shown by the slope of the demand curve. Changes is any of the other determinants have to be shown as a shift in the entire position of the demand curve.

For instance, in Figure 2.4, we show the effect of a higher selling price for the firm's product by shifting the demand for labour curve to the right

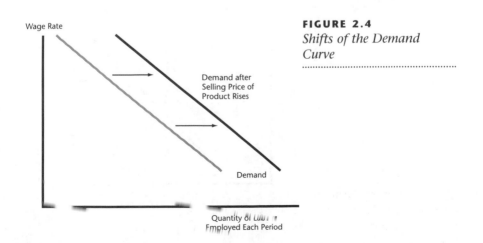

Wage Rate

FIGURE 2.4
*Shifts of the Demand
Curve*

Demand after
Selling Price of
Product Rises

Demand

Quantity of Labour
Employed Each Period

because more labour will be demanded at every wage rate. Similarly, we would show the effect of a lower product price by shifting the demand curve to the left.

The same holds true for the supply curve for labour. The positively sloped line shows that, other things equal, a higher wage rate leads to an increased willingness to work. A lower wage rate leads to a decreased willingness to work. But there are other influences, such as job safety and the level of unemployment insurance benefits. So there are at least four things to talk about on the supply side as well: the wage rate, the level of job safety, the level of unemployment insurance benefits, and the quantity of employment itself. The partial relationship between the wage rate and the quantity of labour supplied is shown by the labour supply curve. A change in any other influence must be shown as a shift in the entire position of that curve. For example, an increase in the safety of working conditions raises people's willingness to work and thus shifts the entire position of the labour supply curve to the right, as shown in Figure 2.5. At each wage rate, more labour is supplied. Similarly, a decrease in the desirability of the working environment decreases people's willingness to work, and we would show this as a shift in the position of the labour supply curve to the left.

Knowledge of these shift factors is useful for evaluating policies that can, over the longer run, increase both the incomes of unskilled workers and their level of employment. For example, by providing training schemes that make workers more productive, the government can induce firms to increase their willingness to hire workers and thus shift their demand curves for labour to the right. Such a development moves the market outcome from point E to point A in Figure 2.6, so that both income per worker (the wage rate) and the number of workers hired increase. It may take a while for policies of this sort

FIGURE 2.5
Shifts of the Supply Curve

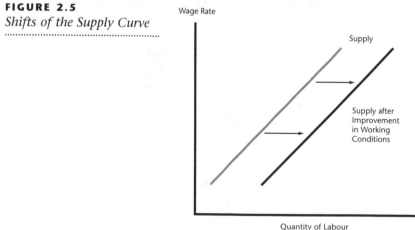

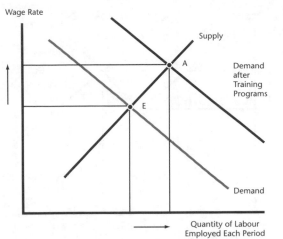

Wage Rate

Supply

A

E

Demand
after
Training
Programs

Demand

Quantity of Labour
Employed Each Period

FIGURE 2.6
*The Effects of Higher
Productivity*
....

to take effect, but at least they do not lead to lower employment the way that a minimum wage policy does.

THE INVISIBLE HAND

Economists apply supply and demand analysis to all markets — those for things such as labour that we call input or factor markets, and those for things produced, such as cars, that we call output or product markets. Supply and demand comprise the basis for understanding free market economies. The alternative to free markets is central planning, and many people think that an economy will be totally disorganized if we do not have central planning. On the other hand, most economists believe that a decentralized system of individual consumers and firms — looking after their own self-interests — does a pretty good job of allocating society's scarce resources.

To see why economists believe this, consider a major change in consumer preferences. Suppose many of us decide that we now want to drive small cars. We used to like big gas guzzlers. Without a central planner, will the economy transfer many of its resources into the small-car industry and out of the big-car industry? Economists say "yes" because the market will adjust itself as if guided by an *invisible hand*.

We can understand how this transfer of resources works by considering supply and demand diagrams for both the small-car and the large-car markets (see Figures 2.7 and 2.8). These **supply and demand curves** are drawn for particular values of all those "other" influences that (if changed) would shift the position of one of the curves. For example, the drawing of the supply curves assumes a given level for the costs of the factors of production used to make cars (e.g., the price of steel and the wage rate paid to auto workers). If tastes change in favour of small cars, then the demand curve for small cars

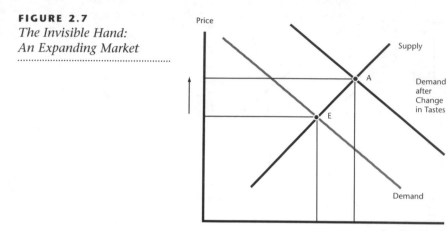

FIGURE 2.7

The Invisible Hand:
An Expanding Market

Price

Supply

A

Demand
after
Change
in Tastes

E

Demand

Quantity of Small
Cars / Time Period

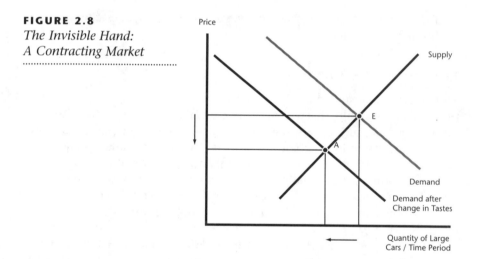

FIGURE 2.8

The Invisible Hand:
A Contracting Market

Price

Supply

E

A

Demand

Demand after
Change in Tastes

Quantity of Large
Cars / Time Period

shifts out to the right. At every price, people now want to buy more of these small cars. Similarly, in the large-car market, the change in tastes means that demand has shifted back in to the left, indicating a decreased willingness to buy. Figures 2.7 and 2.8 clearly show the "before" and "after" outcomes in each industry. For example, in the small-car market, the intersection of the original demand and supply curves (point E) indicates what things were like before the change in tastes. After the change in tastes, A has become the equilibrium point. The lines drawn from points E and A to the axes show the results. The shortage at the original price has driven the price up, and that is what makes it privately profitable for firms to slide up their supply curves, producing more of exactly what people now want. The firms make this adjustment in their own profit interests, without any social directive.

Similarly, in Figure 2.8, with the reduced demand for large cars, the equilibrium point in that sector moves from point E to point A. The fall in the price of large cars means that losses will be incurred by the producers of large cars, so there will be shutdowns and layoffs in this segment of the auto industry. Hence, the resources move from the declining sector to the expanding sector, not because a planner has noticed the change in people's tastes and told the resources to move, but simply because people are looking after their own self-interests. The owners of the firms want to earn as much profit as they can, so they enter the industries where the products are selling better and at higher prices. Thus, firms migrate from the large-car industry to the small-car industry. These firms get resources such as labour to go with them by offering them higher wage rates. All we need to assume is that firms want to maximize their profits and that income earners (households) want to maximize their incomes. These assumptions ensure that resources will be transferred in the very direction that the change in tastes wants them to go. So a decentralized system can do a pretty good job of responding to people's tastes.

Adam Smith, an economist writing some 200 years ago, coined the term **invisible hand**. According to Smith, self-interest is the invisible hand that guides the allocation of society's scarce resources, so that they are placed in precisely those areas where a planner would want them.

Government policy-makers often seem to be unimpressed with the invisible hand since they are concerned with what they regard as "unfair" outcomes of the market system. Policy-makers frequently try to overrule the forces of the market. Often they impose controls to keep prices from rising. If we did so in our car example (i.e., if we kept prices from rising in the small-car industry), then the profit incentive would not be there, and the resources would not get transferred. So high prices for certain items are exactly what we want in the longer run because they provide the necessary profit signals to get the desired resource transfers to occur. But often governments are worried about the short run, and about income distribution or equity problems, not about long-run resource allocation issues. Thus, they impose price controls.

PRICE CONTROLS

A classic example of government intervention to limit price increases is rent control, and to evaluate this policy we turn once again to supply and demand. Figure 2.9 shows both a demand curve and a supply curve for housing units. You might wonder why the supply curve is not a vertical line, indicating that there is a fixed number of apartments available at any point in time. There is some slope to the supply curve because apartment units can be converted fairly quickly to other uses, such as offices or basement rec rooms. If the rent is not high enough, then many owners opt for these alternative uses.

In a free market without rent controls, the equilibrium is at point E in Figure 2.9 because that point shows the only price for which the quantity of

FIGURE 2.9
The Rental Housing Market
....

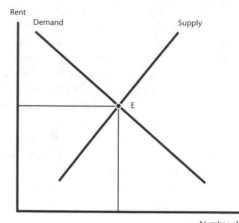

FIGURE 2.10
Construction Subsidies
....

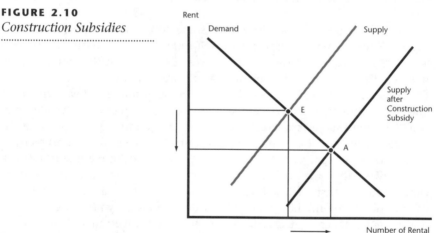

housing units demanded just equals the quantity supplied. But voters and governments are often not satisfied with this outcome because they regard this rent as too high for some people to pay.

One policy that could address this concern might be to subsidize the production of new housing units. This policy would shift the supply curve out to the right, as shown in Figure 2.10, so that the equilibrium would become point A. Figure 2.10 shows that this policy would both lower rents and increase the quantity of housing. Of course, to implement this policy, the government would have to levy taxes, borrow more, or cut back on other programs to come up with the money for the production subsidies.

Policy-makers frequently think that it is less costly not to attempt a shift in the supply curve but simply to pass a law stipulating that no one may charge a rent above the amount indicated by the height of the horizontal line

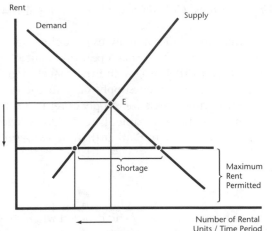

FIGURE 2.11
Rent Controls

....

in Figure 2.11. What are the effects? At this low rent, many people want apartments, so there is an increase in the quantity of apartments demanded. But the owners are not interested in making so many units available. It is not profitable for them to do so at the lower rent, so we see a shrinkage in the quantity supplied (as shown by the arrow along the quantity axis in Figure 2.11). We end up with an excess quantity demanded or a shortage — many people wanting apartments who cannot find them. There was no shortage before the rent control was enacted, but there is afterward.

A shortage like the one illustrated in Figure 2.11 occurs because of policies that refuse to allow a higher price to ration the scarce item. Economists like to summarize the situation this way: when we try to overrule the invisible hand, it fights back, giving us outcomes we do not really want. What happens so often in these cases is that an arbitrary means of allocating the shortage emerges instead. For example, apartment owners discriminate against certain types of potential renters. Or they end up charging "key money" — thousands of dollars just to obtain the key to the apartment. Thus, either the overall cost of renting an apartment is not lower (especially if discrimination or an underground market develops and arrangements such as key money become common) or the law is effective and overall payments to landlords are lower. But in this case landlords will use the space in other ways so that the quantity of rental housing falls and there is an increase in the housing shortage. Neither outcome is what the government intended.

We have now seen that both maximum price laws (e.g., rent control) and minimum price laws (e.g., the minimum wage) cause scarcities. This is not what policy-makers intend, so economists do not recommend such attempts to overrule market outcomes. Economists believe that in many of these areas the market mechanism should be allowed to operate. If some people cannot afford the prices, then we should transfer income directly to them through a general tax and income-support system. This way, those with lower incomes can be protected from market outcomes. Chapter 9 explains in detail how this can be done.

It is important to remember that not all of our analyses have shown that government policy works out badly. We have seen that a policy of educating and training the unskilled can raise both their wages and their level of employment. And a policy of zoning and increased supply of land for low-income housing can both lower rents and increase the supply of rental units. As these examples indicate, it is possible for governments to design policies that *work through* the forces of supply and demand rather than *try to overrule* those forces.

EXCISE TAXES

Governments seem to appreciate the forces of supply and demand when they decide how to raise money through taxation. For example, an excise tax is a charge levied on certain goods — such as a charge for each litre of gasoline you buy. We now explain how supply and demand analysis can clarify which excise taxes yield the greatest revenue for the government.

Figure 2.12 shows the demand curve for a commodity on which the government is thinking of imposing an excise tax. To keep our analysis simple, we assume that this good can be produced at a constant price (given by the height of the horizontal, or infinitely elastic, supply curve shown in Figure 2.12). If an excise tax is levied on the sellers of this good, then they will have to charge precisely that much more per unit to cover the tax (and still pay all their other costs as before). So, with the tax included, the supply curve shifts up by the amount of the tax per unit. This means that the equilibrium moves from point E to point A. The higher price resulting from the tax induces consumers to reduce their consumption, and this reduction is shown by the arrow along the quantity axis in Figure 2.12. The shaded rectangle shows the amount of tax paid by consumers. The height of the rectangle is the tax per unit, the width of rectangle is the quantity purchased after the price increase, and the product of the tax per unit times the number of units (height times width of the rectangle) gives the total taxes paid.

There has been some "tax avoidance" in the sense that buyers have avoided making some of the purchases that they previously made. Clearly, the tax would not generate much revenue for the government if the reduction in the quantity demanded were dramatic. An example of that problem is shown in the right-hand panel of Figure 2.13. For that highly elastic demand curve, the tax causes purchases to drop fairly dramatically, so the tax raises very little revenue (see how small the shaded rectangle is). By comparing the two shaded rectangles in Figure 2.13, we can see that, to maximize its tax receipts, the government should concentrate its taxes on commodities for which the demand is inelastic.

Does the government actually use this analysis? Not completely, since there is no tax on insulin, which has an extremely inelastic demand; how-

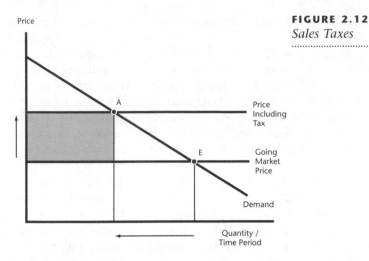

FIGURE 2.12
Sales Taxes

FIGURE 2.13
Sales Tax Revenue and Demand Elasticity

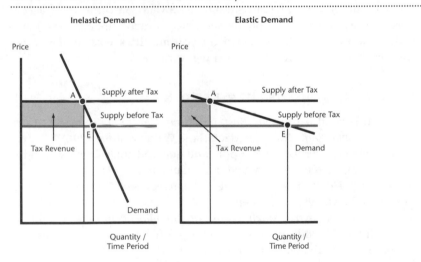

ever, the highest excise taxes in Canada have been levied on gasoline, alcohol, and tobacco — goods that tend to have very inelastic demands. So in the excise tax area, at least, most policy-makers seem to appreciate the principles of supply and demand.

SUMMARY

The analysis in this chapter has shown that the market system can work pretty well and that government attempts to override the forces of supply and demand often lead to unintended and undesirable effects. But there are some areas within our economy where we simply cannot rely totally on market forces. Some government involvement is definitely required to solve problems such as pollution, and Chapter 8 is devoted to these issues. This point is emphasized now so that you do not think this book is dedicated to claiming the market system can do everything. Pollution is just one issue that proves it cannot. The central question is what the market does well and what it does poorly. In any one chapter, space constraints may force us to stress one side of the issue or the other. But, taking the book as a whole, I hope that there is adequate balance to give you the tools to form your own overall opinion.

Here is a review of some of the key concepts covered in this chapter. We have furthered our understanding of the basic economic tools of **supply and demand**, and we have learned how economists use **elasticity** to measure how much demand and supply respond to price. We have discussed some of the factors that cause **shifts in supply and demand curves**. Many individuals think that central planning is needed to avoid economic chaos. But we have seen how the **invisible hand** of self-interest (working in free markets) can duplicate the outcome of an effective planning process and that this automatic guiding of society's scarce resources toward outcomes that accord with people's tastes can break down when **price controls** are imposed. Finally, we have learned that **taxes** levied on **commodities with inelastic demands** yield the **greatest revenue** for the government.

SUGGESTIONS FOR FURTHER READING

D. Foot, with D. Stoffman, *Boom, Bust, and Echo: How to Profit from the Coming Demographic Shift* (Toronto: Macfarlane Walter & Ross, 1996) — an entertaining bestseller that uses supply and demand analysis to explain the wide-ranging effects of the baby-boom generation.

S.E. Landsburg, *The Armchair Economist: Economics and Everyday Life* (New York: Free Press, 1993), Chapters 10–15.

P. Luciani, *Economic Myths: Making Sense of Canadian Policy Issues*, 2nd ed. (Don Mills, ON: Addison-Wesley, 1996) — brief essays on many aspects of the economy that are often misunderstood.

WEB ACTIVITIES

www.cdhowe.org
The Web site of the Toronto-based "think tank" named after Canada's influential cabinet minister who oversaw the country's transformation to a modern industrial society; numerous "commentaries" and "backgrounders" on economic policy issues.

www.economist.com
The Web site of the *Economist* magazine; world news interpreted from an economist's perspective; click on "Library."

CHAPTER THREE
Demand Theory: Household Behaviour

LEARNING OBJECTIVES

After reading this chapter, you should understand
- how the hypothesis of diminishing marginal utility is used to explain both the demand curve's negative slope and consumer surplus — a central concept in benefit–cost analyses;

- how small user charges can generate both large resource savings and small reductions in household utility; and
- how supply and demand analysis is used to determine the extent to which taxes can be passed on to others.

INTRODUCTION

So far in this book, we have justified the slopes of the supply and demand curves simply on the basis of the notion that suppliers like price increases while demanders do not. But more insight can be gained from these tools if we think more carefully about what lies behind the demand and supply curves. So the job for this chapter (and the next one) is to embark on two major excursions. First, we take a closer behind-the-scenes look at the demand curve, and this involves studying what economists call the **theory of household**, or **consumer**, **behaviour**. Second, in the next chapter, we look at the supply curve and study what economists call the theory of the *firm*. Once we have completed these two background studies, we will be able to use the demand and supply tools to ask and answer many more particular questions. So we now begin these excursions with the trip behind the demand curve.

THE LAW OF DIMINISHING MARGINAL UTILITY

As consumers, we make many decisions every day, such as how many pieces of pizza to buy for lunch. Presently, we will use this example to explain the basic assumption that economists make about human behaviour to explain the negatively sloped demand curve. Economists assume that consumers buy goods because they get satisfaction from them and that a consumer's goal is to maximize the satisfaction that can be had from a limited budget. To proceed, we need to know how satisfaction varies as a person buys more or less of any good or service. Our basic psychological assumption is called the **law of diminishing marginal utility**.

Let us focus on each of these words in turn. **Law** is just a scientific word for "assumption." It makes an assumption sound plausible since the professionals within that discipline call it a law. Economists do this since there is a lot of accumulated evidence consistent with this assumption about human behaviour. **Diminishing** means "getting smaller" or "less." The word **marginal** means "additional" or "incremental." **Utility** is the word used by John Stuart Mill, a nineteenth-century philosopher, to talk about "satisfaction." Economists assume that the more people buy of a particular commodity, the more total satisfaction or utility they get from consuming that commodity, but that each subsequent unit of the good adds less to this accumulated total amount of utility. For instance, when you buy pizza, you get a lot of satisfaction or utility from the first slice or two. But once you get full, you do not get as much extra utility from your third and fourth slices. Economists say that this is an example of the diminishing additional or marginal satisfaction provided by the additional units of a good that you purchase.

The assumption of diminishing marginal utility is shown in Figure 3.1. We measure the number of slices of pizza along the horizontal axis and the total or cumulative amount of utility along the vertical axis. We need some unit of measurement for utility, so we measure it in terms of the amount of a person's income that she is willing to give up to have each possible amount of a good. So in this case we are *measuring* the *satisfaction* derived from slices of pizza in *willingness to part with income*.

In the example shown in Figure 3.1, when this person eats one slice, she gets an amount of satisfaction equal to the first shaded rectangle on the left. That is the amount she is willing to pay for the slice of pizza. When she eats the second slice, she gets some more satisfaction. That higher total satisfaction is shown by the second (somewhat larger) rectangle in Figure 3.1. The second rectangle is larger than the first; however, since the second rectangle is not double the size of the first, the amount of additional satisfaction from eating the second slice is not quite as much as from the first one (because the consumer is not so hungry). Then the third slice raises her total utility even higher, but the incremental utility — that is what we mean by marginal util-

FIGURE 3.1
Household Utility
....

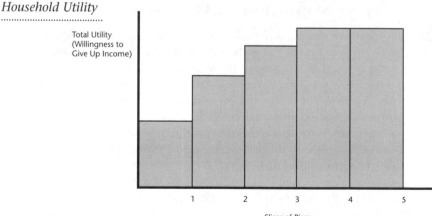

Total Utility
(Willingness to
Give Up Income)

1   2   3   4   5

Slices of Pizza
Purchased Each Period

ity — is even smaller still. The fourth slice is hardly worth eating since it does not add much to the size of the total utility rectangle. Finally, the last (fifth) slice is worth nothing to the individual since the total utility rectangle for five slices is no bigger than that for four slices. So the additional or marginal utility of the fifth slice is zero.

We can show the marginal utility of each slice of pizza by shading (in a darker fashion) the amount by which each slice makes the accumulated total bigger, and this is shown in Figure 3.2. There is no dark part for the fifth slice since its marginal utility is zero. There are two ways that we can tally up how much total satisfaction our consumer gets from five slices of pizza. One is simply to measure the area of the fifth lightly shaded rectangle. The other is to add up all the additional bits of utility, the marginal utilities. When we add up these four darkly shaded areas, we get the same total.

Another thing that we can do is to show marginal utility on the vertical axis in a separate graph, as in Figure 3.3. This just involves transferring the darkly shaded rectangles down so that they are the only things appearing in the graph. Notice how the heights of the rectangles get smaller as more slices of pizza are consumed, illustrating diminishing marginal utility. Since the satisfaction derived from five slices of pizza is given by the sum of the four darkly shaded rectangles (wherever we have located them in Figures 3.2 and 3.3), we see that the area under the jagged marginal utility "curve" in Figure 3.3 measures the total benefits derived from that much pizza.

To explain the assumption of diminishing marginal utility in terms of a common example such as purchasing pizza, the graphs have been drawn so that each slice is represented by a noticeable distance along the horizontal axis. The results it that marginal utility looks like a set of stairs. But when examining economic issues more generally from now on, we will find it easier to smooth out the corners of the steps by considering that each unit of our good can be represented by a tiny distance along the quantity axis. Thus,

FIGURE 3.2
Total Utility

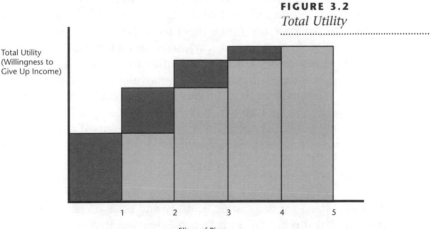

Total Utility
(Willingness to
Give Up Income)

1   2   3   4   5

Slices of Pizza
Purchased Each Period

FIGURE 3.3
Marginal Utility
....

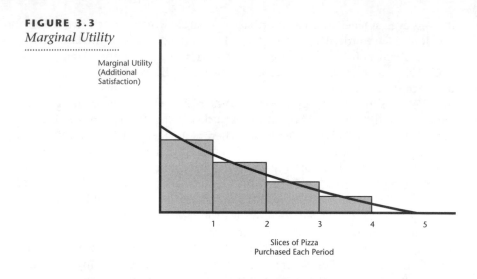

from now on, we will deal with smooth marginal utility curves, like the one that also appears in Figure 3.3.

THE HOUSEHOLD'S OPTIMAL PURCHASE RULE

We have been focusing on pizza as a specific example, but economists believe that people's tastes follow this pattern for essentially all commodities. Except for cases in which addiction, for example, to a drug, is involved, marginal utility falls as the quantity consumed rises. But how does this fact help a consumer to decide how many slices of pizza to buy?

To see what a consumer must do to maximize the utility derived from a limited budget, it is useful to think of her spending that budget one dollar at a time. The first dollar should be spent on a small quantity of the item that has the highest marginal utility. Once that first unit has been purchased, the marginal utility of a second unit will be lower, so perhaps the second dollar should be used to purchase the first unit of some other commodity rather than a second unit of the first item. At each stage, as each dollar is spent, the consumer wants to get the highest marginal utility for that dollar. As long as each item can be purchased in small units, maximum utility will not be achieved, unless the consumer would receive the same additional utility for the last dollar spent — no matter which item it is used to purchase. That is, the marginal utility per dollar spent must be the same for all commodities. For an example involving two goods, this optimal purchase rule is

$$MU_A/P_A = MU_B/P_B,$$

where MU and P stand for the marginal utility and price of each good — A and B. Suppose that this condition is not satisfied and that the consumer's marginal utility per dollar from good A is higher than that from good B

$(MU_A/P_A > MU_B/P_B)$. The consumer could get more satisfaction by cutting her purchase of B somewhat and using the money to buy more A. By assumption, the loss in utility that stems from having less B is dominated by the gain in utility from having more A. The consumer should continue with this reallocation of funds until it no longer pays. With diminishing marginal utility, that point must come. As less B is purchased, MU_B rises — so its marginal utility per dollar spent rises. Similarly, as more A is purchased, its marginal utility per dollar spent falls. Eventually, these ratios converge and become equal. Consumers do not actually think in these terms. But their behaviour must be consistent with this outcome if households do the best they can in their limited circumstances.

Economists have harnessed the logic behind this optimal purchase rule by considering A as the one good contemplated in a particular policy debate and by considering B as all other goods. If expenditure on A is a small proportion of total income, then we can approximate by interpreting B as income itself. Since the "price" of a dollar of income is one, this application makes the consumer's rule simplify to $MU_A = P_A$.

Let us now apply this single-good version of the optimal purchase rule to the question of how much pizza to buy. In Figure 3.4, we see the smoothly drawn version of the marginal utility curve for any commodity, such as pizza. For simplicity, it is shown as a straight line. Each commodity has a going market price, and in this case the price of pizza is given by the height of the horizontal line in Figure 3.4. The price line shows the cost to the consumer of buying more pizza (i.e., of moving to the right in the graph), because for every slice of pizza that she buys, she must pay that price. She must give up that many dollars' worth of other things that she could otherwise buy. So the extra cost to her of consuming more pizza is equal to the going market price. And the addition to her benefits — her satisfaction — is the height up to her additional utility or marginal utility curve. We can compare the heights to

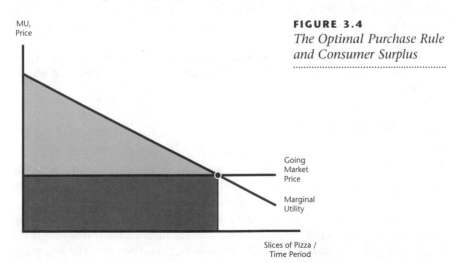

MU,
Price

FIGURE 3.4
*The Optimal Purchase Rule
and Consumer Surplus*

Going
Market
Price

Marginal
Utility

Slices of Pizza /
Time Period

the two lines in Figure 3.4 since utility is being measured in terms of willingness to part with income — that is, in dollars — just like price.

Should the consumer pictured in Figure 3.4 move from zero pizza consumed to a little bit of pizza purchased? Yes, she should, because the height up to her additional benefits line is much greater than the height up to the line showing the cost of purchasing it. For this consumer, buying a bit of pizza is obviously a good deal — so she will move to the right. This reasoning suggests that she will keep buying until she reaches the point at which the additional satisfaction of another slice of pizza is just balanced by the price of buying that slice. Thus, she should increase purchases just to the point indicated by the dot in Figure 3.4. By focusing on this point, we can appreciate the optimal purchase rule for households. They should govern their spending so that the **marginal utility** they get from each item consumed — measured in terms of willingness to part with income — is just **equal to the price** they have to pay for that item.

CONSUMER SURPLUS

In Figure 3.4, we see that this person's total willingness to pay for her optimal amount of pizza is the entire area under the marginal utility curve up to the amount consumed. We must remember from the previous graph with the stairs that, if we add up all the additional bits of satisfaction for having moved all the way over to the optimum point, we get the total utility received. Thus, the total willingness to pay for the chosen amount of pizza in Figure 3.4 is the entire shaded trapezoid (which is partly shaded light grey and partly shaded dark grey). But all that the market is making our consumer pay for each unit of pizza is the going market price. So the total payment is just that price times the number of units consumed — that is, the darkly shaded rectangle in Figure 3.4. So the consumer is getting a bargain. Her total willingness to pay (the whole trapezoid) exceeds what she has to pay (the darkly shaded rectangle), so she gets the lightly shaded triangle for nothing.

Economists call this free bit **consumer surplus**. It is the excess of total benefit over total expenditure. You will see this concept used extensively in later chapters.

THE DEMAND CURVE

The final point that follows from marginal utility theory is that an individual's demand curve and her marginal utility curve can be thought of as the same thing. Remember, back in Chapter 1, when the demand curve was first introduced, we noted that you can think of it as the summary of what an interviewer would get if everyone were asked how much he or she would consume at a whole series of prices. If consumers are successful in arranging their buying so that they maximize their satisfaction, then they must be behaving as if they were following the optimal purchase rule (even if they do not use the economist's language).

So, as the interviewer suggests all possible positions of the going market price line, a consumer who follows the optimal purchase rule answers by indicating all the points on his or her marginal utility curve, as shown in Figure 3.5. Thus, given that we are measuring utility in terms of willingness to part with income, the demand curve is simply the adding together (horizontally) of all these individual demand curves. Thus, when economists statistically measure both the position and the elasticity of that overall demand curve, and calculate the area under it, they have a measure of society's total willingness to pay for any quantity of that item. Indeed, this is how economists measure the total satisfaction provided by any commodity.

For the rest of this chapter, we will see how this theory of consumer behaviour can help us to understand some specific problems. We will focus on two questions: "What are the effects of user fees charged for public services?" and "Who actually pays excise taxes — the producers of goods or the buyers of those goods?"

USER FEES FOR PUBLIC SERVICES

We will consider garbage disposal as an example of a public service. All of us generate a lot of garbage. For some of this litter, the benefit we get from being able to move it away from our homes and our children is high; for other items we throw away, the additional benefits we receive through the municipal garbage collection system are trivial. The costs of options such as composting and reusing containers are low. Despite this fact, we often still opt for garbage disposal since the cost we are charged per item is even lower — it is zero. But our landfill sites are reaching capacity, and our government budgets are overdrawn. For these reasons, it seems reasonable to many economists

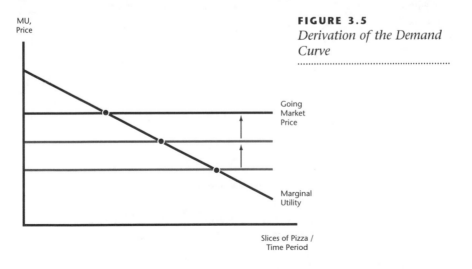

FIGURE 3.5

Derivation of the Demand Curve

that households should be charged a user fee for garbage disposal — that is, the price paid for this public service should depend directly on the number of items set out for collection.

To understand this suggestion, consider Figure 3.6, which shows a demand curve for garbage disposal services. Since we measure utility in terms of people's willingness to part with income, and since the demand curve coincides with the associated marginal utility curve, we can view this demand curve as showing the marginal benefit to society of various levels of garbage disposal services. The optimum purchase rule says that households will consume every item (including garbage disposal services) up to the point at which the marginal benefit is reduced to an extent that it hits the going market price line. If we are not charged for a good on a per-use basis, then the going market price for an additional unit of it is zero, and the market price line coincides with the horizontal axis.

No wonder we demand a tremendous number of these services and have a scarcity of landfill sites when, at the margin, disposing of garbage is free to each individual. We are pricing garbage collection so that reasonable consumers — maximizing their utility — go right out to their optimal consumption points and demand many disposal services.

The marginal benefit curve for garbage disposal is very high for the first few items, but it flattens right out to approach zero at high quantities. This is because some amount of garbage disposal is extremely valuable. It might be difficult to avoid serious disease without this minimal quantity of garbage removed. But of course the last few items that we throw out are not life threatening at all, so the marginal benefit for these units falls to near zero.

What would happen if we raised the user charge (e.g., so much per bag) from zero to some small amount? The marginal benefit curve shown in Figure 3.6 suggests that this pricing policy might result in a dramatic reduction in the quantity of garbage put out each week. As before, people go to the

FIGURE 3.6
User Fees

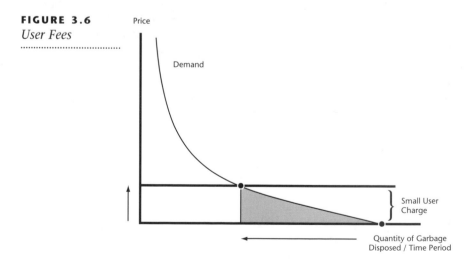

point where marginal utility equals price, but that point is no longer at the right-hand edge of the graph. Such an incentive for increased reusing of containers and for composting would likely make a noticeable difference to our landfill problems (as shown by the large move along the quantity axis in Figure 3.6). Yet the loss in total satisfaction for society would just be the shaded triangle of consumer surplus that is no longer enjoyed. At a zero price, the entire area under the demand curve is surplus. This area may be large. But the loss that follows the introduction of a user fee is small by comparison.

Economists have advocated that user charges be seriously considered for other items, such as medical services. But some of the suggested applications call into question the concept of "universality" in public services. Some people could not afford even a small user charge, and that is one consideration that keeps policy-makers from implementing user charges in areas such as medical care. We really have two problems: an **efficiency** issue — how to avoid squandering scarce resources — a problem that comes from removing the price incentive mechanism when services are offered free on a per-use basis, and an **equity** or income redistribution issue — can all citizens enjoy those services that our society considers necessary? Thus, a user charge generates a "win–lose" outcome: it helps to solve an efficiency problem, but it can worsen an equity problem.

Since we have two policy problems, we really need two policy instruments. First, on the equity side, we need a tax structure and an income support system that can effectively redistribute income in the desired way. Chapter 9 is devoted to this topic. Second, if we can achieve effective income redistribution using this other policy instrument, then we can advocate a wider reliance on user charges. The incentive provided by these taxes makes a major contribution toward solving the problems of resource waste and government deficits, while an income redistribution policy copes directly with the equity issue. By using the two policies together, we can achieve a "win–win" outcome concerning both our efficiency and our equity objectives.

TAX INCIDENCE: WHO REALLY PAYS AN EXCISE TAX — CONSUMERS OR PRODUCERS?

Perhaps this is a good time for a bit of review. We have discussed taxes a couple of times now — excise taxes in Chapter 2 and user charges in this chapter. But the analysis so far has been oversimplified since we have assumed that firms can fully "pass on" the burden of any tax to consumers. Let us now use supply and demand analysis to see whether this assumption is a good one. This analysis allows us to deepen both our understanding of a fundamental tax-policy question and our ability to manipulate supply and demand curves.

In Chapter 2, we saw that, when the supply curve is completely elastic, and a tax is levied, the product price goes up by just the amount of the tax, so firms pass on the tax to consumers. But can firms do this in the more standard case of a positively sloped supply curve? To find out, we will focus on the left-hand panel of Figure 3.7.

Before any tax is levied, the market equilibrium is point E. Now suppose the government taxes firms a certain number of dollars per unit sold. If an interviewer asked the firms after that policy was put in place "What price do you now need to justify each level of production?" the interviewer would receive the obvious answer: "A price that is higher than was needed before the tax." And the margin of increase would be just the per-unit amount of the tax, no matter which level of output is chosen. In other words, just as with the horizontal supply curve case, the supply curve shifts up vertically by the amount of the per-unit tax at every point along the supply curve.

This after-tax supply curve is also shown in the left-hand panel of Figure 3.7. The intersection of the now relevant supply curve and the people's demand curve is point A, and this is the new equilibrium point. We see that an excise tax means higher prices. But with the higher price, consumers buy less of the product, and so we get less output produced and consumed. Notice that the vertical distance between the no-tax and with-tax supply curves is the amount of the per-unit tax but that the amount of the price increase is only a fraction of that distance. This difference means that the firms have passed on the tax to some extent but not completely. The total tax collected by the government is the tax per unit times the number of units still being bought and sold — that is, the sum of the darkly and lightly shades rectangles.

Since the price paid by consumers increases by only a fraction of the tax, the net-of-tax price received by firms falls. Thus, firms are able to pass on only the top, lightly shaded part of the total tax payment, and they have to bear the lower, darkly shaded part themselves. The analysis shows that, in

FIGURE 3.7
Distribution of Tax Burden

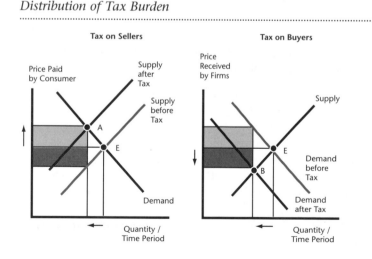

general, taxes will be only partly passed on by firms. How much gets passed on depends on the elasticity of the demand and supply curve. If demand is very inelastic, or (as we saw before) if supply is very elastic, then the upper, lightly shaded part becomes the whole thing. You can verify this result by experimenting with graphs on your own.

In any event, to judge whether a tax is really paid by consumers or producers, we have to talk about particular industries one at a time and statistically estimate the demand and supply elasticities, as economists have done for all major commodities. It is of little help to say, "I think firms are profit maximizers, so they will always pass it on." Consumers are maximizers too, and because they maximize their utility, firms cannot make them buy as much as they did before the price increased. It is not a matter of instinctive belief: the amount of the tax passed on depends on the elasticities.

There is another way of considering the imposition of an excise tax on this commodity. Suppose that, instead of taxing firms every time they sell a good, the government taxes consumers every time they buy the good. In this case, we do not move the supply curve at all because the firm has nothing to do with collection of the tax. When the tax is collected from consumers, it is the demand curve that shifts. The tax decreases consumers' willingness to make payments to firms by the amount of the tax (since that is what must be sent to the government).

In this alternative presentation, shown in the right-hand panel of Figure 3.7, we simply shift down the line representing household willingness to pay (the demand curve) by the amount of the per-unit tax, making the new equilibrium point B. The consumers pass on to the firms some of the tax that was levied on them. As before, the total tax paid is the sum of the two shaded areas, and just as before firms pay only the lower part since the price that they receive net of tax has fallen.

Figure 3.7 allows us to compare the tax on sellers and the tax on buyers. We see that, whomever is formally taxed, the darkly shaded rectangles are the same size in both panels. It does not matter whether the tax is nominally on firms or on households. The distribution of the tax burden is the same. The only thing that matters (concerning who really pays the tax and how much revenue is actually raised) is the elasticity of demand and supply, as the diagrams make abundantly clear.

You may find this conclusion surprising. When people rely on intuition, they often think that taxes should be collected from firms (since firms can afford to pay them) rather than from households (since many households cannot afford to pay them). But our supply and demand analysis has just demonstrated that the actual distribution of tax burdens between households and firms is the same whether the tax is applied to sellers or buyers. With this insight (that some of your intuitive assumptions about economic issues may reflect limited understanding), you will realize that your investment in learning economics is really starting to pay dividends.

SUMMARY

Here is a review of some of the key concepts covered in this chapter. We have studied the **theory of consumer behaviour**, which is the thinking underlying the demand curve. We have examined the **law of diminishing marginal utility**, which helps us to understand households' **optimal purchase rule**. This rule clarifies the logic underlying decisions to buy goods and services. We have seen that one implication of diminishing marginal utility is the existence of **consumer surplus**, and we applied that concept to evaluate **user fees** for public services. A second implication of the optimal purchase rule is that it lets us understand **tax incidence** and how consumers can "pass" the burden of taxation on to firms.

In the next chapter, we will take a similar excursion. We will go behind the supply curve instead of the demand curve and examine the theory of the firm.

SUGGESTIONS FOR FURTHER READING

T.G. Buchholz, *New Ideas from Dead Economists* (New York: Penguin, 1990), Chapters 5, 7.

M. Jevons. *Murder at the Margin* (Princeton, NJ: Princeton University Press, 1993) — a (corny but fun) mystery novel in which the detective uses economic theory to unravel the crime. (See also *The Fatal Equilibrium* [Cambridge, MA: MIT Press, 1985] by the same author.)

WEB ACTIVITIES

http://canada.gc.ca/directories/internet_e.html
The main Web site of the federal government; information on all topics listed by individual departments.

CHAPTER FOUR

Supply Theory: The Behaviour of Profit-Maximizing Firms

LEARNING OBJECTIVES

After reading this chapter, you should understand

- how the law of diminishing returns determines what each factor of production gets paid;

- why firms must equate marginal revenue and marginal cost to maximize profits; and

- how firms react to various levies such as licence fees and excise taxes.

INTRODUCTION

This chapter represents the second of our excursions behind demand and supply curves; this time it's the supply curve's turn. We start off by considering a situation analogous to our *theory of household behaviour*. In that theory, each household was assumed to be a tiny part of the whole market, so that the going market price of each commodity was independent of how much that individual consumer purchased. The analogous situation for firms is called a *competitive industry*. Each firm is such a small part of the overall industry that it cannot affect either the price of the output good that it sells or the price of the inputs that it uses to produce that good. Strictly speaking, this theory is descriptive of only a few Canadian industries, such as the large number of farmers who produce a homogeneous brand or quality of a particular food item. Nevertheless, an analysis of competition is a useful starting point; rest assured, we will consider other forms of industrial structure later. For example, in Chapter 6 we will consider *monopoly*, a situation in which one firm has no competitors, and in Chapter 7 we will consider *oligopoly*, a situation in which there is competition among just a few firms.

THE THEORY OF THE FIRM

To follow the reasoning in this chapter, think as if you are the manager of a simple firm and must decide how many units of an input should be hired to maximize the firm's profit. Profit is simply what is left over after you subtract your input costs from the sales revenue that you obtain by selling your output. We talk about output being produced by inputs or factors of production, and there are all kinds of inputs. For example, there is labour, fertilizer, machines, and factories.

Some factors can be adjusted quickly. Others, such as the size of a plant, can be changed only if considerable time is available. So economists find it useful to talk about the theory of the firm in terms of two different time horizons. The **short run** is a period short enough that only some, and not all, of the factors can be varied. The **long run** is a period long enough that firms can vary the amounts (i.e., the numbers of units used) of all the inputs to the production process.

To keep our discussion simple, let us have just one variable-in-the-short-run factor and one constant or fixed factor, and let us call the easily varied factor labour and the fixed factor in the short run capital equipment, or just capital for short. Figure 4.1 illustrates what we call the *input–output function* for any representative firm in the short run. With a fixed size of plant and equipment, the only degree of freedom that the firm has is to hire more or less labour. And the implications for how much output will be generated by the firm's operations are given by this graph. As we increase our hiring of labour (i.e., as we move out from the origin along the labour input axis), the total output obtained from hiring all workers is shown by the height of each rectangle. Clearly, the height increases; we get more and more output as we hire more and more labour.

But notice something more particular. Output not only increases as we hire more input, but, for a while, also increases at an increasing rate. The second rectangle, which shows the output for two workers, is more than twice the size of that for one worker. Then, as more workers are hired, the increases in output get proportionally smaller.

This pattern is more apparent in the left-hand panel of Figure 4.2, where the darkly shaded rectangles highlight the additional output of each new worker hired, as we first move out along the employment axis. In the early range of hiring, the dark rectangles become larger as we hire more workers. If we have only one worker, we cannot divide up tasks and specialize. But if we

FIGURE 4.1

The Firm's Input–Output Relationship
···

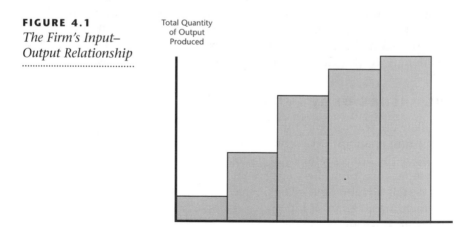

Total Quantity of Output Produced

Quantity of Labour Hired / Time Period

FIGURE 4.2

Total and Marginal Products of Labour

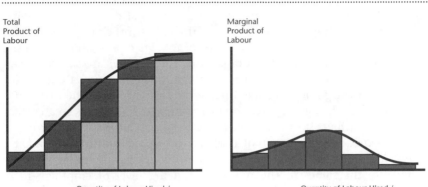

have two or three workers, we can specialize and generate more output than just three times that of the first worker. So output increases at an increasing rate over this initial rate of expansion. But if we keep increasing the number of workers hired, diminishing returns set in. Each dark rectangle becomes smaller. We have more and more workers, and they are all trying to share the one machine. Since each worker has less of a machine to work with, eventually workers get less and less productive. Economists call this effect the **law of diminishing marginal returns** — the proposition that beyond some point, the hiring of more labour brings ever smaller additions to total output.

When developing our theory of consumer behaviour, we found it helpful to focus on marginal utility. The same strategy is very useful in talking about the theory of the firm. The additional or marginal product of each worker is shown by the dark rectangles in the left-hand panel in Figure 4.2, and these marginal product amounts have been transferred down to the axis in a new graph (in the right-hand panel of Figure 4.2), which shows just the marginal product of labour. Once labour has been hired out to the point that its marginal product is falling (i.e., beyond the third worker in this example), we are in the range where diminishing marginal returns have set in. For the remainder of our discussion, we will squeeze the space we reserve for each unit of labour on the horizontal axis so that our total product and marginal product curves can be represented as smooth functions.

You will find this material easier by keeping in mind the strong analogy to our theory of consumer behaviour. For consumers, we assume that households maximize their satisfaction and that there is diminishing marginal utility. Similarly, we assume that firms maximize their profits and that there is diminishing marginal productivity in the short run, as more of one input is hired without a corresponding increase in the other input. That is the basic set-up, and, just as we had an optimal purchase rule for households, the same format leads to an optimal hiring rule for firms.

THE OPTIMAL HIRING RULE

As with any activity, hiring should be expanded up to the point that the marginal benefits are just balanced by the marginal costs of the activity. The benefit of hiring one more worker is the value of the marginal product of that new worker, while the cost is the going wage rate — expressed in the firm's output units, for proper comparison. These curves are shown in Figure 4.3. We must compare the height of the marginal product curve with the height of the going wage rate line. Should the firm hire the first worker? Yes, because the height up to the marginal product curve is greater than the height up the cost of labour line. We can keep adding to our profits if we keep expanding employment until we get to the point that the extra benefit (the marginal product) and the additional cost (the going wage for labour) are the same. So the profit-maximizing level of employment is given by the dot in Figure 4.3.

As occurs in the analogous graph for households, the firm gets a bonus. All the firm has to pay for each unit of labour is an amount of its output equal to the going wage rate, so the total wage bill is equal to the shaded rectangle in Figure 4.3. But the total amount of output the firm gets to sell is the sum of all the workers' marginal products — that is, the whole area under the marginal productivity curve up to the optimum point. So the firm has some **producer surplus**, and, like consumer surplus, it is equal to the area above the going wage line. This surplus represents profits. Since firms try to **maximize profits**, they would be giving up some of this roughly triangular area that represents profits if they did not expand employment all the way out to the amount given by the intersection.

Thus, the **optimal hiring rule** is as follows: Hire any factor up to the point that the value of its marginal product is just equal to the price that must be paid for that factor.

FIGURE 4.3
*The Optimal
Hiring Rule*
....

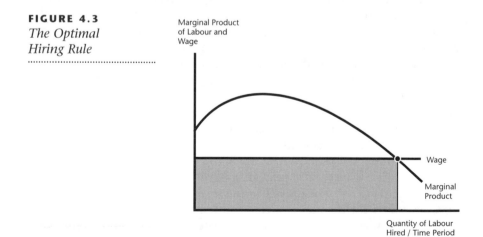

Marginal Product
of Labour and
Wage

Wage

Marginal
Product

Quantity of Labour
Hired / Time Period

THE OPTIMAL OUTPUT DECISION FOR A COMPETITIVE FIRM

So far, our theory of the firm has been limited to determining the optimal level of an input (e.g., labour) to hire in the short run. But given the input–output relationship, once that hiring decision has been made, there is nothing more to choose. The amount of output that can be produced is dictated by the technology that is summarized by the input–output function. So the optimal hiring rule and the optimal output decision represent the same decision. But we can gain many more insights for policy by recasting our theory of the firm to focus on the output decision.

To determine how its profits vary with output, a firm must know how its sales revenue and its costs of production vary with its production level. Let us continue with the cost side and derive what economists call the **total cost curve**. All firms have some capital, the factor of production that is fixed in the short run, and, since there are costs associated with owning that capital, economists call these expenditures **fixed costs**. Firms also have **variable costs**, which in our case simply equal the wage rate times however many workers have been hired.

The best way to appreciate how we should draw the total cost curve is to focus on the input–output function discussed earlier. We measured the input of labour along the horizontal axis and the output of goods along the vertical axis, as is shown in the left-hand panel of Figure 4.4. Now consider flipping and rotating this graph. First, flipping it over so that the labour input axis runs out to the left instead of to the right, we have the middle panel in Figure 4.4. Then, by rotating it 90 degrees clockwise, we end up with the right-hand panel. The graph on the left shows how much output we get for each level of employment; the graph on the right shows the same thing but from the reverse — how much labour input we need to produce any level of output.

FIGURE 4.4
The Required Input Relationship

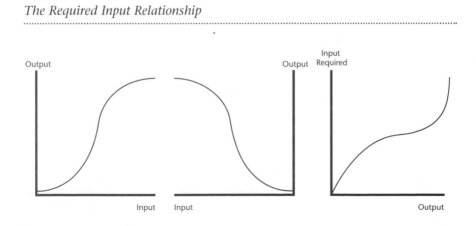

Since labour costs (the variable costs for this firm) simply equal the labour requirement for each level of output times the going wage rate, the variable cost curve is just like the curve in the right-hand panel of Figure 4.4. The height of that curve at each point has to be multiplied by the wage rate for each worker. Thus, the variable cost curve has to have this shape. Variable costs increase, first at a decreasing rate, and then at an increasing rate once diminishing marginal returns set in.

The **total cost** curve looks much the same, as we see in Figure 4.5. It is arrived at by moving the starting point of the variable cost curve up from the origin by the amount of the fixed cost associated with owning the fixed factor (in this case capital).

We started drawing all these graphs so that we could determine the rate of output that will generate the highest possible level of profits for this firm. Since profit is the excess of total revenue over total cost, we need to add a total revenue function to Figure 4.5, so let us take a look at the revenue side of the picture now.

When firms take the going market price as given, the total revenue line is easy to draw. We multiply the total number of units that the firm is selling by the price, and the result is the total amount of sales revenue. So total revenue, when drawn as a function of quantity sold, as in Figure 4.6, is simply a straight line with the slope equal to the price of the product.

Putting the total cost curve and the total revenue curve together, as in Figure 4.6, we can determine the profit-maximizing level of output. What we are looking for is that point along the output axis at which the vertical gap between the total revenue line and the total cost function is the greatest. Clearly, producing next to nothing is not a good level of output to pick because the firm is losing money. Its costs are greater than its revenues. And, at the intersection of the two curves, it is making zero profit since total revenue and total cost equal each other. The biggest positive gap, between revenues and costs, is shown in Figure 4.6.

FIGURE 4.5
The Total Cost Curve
....

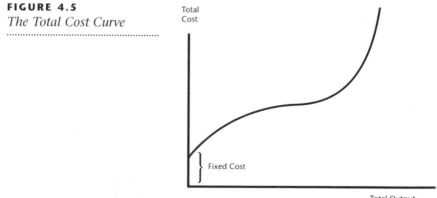

Total Cost

Fixed Cost

Total Output
Produced / Time Period

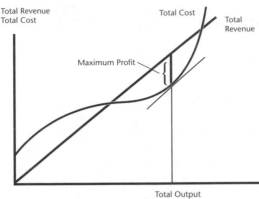

FIGURE 4.6

Profit Maximization

Total Revenue
Total Cost

Total Cost

Total Revenue

Maximum Profit

Total Output
Produced / Time Period

Economists often think of this profit-maximization decision in terms of the slopes of the total revenue and total cost curves. The intersection of the total revenue and total cost curves on the left in Figure 4.6 cannot be the profit-maximizing rate of output because the slope of the total revenue function is very different from the slope of the total cost function. With different slopes, as we move more to the right, the profit gap widens. Similarly, the intersection on the right cannot be a profit-maximizing rate of output because there the total cost line has a much steeper slope than the total revenue line. If we move back and reduce production, then the profit gap widens, again because the slopes are different. In between these two extremes, then, we gain the biggest profits when the slope of the total cost function (as shown by the tangent in Figure 4.6) is equal to the slope of the total revenue line.

Economists define the slope of the total revenue line as **marginal revenue** and the slope of the total cost curve as **marginal cost**. Given these definitions, we can say that profit-maximizing output occurs where **marginal revenue equals marginal cost**.

A **competitive** firm that takes prices as given can sell all that it wants at the going market price. When output is increased by one unit, the additional or marginal revenue for the firm is simply the going market price. The slope of its total revenue curve is just the going market price, so marginal revenue is simply another name for price. For this special case of a small competitive firm, then, the profit-maximizing rule can be restated as follows: Produce that rate of output for which **marginal cost equals price**.

There are many uses for this analysis. For example, governments raise money through a variety of taxes, and some of these taxes are levied on firms. The theory of the firm allows us to compare how firms react to these different kinds of taxes. We often hear firms claiming that, if the government imposes a tax, the firm will have to lower output and lay off some workers. Is this kind of lobbying just a bluff? To have an informed opinion about tax policy, we must appreciate which taxes are appropriate in different circumstances.

WHICH TAXES CAUSE FIRMS TO CUT PRODUCTION IN THE SHORT RUN?

One tax that governments impose on firms is a licence fee. For example, this tax is used when a restaurant is allowed a franchise along a highway with limited access. The firm often has to pay an annual fee for being allowed to be the only restaurant available to motorists in that region. This type of fee the firm pays just for being there. It is not a fee that varies with the level of sales. It is a one-time payment that is part of the firm's fixed costs. It is just like the fee for a licence plate for your car — the amount charged does not vary with the amount you drive.

The imposition of a licence fee is shown in Figure 4.7. Since it increases fixed costs, the fee simply moves the total cost curve up by the same distance at every point. So the point at which we have the biggest profit gap remains at the same rate of output as before. It will be a smaller gap, so the firm will not like it, but the firm is not going to cut its output since doing so would lower profits even more. The analysis shows that, as long as our assumptions of diminishing returns and profit maximization are reasonable, any threat by a firm to lay off workers in response to this type of licence fee is likely to be a bluff. Firms may use such a threat to try to discourage the government from imposing the fee, but if the government does impose it, a profit-maximizing firm will not want to worsen its profit picture in the short run by moving away from the profit-maximizing rate of output.

But other taxes do cause short-run adjustments. For instance, if an excise tax is imposed, under which the firm pays a certain amount per unit of output, then the total cost curve rotates upward and counterclockwise, as shown

FIGURE 4.7
A Licence Fee

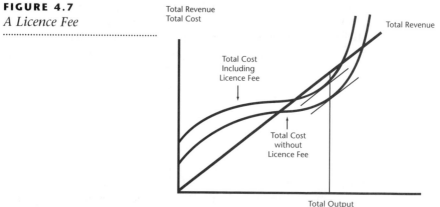

Total Revenue
Total Cost

Total Revenue

Total Cost
Including
Licence Fee

Total Cost
without
Licence Fee

Total Output
Produced / Time Period

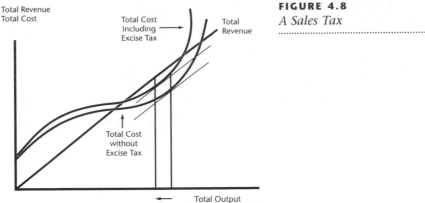

FIGURE 4.8

A Sales Tax

in Figure 4.8. The excise tax does not change fixed cost at all because it is a tax per unit of output, and, if the firm does not produce anything, then of course it does not incur any tax. So the intercept of the total cost curve does not move up at all. But the greater the output produced and sold, the more taxes the firm has to pay, and the distance between the old cost curve and the new one increases as output increases. Clearly, this policy raises the slope of the total cost curve at every quantity. The result is that the maximum profit gap must occur at some point farther to the left. So with an excise tax we find that firms do cut their outputs because doing so is in their profit interests. This tax does result in immediate layoffs.

Economic analysis shows that not all taxes are the same. Some are good for one purpose and bad for another. Which tax should be used depends on the goals of the government. If the government is concerned about income redistribution and the tax is designed to take some profits away from the owners of firms (and transfer the funds to the less well off), then the licence fee is a good idea. We get income transferred without any layoffs. But if the reason for the tax is to reduce a certain activity, such as an industry that causes of lot of pollution, then we do want a reduction in output, so the excise tax is desirable.

AVERAGE COST AND MARGINAL COST CURVES

Just as we found it useful in our analysis of household behaviour to move away from the total utility function to look at the marginal utility function, it is useful to move away from the total cost curve to look at the **marginal cost curve** (and, while we are at it, the **average cost curve**).

To do this, we start with the standard total cost curve shown in the left-hand panel of Figure 4.9. Next we draw the line that goes through the origin of this graph and is tangent to the total cost curve. Average cost is simply the

FIGURE 4.9

Derivation of Average Cost

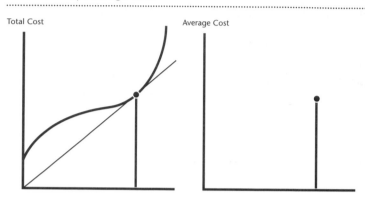

Total Cost

Average Cost

Total Output
Produced / Time Period

FIGURE 4.10

The Average Cost Curve

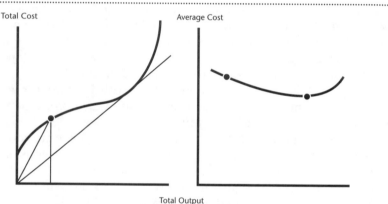

Total Cost

Average Cost

Total Output
Produced / Time Period

ratio of total cost to the quantity of goods produced. For the output level highlighted in the left-hand panel of Figure 4.9, it is the ratio of the height of the large dot to the distance of the dot from the right of the origin. We graph this ratio as the height of the large dot in the right-hand panel of Figure 4.9. That dot is one point on the average cost curve. At output levels below and above this one, the ratio of total cost to output is higher since the ray to the origin in the left-hand panel is steeper. Thus, the average cost curve must be U-shaped, as shown in Figure 4.10.

As noted earlier, marginal cost is the slope of the total cost curve. As indicated by the tangents in the left-hand panel of Figure 4.11, this slope is high at low output levels. As output increases, this slope falls and then rises again. And so, when we record the value of this slope as a height in the right-

FIGURE 4.11

Average and Marginal Cost

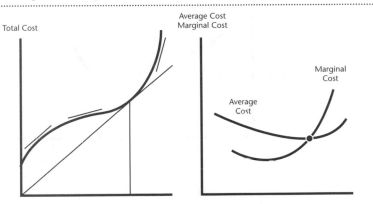

hand panel in Figure 4.11, the marginal cost curve must also be U-shaped. Also, since the tangent and the ray through the origin in the left-hand panel must coincide when the ray is at its smallest slope, average cost and marginal cost must be the same amount at this output. Thus, the marginal cost curve must cut the average cost curve at its minimum point.

THE LONG RUN

The long run is a time horizon during which firms can change not only the amount of labour they hire but also the amount of capital equipment they use. When the amount of capital is varied, the entire position of all the short-run cost curves (which we have just derived) is shifted. If larger amounts of capital equipment permit more automation, then the firm's cost curves are lower.

We see two such positions of the firm's short-run average cost curve in Figure 4.12. A curve that summarizes these and a host of other possibilities appears as well. Economists call this summary the firm's **long-run average cost curve**. There are three general possibilities for the shape of this long-run average cost curve.

For many industries, firms can achieve the economies of large-scale operation fairly quickly without reaching a high rate of output. Then they can continue to expand simply by replicating their existing plants. The result is that doubling both the labour and the capital inputs doubles the rate of output. Economists call this **constant returns to scale**, and it is characterized by a horizontal long-run average cost curve. For some industries, however, a firm's attempt to expand involves a severe problem of co-ordination within the firm (as the enterprise becomes very bureaucratic), and costs rise as output expands. Economists call this a **decreasing**

FIGURE 4.12
Long-Run Average Cost
....

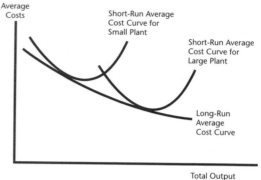

returns to scale industry, and it is characterized by a rising (or positively sloped) long-run average cost curve.

Finally, for other industries, the long-run average cost curve declines over the entire relevant range of output (as shown in Figure 4.12). Any industry that has large set-up costs, such as a telephone network or a public utility with a grid of pipes or power lines, is in this position. We call this type of industry an **increasing returns to scale** industry, and such returns often lead to what we call **natural monopoly**. Such an industry cannot remain competitive; once one firm gets bigger than the others, it achieves lower unit costs. It underprices the other firms and eventually drives them out of business. So we simply cannot talk about this kind of long-run average cost curve in a competitive environment.

Whatever the shape of the long-run average cost curve, this relationship represents the supply curve for that commodity in a long-run time horizon.

SUMMARY

Here is a review of some of the key concepts covered in this chapter. I have outlined the theory of the firm based on the assumption of **profit maximization**. This theory allowed us to understand two alternative ways of stating what competitive firms must do to maximize profits. First, the **optimal hiring rule** is what managers use when adjusting input levels. Each input is hired up to the point that its **marginal product** is pushed down to the level of its price. Second, we recast this hiring rule so that we could indicate how a manager can determine the optimum output level for a competitive firm. Output is expanded up to the point that **marginal revenue** is equal to **marginal cost**.

We considered several ways to illustrate a firm's revenue and cost data by deriving the marginal revenue curve and the average and marginal cost curves. To illustrate why policy-makers need to be aware of this analysis, we used the theory to explain which **taxes** cause firms to cut production in the short run and which do not cause layoffs.

Finally, we discussed why some industries are characterized by constant **returns to scale** in the **long run** and why others involve decreasing and increasing returns to scale.

In the next chapter, we will focus on industries that have constant returns to scale, and we will compare a competitive market economy to a centrally planned one. Then, in Chapter 6, we will consider industries that have increasing returns to scale (i.e., monopolies), and we will discuss competition and regulation policies. Finally, in Chapter 7, we will consider competition among just a few rival firms. In this situation, firms must guess what their rivals' reactions may be — before their own optimal behaviour can be defined.

SUGGESTIONS FOR FURTHER READING

S.E. Landsburg, *The Armchair Economist: Economics and Everyday Life* (New York: Free Press, 1993), Chapters 16–21.

WEB ACTIVITIES

www.cabe.ca
The Web site of the Canadian Association for Business Economics; information from the perspective of economists employed by private firms.

www.cfee.org
The Web site of the Canadian Foundation for Economic Education; information on many topics, including economics in grade school and starting your own business.

CHAPTER FIVE
Competition and the Invisible Hand

LEARNING OBJECTIVES

After reading this chapter, you should understand

- how the theory of the firm provides the underlying explanation behind market supply curves;

- how a competitive industry operates; and

- why a competitive industry duplicates the decisions of an optimal social planner.

INTRODUCTION

In this chapter, we discuss the operation of a perfectly **competitive industry** in some detail. This is not because economists think there are a number of industries that are perfectly competitive; indeed, they do not. It turns out that the model of a perfectly competitive industry forms an ideal against which we can evaluate all other outcomes. Out first job in pursuing this goal is to establish how the theory of the firm that we examined in the previous chapter is used to derive the supply curve of a commodity in the short run.

THE SHORT-RUN SUPPLY CURVE IN A COMPETITIVE INDUSTRY

We begin with a reminder from Chapter 4. Perhaps you should glance back at Figure 4.11 on page 49. The short-run total cost curve for a firm involves, first, an increasing returns region and, then, a decreasing returns region at higher levels of output. As a result, costs increase at a decreasing rate over the low-output range of production but then increase at an increasing rate at higher output levels. This pattern is represented by the average and marginal cost curves. Both curves are U-shaped because there are increasing returns in the early phase of operations, with diminishing returns setting in at higher outputs. This fact makes per-unit costs first fall and then rise. In this chapter, we focus on the average and marginal cost way of picturing the behaviour of a firm's costs.

Economists argue that every activity should be carried on to the point that the marginal benefits of the activity are brought down to just equal its marginal costs. In the case of a firm, the marginal benefits of selling more output are the additions to total revenue. Recall that we have named these additions *marginal revenue*. And, for a competitive firm, marginal revenue is just the going market price for which the firm can sell the product.

So the market price line shown in Figure 5.1 represents the additional benefits line or marginal revenue line associated with increasing output. The

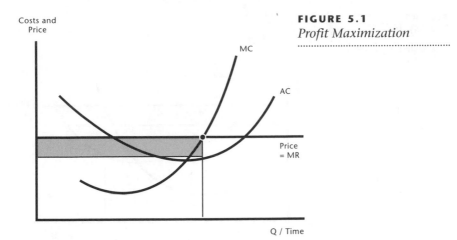

Costs and
Price

FIGURE 5.1
Profit Maximization

MC

AC

Price
= MR

Q / Time

marginal cost curve shows the additions to total cost. The firm will maximize its profits if it keeps choosing a higher level of output — that is, if it keeps moving to the right in Figure 5.1 — so long as the additions to revenue more than make up for the additional cost of that expansion. As long as the height up to the additional revenue line is greater than the height up to the additional cost line, the firm should expand. Similarly, if the height up to the marginal cost curve is greater than the height up to the going price line, then the firm must have expanded too much, because the last unit produced has added more to its costs than to its revenue (thus decreasing its profits). So to maximize profits, a competitive firm must operate where marginal benefit — that is, the going market price — is just balanced by the marginal cost of production, and that is right at the dot in Figure 5.1.

Now glance back at Figure 4.6 on page 45. When discussing that graph, we said that profit maximization occurs at the point where the slope of the total revenue curve and the slope of the total cost curve are the same, since that point gives the firm the biggest profit gap. But in Figure 5.1 here, we are showing marginal cost and marginal revenue not as slopes but as heights in a diagram on their own. That is why it is the intersection of marginal revenue and marginal cost that illustrates the same profit-maximizing level of output for the firm.

Why is the average cost curve shown in Figure 5.1? Because with it we can measure exactly how much profit the firm is making. Since revenue per unit is the height up to the price line and cost per unit is the height up to the average cost curve, profit per unit is the difference between those two heights. The height of the shaded rectangle indicates the profit per unit, and the width of that rectangle is the number of units involved. Thus, the area of the shaded rectangle is total profit.

When the supply curve was first introduced in Chapter 1, we said that it can be thought of as the tabulation that an interviewer would record after

FIGURE 5.2
The Supply Curve of a Competitive Firm
....

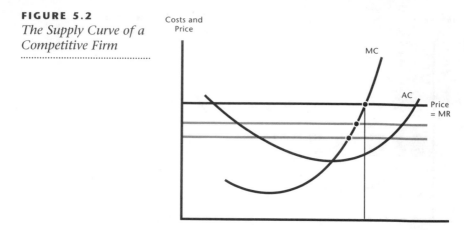

talking to all firms and asking them a series of if–then questions. "If the price is high, how much would you want to produce?" "If the price is lower, how much would you produce?" And so on. Now we know that a profit-maximizing, perfectly competitive firm would arrive at its answer by drawing in a price line for every different output price that the interviewer asks it to consider, as shown in Figure 5.2. The firm states the quantity of output that corresponds to the point where the price line cuts its marginal cost curve. So, when the firm answers the interviewer, all the firm is really doing is tracing out points on its marginal cost curve. The firm's **short-run supply curve** is therefore nothing more than the relevant range of its marginal cost curve.

The overall market supply curve in the short run is constructed by adding the quantities supplied by each individual firm (at each price), so it is simply the horizontal summation of all the individual firms' marginal cost curves.

HOW FIRMS REACT TO LOSSES

So far, we have focused on prices that are high enough to ensure that firms make a profit. But what happens at lower prices? Figure 5.3 shows the price equals marginal revenue line below the minimum point of the average cost curve. If the firm were to produce goods at all, then the level of output given by the dot would be its best rate of output. By extending a vertical line through this point, we can assess whether the firm will produce goods at all.

Its cost per unit is given by the height up to the average cost curve, and this is greater than its revenue per unit (the height up to the price line). So the firm is suffering a loss on each unit of the good produced equal to the height of the shaded rectangle. That per-unit loss means a total loss on all units equal to the area of the shaded rectangle.

Why should the firm operate if the best it can do is incur this loss? The simple answer is that the firm will not stay in this business very long if it can

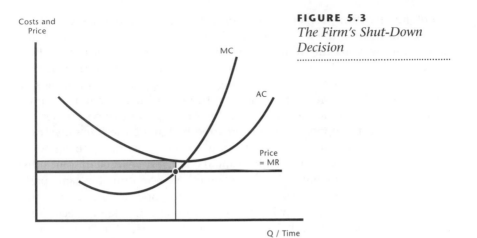

Costs and
Price

MC

AC

Price
= MR

Q / Time

FIGURE 5.3

*The Firm's Shut-Down
Decision*
....

move its capital into another industry. But remember that our graph shows
the short run. We cannot vary or move capital until the long run, when capital becomes a variable factor of production, along with all the other inputs.

In the short run, the firm is stuck with having to pay its fixed costs —
that is, the costs associated with owning or leasing its capital equipment. If
it chooses not to operate in the short run, it still has to pay these fixed costs.
Thus, in the short run, the firm shown in Figure 5.3 should pick the outcome
that involves the smallest losses. If it shuts down, its losses will equal its fixed
costs. If it operates at the quantity given by its price equals marginal cost intersection, its losses will equal the shaded rectangle. So, for prices just a little
below the minimum point of the average cost curve, the firm will still operate in the short run. But, for prices below the minimum point of the average
cost curve by a wide margin, the firm will shut down because its losses would
exceed its fixed costs. It would do better just to shut down and lose only its
fixed costs.

You must remember, though, that all of this is for the short run. In the
long run, if a loss is incurred, a firm will not stay in the industry. It would
rather employ its capital in some other industry in which profits can be
earned.

How can we define full **long-run equilibrium** in a competitive economy? We say that firms do not reach the end of their migration from one industry to another until all firms are making the same rate of profit in every
industry, since only then will firms no longer have any incentive to move. So
having the same profits earned everywhere defines long-run equilibrium.

Economists use profits in a little different way from how accountants and
everyday people do, and we should clarify this difference now. The way of
defining profits according to standard accounting methods is simply to take
total sales revenue minus all the costs that firms actually pay out for the factors of production that they are using and do not already own. But economic

profits involve the notion of opportunity cost. Economic profits are accounting profits minus what the firm is forgoing by not renting out the factors of production it owns to other firms. If the owner of the firm uses her own labour time and some machines that she owns, she does not have to pay herself to use them. But by using them, she is forgoing the opportunity of being paid by someone else. To make the correct profit-maximizing decision, she must realize that she has incurred these costs by forgoing those opportunities.

So what is the opportunity cost incurred by having the firm's own capital being tied up in this industry? The firm's owner is giving up the opportunity of earning those profits that her capital could have earned in some other industry. In the full equilibrium of a competitive economy, the same profit rate is earned everywhere. This means that the forgone earnings in potential profits elsewhere are exactly what the firm's capital earns here. So **economic profits** will be profits that she's earning here minus the profits that she could be earning elsewhere — in other words, zero. So another way of stating what we mean by equilibrium in a fully competitive economy is that all firms earn economic profits of zero, or just a normal rate of return on their invested capital. We have included all these opportunity costs when drawing all cost curves, so we are using the economist's way of defining profits.

THE INVISIBLE HAND IN A COMPETITIVE INDUSTRY

We discussed the **invisible hand** in Chapter 2. This expression summarized the notion that self-interest can provide the necessary incentive for individuals and firms to behave so that outcomes in the economy are the same as those that an all-knowing central planner would try to accomplish. We can now describe this process in more detail.

Figure 5.4 depicts a competitive industry — the whole industry in the right-hand panel, and the situation for any one representative firm in the left-hand panel. Initially, the industry is in long-run equilibrium. Demand and

FIGURE 5.4
A Competitive Industry

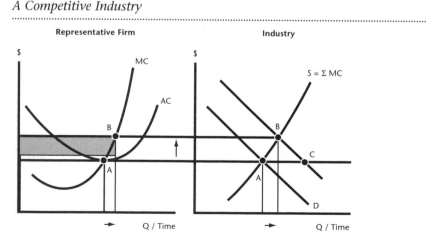

supply intersect at point A in the right-hand panel, and the height of point A determines the going market price. The market price line is extended over to the left-hand panel, where it is interpreted as the marginal revenue line. Each firm is at its marginal cost equals price outcome at point A in the left-hand panel, earning zero economic profit. So we begin with a long-run, competitive equilibrium — with the market clearing, no economic profits being made, and the optimal output-setting rule (price equals marginal cost) being obeyed.

[handwritten margin note: 3 criteria]

Now let us assume that there is a change in taste. If the change is in favour of this commodity, then the demand curve in the industry part of the graph moves to the right. In the short run, we move from point A to point B — the intersection of the now relevant demand and supply curves in the right-hand panel of Figure 5.4. For every firm in the industry, the price line is now the higher horizontal line in Figure 5.4. So the profit-maximizing point for each firm is the intersection of marginal revenue and marginal cost at point B in the left-hand panel of Figure 5.4.

Each firm increases output, and this adjustment is shown by the arrows along the quantity axis in Figure 5.4. In the short run, all of this new output has to come from existing firms, for there is not enough time for capital to be adjusted within these firms or for new firms to enter this industry.

But the shift to point B is not the end of the story. At point B, revenue per unit is greater than cost per unit, so firms receive positive economic profits (shown by the area of the shaded rectangle in Figure 5.4). Positive economic profits mean more profit than anybody else is earning in any other competitive industry. Thus, in the long run, more firms enter the industry. Hence, there are more marginal cost curves to add up to get the industry supply curve, which shifts out to the right.

How far does the supply curve shift? For simplicity, we assume that this industry is characterized by constant returns to scale in the long run. This means that the supply curve will have to move out to the point that the market price gets competed down to precisely where it was before (as shown by point C in the right-hand panel of Figure 5.5). If the price does not fall all the way to where it was before, then the intersection of the price line and the marginal cost curve will still be above the average cost curve, and there will still be a positive profit rectangle (like the one pictured in Figure 5.4, only smaller). And, if above-normal profits still exist, then there will still be an incentive for more firms to enter the industry.

So the full long-run competitive equilibrium occurs when enough firms enter the industry to force the price all the way back down to where it was in the first place. We get more industry output, but each firm will have returned to its lower level of output and be at zero economic profit again. There will simply be more firms.

THE ADVANTAGES OF COMPETITION

The foregoing analysis makes one thing clear. The way in which a decentralized system of free markets works is that **temporary profit opportunities**

FIGURE 5.5
Long-Run Equilibrium

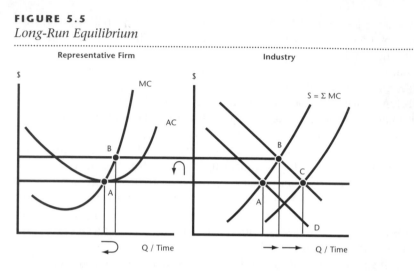

open up in the areas that people want expanded. Then the selfish pursuit of those profits causes the resource reallocation that the people wanted to occur.

While resource reallocation requires profit incentives, it does not involve permanent income redistribution. This is because the profit rectangles appear only in the short run, and they are competed away in the long run. Nobody is in a position of permanently receiving above-normal profits, and that is an outcome that many people seem to like.

The second desirable feature of a competitive industry is that the outcome is **efficient**. When we reach full equilibrium, society gets the commodity for the minimum possible unit price. Point A in Figure 5.5 is the lowest point on the unit cost curve, and that is efficient. We are tying up the least amount of society's scarce resources to produce each unit of each good.

The third appealing feature of this outcome is that, even without a central planner, the outcome coincides with what a perfect, all-knowing planner would do if one really could perform such a job. If the planner actually had all the data and the computer ability to do a perfect job of planning, then it would end up replicating this competitive outcome.

Here is why a planner can do no better. In a competitive economy, consumers go about their selfish ways obeying the optimal purchase rule — making their purchases so that

marginal utility equals price (MU = P).

Firms know nothing about these people's tastes directly, just as households know nothing about the production processes of the firms. The firms just selfishly go about setting their output decisions so that

price equals marginal cost (P = MC),

because doing so is in their best private interests. But since the price that the firms receive and the price that the households pay are the same thing, we have

marginal utility equals marginal cost (MU = MC),

even though no firm or household has attempted to ensure this outcome.

The outcome of marginal utility equals marginal cost is exactly what a perfect planner would want to achieve, because a planner must keep expanding any industry for which the extra benefit that somebody in society receives from the last unit produced is greater than the value of the resources that the economy used to produce that last unit. But further expansion drives up marginal cost, which is the value of the forgone resources, and drives down marginal utility, which is the extra benefit that someone receives from consuming the last unit. Thus, the planner's rule is marginal utility equals marginal cost, and that is automatically satisfied in a competitive economy.

Economists use the optimal planner's rule as a benchmark against which to judge all departures from the competitive ideal. We say that any industry for which marginal cost is greater than marginal utility is overexpanded. Similarly, if marginal utility is greater than marginal cost, we say that we do not have enough of that activity occurring. This theme is pursued in the next several chapters. As you will see, by viewing varied issues such as monopoly and pollution as examples of the same generic problem (a gap between marginal utility and marginal cost), economists have developed a unified approach to problems of economic policy.

But why do economists want a system that can replicate a perfect planning outcome? Why not just adopt a centrally planned system in the first place?

THE ROLE OF GOVERNMENT

To appreciate how impossible efficient **central planning** is, consider an economy with just three goods: steel, coal, and electricity. To set the output levels of these industries efficiently, the planner needs at least twelve pieces of data. First, the planner must know people's tastes to determine the desirable amounts of the three goods to be made available to consumers. Second, the planner must know how much coal is needed to produce each unit of coal itself, each unit of electricity, and each unit of steel; then how much electricity is needed to produce each unit of coal, electricity, and steel (and so on); and there are three times three or nine data requirements here.

Now consider an economy with a million items, and this is still a gross underestimate of the number of different products available in the real world (think of all the different sizes of nuts and bolts and how useless these items are unless they are properly matched). For this economy, there are one million times one million, or one trillion, pieces of data for the planner to collect! That a competitive *de*centralized system can replicate the job of an all-knowing planner without anybody having to collect all this information and know how to use it is a *very* powerful result. There seems to be little option but to try making our actual economy approach this competitive ideal.

Given that so many countries have tried and rejected central planning, there seems to be fairly strong support for the strategy of trying to fix what a market system does poorly, rather than giving up on the market completely, as a planned system does. This is the approach adopted for the remainder of this book.

We have just spent several chapters extolling the virtues of the market. Back in Chapter 2, we learned how attempts to "repeal" the laws of supply and demand through legislation can backfire. In Chapters 3 and 4, we explored the logic behind supply and demand curves so that the invisible hand feature of markets can be appreciated. It is fully understood that — with countless thousands of people involved in the production and distribution of items and with no central co-ordinators — we can buy things such as high-quality cameras and food from anywhere in the world at such low prices.

The market system works on the basis of *voluntary exchange* among *self-interested* individuals. But we must remember that, just because self-interest removes the need for central planning, voluntary exchange works well only if there is a well-defined system of property rights, reliable information, and effective methods of communication. Government is still needed to provide and enforce the fundamental institutions that meet these needs: a legal and judicial system and basic infrastructure. So, while it is important to appreciate the market's strengths, we must also appreciate its limitations. Since we have just spent four chapters focusing on the market's positive features, this balance will be provided by our devoting the next four chapters to considering some of the market's shortcomings. Each problem stems from the fact that there are differences between the competitive ideal and the real world. Some firms have market power, many individuals have less than complete information, it can be impossible to establish private ownership for some goods, some production methods create pollution, and some individuals may be unable to secure employment or an adequate income. All these issues are discussed in the next four chapters. Then, in case you have forgotten the positive side of the debate, we will end the microeconomics half of the book with an analysis of free trade.

SUMMARY

Here is a review of some of the key concepts covered in this chapter. We have derived the **short-run supply curve** for a **competitive industry**, and we have seen what determines **long-run equilibrium**. We used these concepts to provide a more detailed account of the **invisible hand**. We identified some of the desirable features of this competitive outcome, one of which is that it duplicates what an efficient **central planning** system tries to achieve — that is, to have **marginal utility equal marginal cost** for each commodity. We saw why efficient central planning is impossible.

In the next chapter, we will consider industries in which competitive forces do not exist — a situation that we call **monopoly**. We will evaluate government attempts to regulate monopolies and to control their behaviour through the Competition Act.

SUGGESTIONS FOR FURTHER READING

R. Barro, *Getting It Right: Markets and Choices in a Free Society* (Cambridge, MA: MIT Press, 1996) — challenges those committed to government as the solution to many problems.

T.G. Buchholz, *New Ideas from Dead Economists* (New York: Penguin, 1990), Chapter 6.

R. Douglas, *Unfinished Business* (Auckland, New Zealand: Random House, 1993) — a detailed account of New Zealand's abrupt shift to free market principles in the 1980s.

M. Friedman, *Capitalism and Freedom* (Chicago: University of Chicago Press, 1953) — a classic defence of free markets.

WEB ACTIVITIES

www.ebrd.com
The Web site of the European Bank for Reconstruction and Development, an institution developed for easing the transition from central planning to the market; see the *Annual Transition Report.*

www.fraserinstitute.ca
The Web site of the Fraser Institute; numerous publications from a conservative institute dedicated to free markets and smaller government.

www.policyalternatives.ca
The Web site of the Canadian Centre for Policy Alternatives, a group that advocates a larger role for government and more income equality; each year the centre posts its *Alternative Federal Budget.*

CHAPTER SIX
Monopoly

LEARNING OBJECTIVES

After reading this chapter, you should understand
- how government-created monopolies can hurt consumers without helping producers;

- why taxing a monopolist can simultaneously reduce profits and worsen the inefficient allocation of resources; and
- why it is difficult to regulate a natural monopolist.

INTRODUCTION

In the previous two chapters, we saw what the market system does well. The basic message was that, if there are many buyers and sellers for each commodity, then competition forces firms to arrange society's scarce resources in just the way that a perfect planner would, without any need for the impossible calculations that central planning involves. But in some industries in our economy there are not many firms, so there is limited competition. This lack of competition is the problem we explore in this chapter. We focus on the extreme case that economists call monopoly — a situation in which there is only one seller of a commodity. In the next chapter, we will consider an intermediate case, oligopoly — competition among just a few firms.

There are two ways in which a monopoly can develop: through deliberate government policy and (without government intervention) through one private firm taking over all competitors through a series of mergers. We start by considering a common form of government-created monopoly — a marketing board.

MARKETING BOARDS

Some of the most competitive industries that we could have in Canada are in the farming sector. For example, consider the egg industry, in which there is a large number of farms, each producing a homogeneous product. For years we have had provincial marketing boards for eggs and other products. All producers within a province must sell their eggs to the marketing board. The board then acts as a monopolist and sells the eggs to the rest of the community, after making sure that it withholds enough supply to keep the price up. The rationale is to raise the income of farmers.

Figure 6.1 clarifies how a marketing board works. Initially, we assume perfect competition. In the industry part of the graph (the right-hand panel), demand and supply intersect to determine the going market price. This price

FIGURE 6.1

A Marketing Board

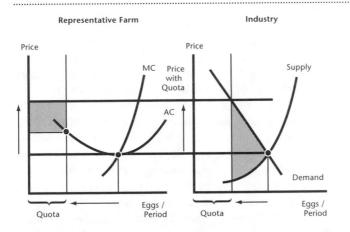

is taken as given by each farmer, who is pictured in long-run equilibrium in the left-hand panel of Figure 6.1.

Now suppose a marketing board is created, and it assigns a quota to each producer that limits output. In the overall industry, with the total number of eggs being reduced by the quota, market price rises by a large amount. Each firm (farm) is allowed to sell eggs at this price per unit, but each farm is limited by its share of the overall quota.

Total revenue is the new high price shown in Figure 6.1 times the number of units allowed by the quota. This revenue is represented by the area below the high price line and to the left of the quota line in the left-hand panel of Figure 6.1. Total cost is the cost per unit (given by the intersection of the average cost curve with the quota line) times the same number of units allowed by the quota. Total revenue exceeds total cost by an amount given by the shaded rectangle in Figure 6.1. Thus, with the marketing board, each farmer makes positive economic profit equal to the shaded rectangle each period.

This outcome is bad for consumers because they get less output at higher prices. In the competitive outcome without the marketing board, society obtained this good at the lowest conceivable price since each farm operated at the minimum possible point on its average cost curve. That was an efficient outcome. Now we see that, by producing fewer units through the monopoly selling arrangement, average cost is higher than its minimum point. So, from society's point of view, a monopoly of this kind is less efficient than a perfectly competitive industry. Also, it causes equity concerns as poor people pay more for food to increase the profits of farmers.

Another way of appreciating this inefficiency is by focusing on consumer and producer surplus. Society loses the amount of eggs indicated by the arrow along the quantity axis in the right-hand panel of Figure 6.1 each period as a result of the quota policy. The area under the consumers' demand curve for the product is their willingness to pay for the output that they are no longer getting to consume. So the total loss to consumers due to this restriction on the rate of output is the whole area under the demand curve over that range of output. But society has saved some resources by curtailing the output in this industry, and the area under the marginal cost curve (over this range of output) is the value of the alternative uses of these resources. So society gains the area under the marginal cost curve. But society's loss (the area under the demand curve) exceeds society's gain (the area under the marginal cost curve) by the shaded triangular area in the right-hand panel in Figure 6.1. This area is the annual net loss to society of having the marketing board.

This loss each year is what convinces many policy analysts that marketing boards should be eliminated. While acknowledging this inefficiency, others defend the policy since they believe that income redistribution toward farmers is good. That is, they support the policy on the ground that this equity gain is worth the loss in efficiency. But is there really a redistribution to farmers? The answer is "yes," but only to those farmers who were in operation when the marketing board was originally established.

The reason is that the quota — the right to sell a specified number of eggs — was originally given to each farmer in the industry at the time. This quota has a value, and it can be bought and sold. It adds to the value of what the farmers own in the same way that a house or barn does. For new producers to enter the industry at a later date, they must buy both a farm and a quota. The additional payment for the quota raises the fixed costs (but not the marginal costs) for the new entrant. Competition among new entrants to acquire the above-normal profits forces the price of the quota (and therefore fixed costs and the position of the average cost curve) to increase to the point that the average cost curve cuts through the intersection of the quota line and the going market price line. Once this has occurred, the excess profits are completely eliminated. In full *long-run* equilibrium, then, farmers (as producers) gain nothing from the marketing board. All that it creates is a once-and-for-all capital gain for the original set of quota owners.

MONOPOLY WITHOUT GOVERNMENT INTERVENTION

A marketing board is a monopoly that could not have existed without government intervention. Now we consider a monopoly that exists without legislation to see whether government intervention can improve the outcome from the consumers' point of view. We focus first on the demand curve of a monopolist.

With a complete monopoly, there is only one seller of a commodity. This means that there is no distinction between the demand curve for the entire industry and the demand curve for the product for that one firm. The downward-sloping demand curve means that, to get people to voluntarily purchase a bigger quantity of the good each period, the monopolist must reduce the price on all units of the product that are sold, since in most cases the mo-

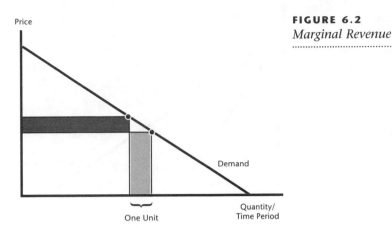

FIGURE 6.2
Marginal Revenue

nopolist cannot separate one buyer from another. This means that, when the firm increases its output, the extra revenue that comes in is less than the market price.

To see this, we focus on the demand curve in Figure 6.2. Suppose the firm considers increasing output and sales by the one unit shown in Figure 6.2. The extra revenue obtained is not just the lightly shaded rectangle on the right, whose height is the going market price. To get the extra sale, the firm has to reduce the price a bit, so it loses a bit of revenue on all the other units already being sold at the higher price. This loss in revenue is shown in Figure 6.2 by the flat but wide dark grey rectangle. The net additional revenue, what economists call marginal revenue from increasing sales by this one unit, is the going market price (the lighter grey rectangle) minus the little bit of lost revenue on all the other sales (the darker grey rectangle). So marginal revenue is less than price, and it can even be negative.

The gap by which marginal revenue is less than price is larger at higher levels of output. If the firm increases output just above zero, the dark grey rectangle hardly exists; however, as the firm moves to the right in the graph, the dark grey rectangle becomes large, and the light grey rectangle becomes ever smaller. This means that the marginal revenue line is almost as high as the demand curve near the zero sales level, but it falls farther and farther below the demand curve at larger and larger levels of sales, as shown in Figure 6.3.

HOW A MONOPOLIST OPERATES

Now we combine these marginal revenue and demand curves with the marginal and average cost curves we derived in Chapter 4. All four curves are shown in Figure 6.4. We learned in previous chapters that any activity should be expanded up to the point at which the marginal benefits are just balanced

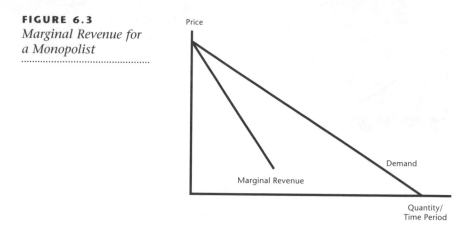

FIGURE 6.3
Marginal Revenue for a Monopolist
....

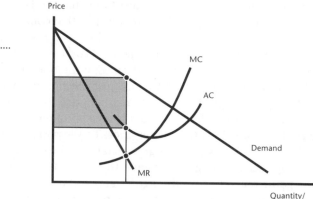

FIGURE 6.4
Profit Maximization with Monopoly
....

by the marginal cost of expanding the activity. In the monopolist's case, the marginal benefits are the additional revenue as shown by the marginal revenue line, and the additional costs are given by the marginal cost curve. So the profit-maximizing rate of output is given by the intersection of marginal revenue and marginal cost, and this level of output is highlighted in Figure 6.4. A vertical line drawn in at this level of output is extended up to the demand curve to see households' maximum willingness to pay for this quantity. The monopolist charges this price. Even though a monopolist has no competitors and could charge an even higher price, it will not do so. If it did, people would buy less, and the firm would operate at a level that generates lower profits.

The height up to the demand curve is the revenue per unit that the firm receives, and the height up to the average cost curve is the cost per unit. The gap between these two heights is the profit per unit, and since the firm is earning this profit per unit on each unit, the shaded rectangle represents the total profits earned. The economic reasoning that we have just used, that profit-maximizing output is given by the intersection of the marginal cost and marginal revenue curves, is the same as we used to analyze perfect competition. The only difference is that, for the monopolist, the marginal revenue and demand curves are distinct.

THE INVISIBLE HAND BREAKS DOWN WITH MONOPOLY

In the previous chapter, we saw that the invisible hand works well in a competitive environment. In that case, consumer tastes were the ultimate authority in deciding the allocation of society's scarce resources. But without competition, a monopolist does not have to serve consumer interests so directly.

Recall that the invisible hand relies on three things:

1) that self-interest leads households to arrange their purchases so that marginal utility equals price:

$$MU = P;$$

2) that self-interest leads firms to set output so that marginal revenue equals marginal cost:

$$MR = MC;$$

3) and that for competitive firms marginal revenue and price are the same:

$$MR = P.$$

These relationships imply that marginal utility equals marginal cost:

$$MU = MC.$$

Thus, for the last unit produced of any good, the additional benefit for someone in society is just equal to the value of the resources that society has to use up to produce it.

When a good is produced and sold by a monopolist, households still set marginal utility equal to price:

$$MU = P;$$

and the firm still sets marginal revenue equal to marginal cost:

$$MR = MC.$$

But since price exceeds marginal revenue,

$P > MR$,

the three relationships imply that marginal utility is greater than marginal cost:

$MU > MC$.

Society gets too little of any good produced by a monopoly since at the margin, society values that commodity at an amount greater than the value of the resources needed to produce it.

We can see this result by comparing the output for which $MR = MC$ with the output for which $MC = P$ in Figure 6.5. Marginal utility exceeds marginal cost at the monopoly output, and the net loss to society of keeping output below the social optimum is (as with a marketing board) the shaded area. Consumers lose the trapezoid under the demand curve, but some resources are saved when the monopolist operates at a lower rate of output, and the saving is the area under the marginal cost curve. The net loss to society is the shaded triangular area. This loss is incurred every period.

We refer to this loss as the *efficiency* aspect of the monopoly problem. The other element of monopoly, which we call the *equity* aspect of the monopoly problem, is the fact that above-normal profits (the economic profits shown in Figure 6.4) are being earned. Some individuals are uncomfortable with the knowledge that others are earning above-normal profits, especially in the case of a monopoly, in which no new entrants may appear to compete away these profits. Also, the existence of the above-normal profits can lead to a further waste of resources. Individuals become tempted to engage in takeover battles and lobbying efforts as they compete to become the ones

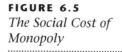

FIGURE 6.5
The Social Cost of Monopoly

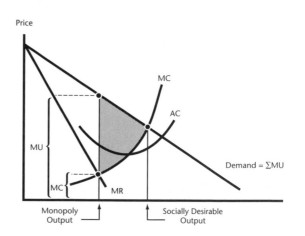

who receive this extra income. This so-called **rent seeking** involves labour being diverted from productive activities (which could create more goods) toward those that are unproductive from society's point of view (since they involve fighting over the goods that already exist).

What can a policy-maker do about these problems? Some people think that the answer is obvious — just tax the monopolist. If all we are concerned about is the equity problem, then a tax might be fine. For instance, if we impose an excise tax on the sales of this good, then it will shift both the marginal cost and the average cost curves up by the amount of the tax, successfully taking away some of the monopolist's profits. But, as can be seen in *Excise* Figure 6.6, this makes the profit-maximizing rate of output occur even farther to the left. The loss of efficiency increases from just the dark grey area to the sum of both darkly and lightly shaded areas in Figure 6.6. Thus, the trouble with using an excise tax to reduce a monopolist's profits is that, while making progress on the equity dimension of the monopoly problem, we worsen the efficiency aspect of the monopoly problem.

The result is quite different if we impose a licence fee on a monopolist. *Licence* In this case, the tax adds to fixed costs, so the average cost curve shifts up, while the marginal cost curve does not. The size of the profit rectangle is reduced, while the size of the efficiency loss triangle is not increased. Thus, if it were not for the fact that higher fixed costs create a bigger barrier to entry for would-be competitors, a licence fee is an effective tool for reducing monopoly profits.

Because excise taxes worsen the efficiency dimension of the monopoly problem, and because licence fees make it harder for new firms to enter an industry to compete with a monopolist, public policy-makers have considered other approaches, such as direct government regulation of monopolies and the passing of the Canadian Competition Act. But before we evaluate these policy measures, it must be emphasized that all we have considered

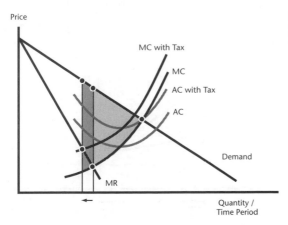

FIGURE 6.6
Taxing a Monopolist

about monopoly so far is how the firm's demand curve differs from that of a perfect competitor. As we will see in the next section, it is possible that the structure of production costs differ for monopolists as well.

One final point concerning the revenue side of a monopolist's operations is worth noting. The firm can make more profit than is illustrated in Figure 6.4 if it can keep buyers separated from one another. If separation is possible, then the firm can sell at different prices to different buyers — charging a high price to individuals who have an intense desire to consume the product and a lower price to others. This is called **price discrimination**. A discriminating monopolist is able to capture part of what would otherwise be consumer surplus. A perfectly discriminating monopolist would charge every buyer her maximum willingness to pay — totally eliminating consumer surplus. No monopolist can price-discriminate to this extent, but many firms vary the sizes of their items to accomplish a significant degree of price discrimination. For example, the "economy" box of laundry detergent that is twice the size of the "family" box sells for less than double the price of the latter. The lower price per gram is then offered only to a subset of the market.

THE COST CURVES OF A MONOPOLIST

Often an industry becomes monopolized because there are large fixed costs involved. Think of the major monopolies in our economy, such as a public utility like the electricity system. Such operations involve major set-up costs to get the grid of wires in place and rather low (basically constant) marginal costs to add new users to the network. The large fixed cost makes it very difficult for a new entrant to come into the industry in a step-by-step fashion.

This typical cost structure is shown in Figure 6.7. There is a low and constant marginal cost curve, and an average cost curve that starts off high because there is a large fixed-cost component. The average cost curve becomes

FIGURE 6.7
A Natural Monopoly

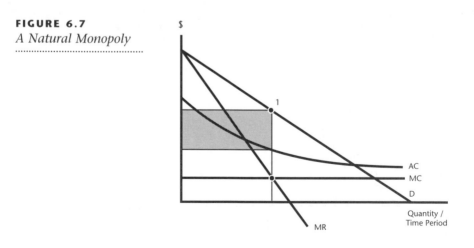

lower and lower as output increases, because the fixed cost is spread over more and more units to calculate average cost. And it never turns up because the marginal cost is constant.

This pattern of costs creates what is called a **natural monopoly** — a situation in which average cost falls over the entire range of output. Once such a firm becomes large, it can underprice all smaller would-be competitors and become, or remain, a monopolist.

Broadly speaking, there are three approaches to coping with monopoly power. One is to have direct government **regulation** of monopoly, as we used to have in the airline industry. A second is to rely on prosecutions through our **Competition Act**. And the third is to rely on the discipline imposed by **foreign competition** when free trade is allowed. We consider each alternative in turn, discussing regulation and the Competition Act in this chapter, and free trade in Chapter 10.

REGULATION OF MONOPOLY: THE THEORY

What are the pros and cons of regulating natural monopolies? Until the 1980s, many people thought that regulation was a good idea, but since then many analysts are less convinced. We now consider this debate.

Before we use our graphs to evaluate a policy of government regulation of natural monopoly, we should remind ourselves where a monopolist would operate without any regulation. As before, the intersection of marginal revenue and marginal cost determines the profit-maximizing rate of output if the firm is not subject to any regulation. We extend this line up to the demand curve, to point 1 in Figure 6.7, to get the profit-maximizing price. Revenue per unit is that price, and cost per unit is the height up to the average cost curve. So profit per unit is the height of the shaded rectangle, and total profits earned by the unregulated monopolist are represented by the shaded area.

Compare this outcome with the most efficient outcome from society's point of view, that given by MU = MC. Since the demand curve shows marginal utility, it would be efficient for production to be expanded all the way to the point where the demand curve crosses marginal cost at point 2 in Figure 6.8. With this much more output, society would achieve extra satisfaction equal to the area under the demand curve between points 1 and 2, and society would incur extra cost equal to the area under the marginal cost curve over this range of output. Thus, the shaded triangle in Figure 6.8 is the extra net benefits that society is throwing away by letting the monopolist maximize its profits in an unregulated fashion.

It is appealing to set up a regulatory board that can collect data and then require that this firm not charge a price any higher than its marginal costs. The problem is that this policy cannot force a firm to operate at the socially optimal point. To see why, consider how much profit the firm would earn if it actually operated at point 2. This is shown in Figure 6.9. The price per unit would be the height up to the demand curve, while the cost per unit would

FIGURE 6.8
*Inefficiency with
No Regulation*

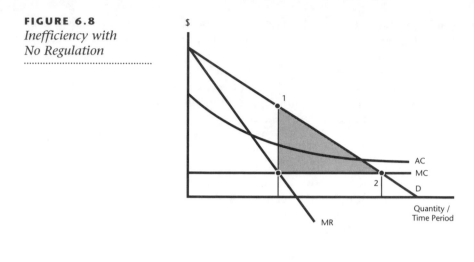

FIGURE 6.9
*Regulation with
Marginal-Cost Pricing*

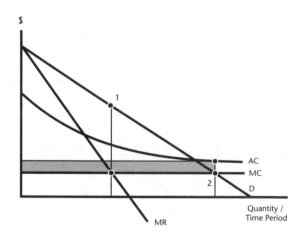

be the height up to the average cost curve, which is higher. So there would be a loss per unit equal to the difference between these two heights. Multiplied over the total number of units, total losses equal the shaded rectangle if we regulate the monopolist in this way. Clearly, this monopolist will not stay in business only to suffer these regulation-induced losses. With this regulation policy, this firm will quit the industry, and society will get none of this commodity.

The general approach in the history of regulation is to try to push the firm as much from point 1 toward point 2 as possible without forcing the firm out of business. With this goal in mind, we can go no farther than the point where the average cost curve intersects the demand curve, because at this point, point 3 in Figure 6.10, the height up to the demand curve and the height up to the average cost curve are equal, making economic profits zero.

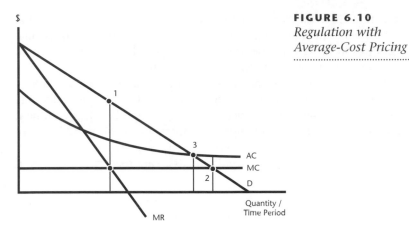

FIGURE 6.10
*Regulation with
Average-Cost Pricing*
···

So essentially regulators have tried to calculate which price would yield the firm a "fair" rate of return — a profit rate equal to what can be earned in competitive industries — and to impose the corresponding regulation on price. Thus, trying for point 3 through regulation is a compromise, getting as close to point 2 as we can without driving the firm out of business.

REGULATION OF MONOPOLY: THE EXPERIENCE

There are two issues that the basic theory of regulation overlooks: that the process of regulation may affect the monopolist's productivity and that the monopolist may be able to limit the technical information that the regulator acquires, with the result that regulation may actually further the monopolist's own interests. We will consider each issue in turn.

What does regulation do for the firm's incentive to invest in cost-saving technology? Normally, firms invest in new techniques to lower costs and thus create extra profits. But if regulation pushes down the allowable price every time costs are reduced, then the firm will get no payoff from investing in cost-saving techniques. One way that our policy-makers have tried to limit this low-productivity problem is to permit patents. Another is to have a lag in the regulatory process. The lag is intended to be long enough to make it worthwhile for the firm to invest in new technology but not so long that the small group of individuals who are the majority shareholders of these firms can reap vast profits.

Have regulators become captives of the regulated firms? The best way to answer this question is to see what happened during the process of deregulation during the 1980s. In many deregulated industries, the number of firms increased and prices fell. According to Figure 6.10, the removal of regulation is supposed to cause a move from point 3 back up to point 1. That prices fell with the removal of regulation can mean only one of two things. First, it could mean that the cost savings that come from new investment, and that are ignored in basic theory of regulation, are substantial and that the regulatory process was limiting this investment to a large extent. Second, it could mean that many of the industries that were regulated were not natural monopolies at all. This second explanation is supported by the fact that many new firms entered a number of the deregulated industries. What really may have happened with regulation, then, is that it provided a government agency that served the monopoly, not consumers, by keeping out new entrants and keeping prices high. The result of this experience is that many economists are now sceptical about regulation as an approach to competition policy.

THE COMPETITION ACT

The second approach to monopoly problems, which also has a long history, is to pass laws such as our Competition Act. This legislation defines many business practices, such as rigging prices and misleading advertising, as unlawful. Ever since 1889, Canada has had some form of the Competition Act, but these laws have had limited accomplishments. For one thing, the fines have been trivial compared with the benefits that firms could derive from breaking the law. A second problem was that early interpretations of the act set the precedent that a guilty verdict was warranted only if competition was completely eliminated, not just lessened. A third problem was that the act was part of the criminal code, not the civil code. Since a conviction under the criminal code requires no reasonable doubt and the courts have limited knowledge concerning particular industries, there frequently was some reasonable doubt, and convictions were rare.

There was a major revision of the Competition Act in 1986. Fines and prison terms for company executives were made much stiffer, and many offences were transferred to the more flexible civil code of law, involving a new competition tribunal to replace the standard courts. The authority of the tribunal was challenged in a series of Supreme Court cases; however, since the government won all these cases in the early 1990s, many economists have recently acquired a renewed but cautious optimism concerning this legal approach to competition policy.

SUMMARY

Here is a review of the key concepts covered in this chapter. We have studied how the invisible hand breaks down when competition is limited. We discussed **monopoly** and saw that it results in **inefficiency**. When monopoly is government-created, as with **marketing boards**, inefficiency can be eliminated by dismantling the marketing board. With a **natural monopoly**, however, it is very difficult to eliminate inefficiency. There are three ways of trying to do so. First, we can have government **regulation** of the monopoly;

second, we can apply the **Competition Act** through the courts and the competition tribunal; and, third, competition can be enforced by dropping tariffs to permit new market entrants from other countries.

Given the limited success of regulation and the legal approach to monopoly problems, many economists favour relying on the discipline of the market — which can be made more effective through free trade. (See Chapter 10.) But before examining this alternative, we will consider oligopoly — a market structure that lies between the extremes of perfect competition and complete monopoly — and will look at other reasons why free markets can fail to operate efficiently.

SUGGESTIONS FOR FURTHER READING

W. Block and G. Lermer, *Breaking the Shackles: Deregulating Canadian Industry* (Vancouver: Fraser Institute, 1989) — essays on the history of business regulation in Canada.

F. Mathewson, M. Trebilcock, and M. Walker, *The Law and Economics of Competition Policy* (Vancouver: Fraser Institute, 1990) — essays on the history of competition policy in Canada.

D. McFetridge, *The Economics of Privatization* (Toronto: C.D. Howe Institute, 1997) — an analysis of the privatization of government monopolies.

WEB ACTIVITIES

www.ct-tc.gc.ca
The Web site of the competition tribunal; full details of recent cases concerning monopolistic business practices.

CHAPTER SEVEN

Co-ordination Failure and Incomplete Information

LEARNING OBJECTIVES

After reading this chapter, you should understand
- how game theory can determine the best way to react in uncertain environments;
- why firms offer incentives for high worker productivity and why this practice generates unemployment; and

- why institutions that help us to deal with uncertainty represent incomplete solutions: insurance involves problems of adverse selection and moral hazard, and the median voter can dominate choices in the public sector.

INTRODUCTION

Monopoly is not the only reason why markets operate imperfectly; problems also occur when individuals or firms have incomplete information. One simple example can illustrate the general problem. Consider two candidates — one male and one female — applying for a job. Both are married, and neither plans to have children. As a result, neither candidate plans to withdraw from the labour force for any period during his or her career. However, the employer knows that statistically there is a higher probability of career interruptions for child care with female employees. As a result, there is a bigger risk that the employer's investment in training will not pay off to the same degree with the female candidate. Hence, the male candidate is offered the job, and the female applicant suffers from what is called statistical discrimination. Competition among employers does not eliminate this discrimination, since all employers read the same statistical studies concerning child care. Individual women cannot convince employers that the statistical regularity does not apply to them.

In this chapter, we will see how incomplete information complicates the operation of both product and labour markets and how various institutions — including government — may help us to deal with uncertainty.

STRATEGIC BEHAVIOUR

	BG	B NG
AG	2,2	-4, 6
ArG	6,4	0,0

A major source of uncertainty for many firms is how competitors may react to their initiatives. Such strategic reactions can be ignored when a firm has no competitors (pure monopoly) or when it is too small to affect others (pure competition). But with a small number of firms in an industry, each firm must try to guess the reactions of the others before it can even begin to guess what the demand function for its own output will be. The MR = MC rule for profit maximization is of little use if MR cannot be calculated. Economists use a tool called **game theory** to explore the implications of this uncertain environment. As we shall see, the "players" in the game often end up in a wasteful outcome. The reasons for this co-ordination failure are best clarified with a simple example involving households, not firms.

Consider the behaviour of two individuals, A and B, trying to limit crime in their neighbourhood. Each individual knows that crime can be reduced by giving money to charity, and each knows that the payoff from the donation will depend on whether the neighbour contributes as well. Suppose that, if both neighbours give $10 to charity, crime falls by an amount that each homeowner regards as equivalent to an increase in income of $12. The net payoff for each individual is $2 in this case. But if just one neighbour makes a $10 contribution, only half the crime is eliminated, so the net benefit drops to the equivalent of $6 for the neighbour who makes no contribution to charity and to ($6 – 10), or –$4, for the individual who does. If neither individual gives to charity, there is no cost or benefit for either individual compared with the status quo. Since both individuals can either give to charity or not, there are four possible outcomes, as summarized in Table 7.1.

B can determine her optimal strategy by considering the table. She reasons as follows: "If A gives to charity, it is better for me not to give — since I prefer a $6 return to a $2 one. If A does not give to charity, it is still better for me not to give — since a zero return beats a loss of $4." A reasons in the same way, so neither individual makes a contribution. The two-person society is caught in an inferior outcome. Everyone would be better off if the fourth line in the table emerged as the equilibrium instead of the first line. The inferior outcome is referred to as a **prisoner's dilemma**. Both "players" in the "game" are driven to the inferior outcome since both are prisoners of their inability to trust the other player.

In this example, we would expect the individuals to stop playing the game and to co-operate instead. It would be easy for both individuals to verify that the other did, in fact, follow through on a promise to give to charity. But with many individuals in a large community, it is impossible to "police"

TABLE 7.1 *The Payoff Matrix for Charitable Donations*

A's Options	*B's Options*	*A's Net Payoff*	*B's Net Payoff*
no charity	no charity	0	0
no charity	gives to charity	+$6	–$4
gives to charity	no charity	–$4	+$6
gives to charity	gives to charity	+$2	+$2

such an agreement. As a result, most individuals support the proposition that a free market in charitable donations results in "too little" charity, and they support some government redistribution through taxes and transfers.

OLIGOPOLY

Now let us apply game theory to firms instead of households. **Oligopoly** means competition among the few, and it is a fairly common market structure. To keep things simple, we consider an industry that contains just two firms. One option is that they can co-operate by setting the monopoly price and sharing the profits. The other option is that they can cheat on the agreement by offering price discounts. If one firm maintains the high price, discounting by the other pulls most of the customers to it, and profits for the firm that offers discounts are highest in this case. But if both firms discount, most of the monopoly profits are eliminated, and both firms lose. Clearly, the table given above could apply to this interaction if the "gives to charity" and "no charity" labels were changed to "honours the price-fixing agreement" and "offers discounts," respectively. So these firms are caught in a prisoner's dilemma as well, and this is why many price-fixing cartels break down. All participants have a powerful incentive to cheat on the agreement. This co-ordination failure is good news for consumers, but clever firms look for ways to avoid this outcome.

There is a way out — as long as the game is *repeated for many periods*. In this case, firms find it profitable to pursue a strategy that can alter the options for the other player. One option is for one firm to announce that it will play a "tit-for-tat" strategy by promising always to do whatever the other player did in the previous period. Let us use the table to explore the implications of this announcement. Suppose the players have been co-operating (each receiving $2 each period). Player B considers cheating. If she does, she will receive $6 in the first period; she is better off by $4. But then A will cheat as well the next period, so B will get zero every period thereafter. A net gain of $4 for just one period is not worth a loss of $2 every period for many periods, so B would reject this strategy. What about cheating for one period and then co-operating again thereafter? This strategy brings $6 in the first period, then –$4 in the second period (while A cheats), and then the standard $2 each period again. Temporarily cheating brings ($6 – 4), or $2, for the first two periods, while never cheating brings ($2 + 2), or $4, in the first two periods. In short, A's promise forces B not to cheat. Given that the promise "works," there would never be any reason for A to renege on the promise, so it is a credible one.

So the key to avoiding co-ordination failure is that players must make credible threats. But how can this be done when formal price-fixing agreements are ruled out by competition laws? One way is by making a promise to customers — not to competitors. Firms often promise that they will "meet the competition," making it impossible for the other firms to steal customers by dropping prices. With the "I cheat, but my competitor does not" option eliminated, firms do not cheat. Individual consumers often interpret such **lowest price guarantees** as evidence that the market is operating competitively. But this is far from the truth. In fact, when they bring news of a discount at another firm, individual consumers are acting as zero-cost police for the industry. They are the agents who maintain the collusive arrangement.

Game theory is also useful for understanding why some firms choose to operate with **excess capacity**. The direct effect of building too big a factory is that profits are lower than they would otherwise be. But as a defensive strategy, the big plant can still make sense. The firm wants to threaten others that are contemplating entry to this industry — a threat such as "I'll increase my production and flood the market — to drop prices — if you enter." Faced with such a threat, would-be entrants could not recoup their entry costs. Is such a threat credible? Yes, but only if the firm has the excess capacity in place.

What general conclusion can we draw from our application of game theory to product markets? On the one hand, the message seems to be that some competition may be no better than pure monopoly. Given incomplete information concerning competitors' reactions in an oligopoly, firms may waste (from society's point of view) scarce resources in excess capacity. On the other hand, game theory suggests that even a monopolist may be forced to act competitively. Even when there is only one firm in an industry, there is another "player" in the game, since entry by others is often feasible at relatively low cost. Given the threat of entry at low cost, the monopolist finds it in her selfish interest to limit monopoly profits to an amount that just keeps the other player (the potential entrants) out of the market. Economists call such a situation a **contestable market**, and they regard such markets as approximately competitive. This analysis suggests that free trade is a good policy for promoting competition. The threat of entry from more (foreign) firms makes the apparently uncompetitive domestic markets more contestable.

One final remark concerning strategic behaviour is worth making. It is often wise for individuals to be unpredictable, and this fact can be appreciated by considering a tennis match. Player A's forehand is more reliable than his backhand. Without thinking too deeply, player B decides to make all shots to A's backhand. But A can anticipate this strategy and, by always moving quickly to that side, do very well returning B's shots. Of course, B can figure this reaction out as well and can try an alternative strategy — making all shots to A's forehand. But A will quickly adjust his style to make this a silly strategy as well. B must adopt what is called a **randomized strategy** so that the higher probability of his playing to A's backhand on each return just balances the higher probability that A returns the ball successfully on his forehand.

The lesson of this section of the chapter is that the invisible hand breaks down when market participants find themselves in a strategic relationship with each other. In most instances, social welfare is decreased by the existence of uncertainty. And we cannot expect the market to solve this problem on its own since, as we have just seen, the pursuit of private interest often favours a randomized strategy, and this behaviour *creates* uncertainty.

CO-ORDINATION FAILURE IN THE LABOUR MARKET

We now shift our focus from product markets to labour markets. We find that incomplete information leads to market failure here as well, in the form of unemployment. Here is one scenario that illustrates how co-ordination between employers and employees breaks down. In a complicated production environment, it is very difficult for supervisors to know which workers are operating with a low level of effort. For one thing, often group output alone can be objectively measured; for another, it is impossible to verify whether individual employees can be believed when they call in sick. In these cases, there is *asymmetric information*; only the worker knows whether he or she is shirking duties; the employer does not.

Firms can lessen this worker-productivity problem by making it more expensive for employees to lose their jobs. By paying a wage that exceeds the worker's alternative option, the employer can ensure that its employees work hard to avoid being fired. In a sentence, "a happy worker is a good worker." But when all firms raise payments in this way, the overall level of wages exceeds what would obtain in a purely competitive market. With labour more expensive, firms hire fewer workers in total, and there is unemployment. Unemployment exists because there is only one market price (the wage rate), and there are two markets that require an adjustment in that price to reach equilibrium. There is the market for individuals wanting work, and there is the market for the amount of effort devoted by each worker while on the job. The asymmetric nature of the information forces firms to rely on the wage to "clear" the effort-per-worker market, so the wage is not available to clear the workers' market. Again, the invisible hand breaks down; selfish profit maximization does not lead to full employment.

It is worthwhile formalizing this model of the labour market. Let w and x stand for the wage that a worker receives from her employer and what she can expect to receive if she leaves that firm. With the firm's incomplete monitoring process, the worker can be fired for shirking duties. She can reduce that probability by putting forth more effort, but this effort decreases the utility that she receives at work. Let fraction a times the wage represent the income equivalent of the loss in utility that stems from this extra effort on the job and the uncertainty concerning termination. With this notation, we can outline the situation as follows.

The worker faces two options: either she stays on the job with a net return of $(1 - a)w$, or she is fired, in which case she receives x. Firms will get

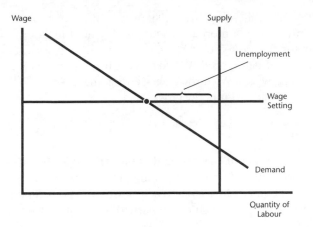

Wage

FIGURE 7.1
*Unemployment
Caused by Incomplete
Information*

solid efforts from workers as long as $(1 - a)w$ is greater than or equal to x. But in the interest of minimizing wage costs, firms do not want to meet this constraint with any unnecessary payment, so they set

$$w = x/(1 - a).$$

Since a is a fraction, this equation verifies the statement given in the previous paragraph: firms set wages above the workers' alternatives. Figure 7.1 shows the unemployment that results.

How is x, the workers' alternative, determined? Again there are two options. A fired worker may be employed by another firm (and the probability of this outcome is the economy's employment rate [1 − u]), or she may go without work (and the probability of this outcome is the unemployment rate u). In full equilibrium, all firms have to pay the same wages to keep their workers. Finally, for simplicity, let us assume that there is an employment insurance program that pays workers fraction f of their former wage if they are out of work. All this means that

$$x = (1 - u)w + u(fw).$$

When this definition of the alternative option is substituted into the wage-setting rule,

$$w = x/(1 - a),$$

the result can be simplified to

$$u = a/(1 - f).$$

This expression indicates that the co-ordination failure — the unemployment problem — is accentuated by a more generous employment insurance program (a higher value for f). The reason? More generous support for unemployment lowers the cost of being fired. Workers react by shirking duties more, so firms react by raising wages. With the wage-setting line in Figure 7.1 moving up, firms find it profitable to hire fewer workers.

UNEMPLOYMENT AND TAXES

Let us extend this model of the labour market to allow for the taxes that are necessary to finance employment insurance. We assume that wage income is taxed at rate t and that employment insurance receipts are not taxed. Since workers keep only proportion (1 – t) of each dollar earned on the job, the revised expressions are

$$w(1 - t)(1 - a) = x$$

and

$$x = (1 - u)w(1 - t) + u(fw).$$

These relationships lead to a revised expression for the unemployment rate:

$$u = a(1 - t)/(1 - f - t).$$

So the unemployment rate depends on the tax rate. Higher taxes lower the return from work. To counteract the resulting increased propensity of employees to shirk duties, firms raise wages, and fewer individuals find jobs.

An important insight can be gained by inserting representative numerical values for each term in the unemployment rate equation. Initially, let us assume a tax rate of 15 percent (t = 0.15), an unemployment support program that pays each former worker half of what she previously earned (f = 0.5), and a shirking parameter value (a = 0.02) that yields a representative value for unemployment of 5 percent (u = 0.05). Now we investigate how much the unemployment rate rises as the tax rate increases (and the other parameters, f and a, are fixed). As the tax rate rises by equal amounts, first from 15 to 25 percent and then from 25 to 35 percent, the unemployment rate rises, first by one percentage point, from 5 to 6 percent, and then by two and two-thirds percentage points, from 6 to 8.67 percent. Clearly, the unemployment rate rises much higher when taxes are already high.

This analysis shows that one does not need to be an extreme right-winger to support low tax rates. Advocates for the unemployed should be just as keen on achieving efficiency within government, since — by minimizing waste — important public services can be provided at lower tax rates. Without that efficiency, we face a discouraging trade-off: more social programs mean higher unemployment.

THE SECOND-BEST THEOREM

One final issue is well illustrated by this labour market analysis of co-ordination failure. Back in Chapter 1, we considered minimum wage laws in the context of a competitive labour market. A review of pages 9–11 will remind you that, in a competitive, full-information setting, no unemployment exists until the minimum wage is introduced. In short, minimum wage laws cause unemployment. We now ask whether the minimum wage receives such a negative verdict in a more complicated setting characterized by market power and incomplete information.

With some monopoly power in the product market, the firm faces a total revenue curve like that shown in Figure 7.2. With labour as the only variable factor, no fixed costs, and no market power in this input market, the labour cost curve is simply the straight line in Figure 7.2. The profit-maximizing level of employment is OA since that level generates the biggest gap between revenues and costs. If the firm is forced to pay a higher wage, through the introduction of a minimum wage law, then the labour cost line pivots up counterclockwise, and employment is pushed down as a result. Thus, monopoly power is not enough to threaten the earlier negative conclusion concerning minimum wages.

Quite a different outcome can emerge if the firm's labour cost relationship is a curved line, as shown in Figure 7.3. This curvature is plausible in a setting of incomplete information since the larger a firm's workforce, the larger the monitoring costs as a proportion of total labour costs. Without a minimum wage law, the firm chooses employment level OA. But with the minimum wage, the labour cost curve becomes ODFH, not

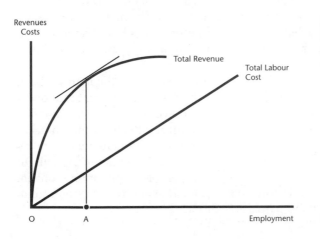

Revenues
Costs

Total Revenue

Total Labour
Cost

O   A   Employment

FIGURE 7.2
*Minimum Wage Laws
with Monopoly*

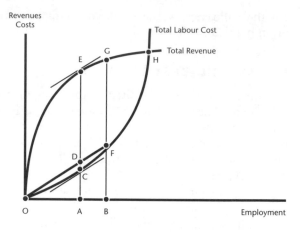

FIGURE 7.3
*Minimum Wage Laws
with Asymmetric
Information*
....

OCFH. The maximum profit gap could easily then be FG, so employment level OB is chosen. In this situation, then, the law can raise both wages and employment.

The intuition behind this more favourable verdict on minimum wages runs as follows. In perfect markets, what economists call a first-best situation, prices convey all the information that individuals and firms need to make decisions that, while selfishly motivated, turn out to serve the public interest. A minimum wage law distorts at least one of those market signals from what had been the "right" value. But when there are some other reasons for markets to be distorted in the first place, as is the case here with monopoly power and asymmetric information, some market price signals are "wrong" initially. It is then possible for "two wrongs to make a right." In this case, we welcome an additional distortion since it moves the economy away from its initially distorted set of signals to another set that could more closely approximate the target outcome of a perfect social planner. Economists say that, when starting in a second-best position, a policy that distorts market signals can be recommended after all. Thus, economists have had to rely on empirical studies to determine whether minimum wage laws raise or lower unemployment.

There are additional applications of the second-best theorem in other chapters of this book. For example, in Chapter 6 we learned that monopoly forces price above marginal cost and that this outcome entails a social loss if we start from the first best. But the interpretation is different if that industry is a heavy polluter. In that second-best setting, society benefits from a reduced level of output, so the same outcome can be "good news" after all. In this case, the monopoly distortion cancels out part of the pollution problem. There is a simple moral to this story: in policy analysis, always look (for second-best situations) before you leap (to a conclusion).

INSTITUTIONS FOR DEALING WITH UNCERTAINTY

In the final two sections of this chapter, we consider some of the ways in which society has tried to cope with asymmetric information and co-ordination failure. Banks and stock markets help to distribute society's limited supply of savings to firms whose investments will be the most productive for society, and they allow **diversification** of risk for individual savers in the process. However, these institutions do an imperfect job of providing these services (as we shall see in Chapters 15 and 18). **Insurance** offers another way to deal with incomplete information, but issues of **adverse selection** and **moral hazard** cause co-ordination failure here as well.

Insurance firms cannot know precisely who their low-risk and high-risk clients are, but they do know that they overcharge the former and undercharge the latter. As a result, they know that the higher they set insurance rates, the more the better-risk clients withdraw their business. Clients self-select so that the insurance company is stuck with only high-risk candidates. In the end, this adverse-selection problem means that it is not profitable for private firms to supply the socially optimal amount of insurance.

There is a second problem. Once a person has insurance, she has reduced incentive to behave in such a way as to avoid the outcome for which the policy offers protection. For example, once her jewellery is insured, she has less incentive to inconvenience herself with attempts to prevent it from being stolen. Insurance companies know this, and they react by providing only limited amounts of insurance unless contracts are structured to reduce this incentive. One way to accomplish this objective is to have a noticeable deductible feature in the policy; with this arrangement, the policy does not cover the first part of the loss (say, $500). Another arrangement is co-insurance, in which the policy covers only some proportion of the loss.

Two applications of the adverse-selection and moral-hazard problems have been prominent in the news in recent years. The first is deposit insurance, which governments offer to ensure that depositors do not lose their savings if their financial institution takes on too many risky ventures and goes bankrupt. But once depositors face no risk of loss, they exercise no care in deciding where to lend their money. If deposit insurance is extended to financial institutions that are not regulated at all, then it leads to an increase in the number of bankruptcies in the financial sector.

Canada's health care system provides a second example of the applicability of these problems. Individuals face no user charge for each visit to a doctor, and they have very incomplete information concerning their needs. As a result, they are willing to undergo almost any treatment that the doctor suggests. Since each doctor's income is proportional to the number of visits and procedures completed, the system involves an incentive for the doctor to "play it safe" and to pursue tests and procedures that offer only small chances of contributing to a cure. Also, there is no incentive to invest in preventative medicine.

In the United States, experiments with health maintenance organizations (HMOs) have been set up with the intention of reducing these adverse incentives. An HMO is a group of doctors, nurses, and others who provide medical care for their clients. Individuals have the right to choose a particular HMO. It receives an annual per-person grant from the government for each of its patients. Since the grant is per person, not per visit or per procedure, the healthier the HMO can keep its clients, the more money it can make. Preventative medicine is encouraged, and waste is discouraged. While moral hazard is limited, however, there is still an adverse-selection problem. HMOs have an incentive to discourage unhealthy individuals from applying to their group practices. So HMOs cannot be a complete answer to reforming the health care sector.

INCOMPLETE INFORMATION AND GOVERNMENT

Since incomplete information limits the market's effectiveness, and since there are large economies of scale in acquiring information, it makes sense for the government to help finance society's creation and dissemination of knowledge. Identifying hazardous substances and establishing rules of safety are therefore sensible and necessary activities for government in an otherwise market-oriented economy. But while incomplete information represents the justification for some government involvement, it also complicates the formulation of government policy — making intervention less effective than it otherwise would be.

An example of this latter problem is the provision of **welfare**. The government needs to limit support to only the less able individuals in society. But since ability cannot be observed directly, the government looks for some characteristic that can be measured and that may be strongly correlated with ability. The obvious candidate is income — with the assumption being that low-income individuals have low ability. The problem, in a setting of incomplete information, is that somewhat higher-ability individuals can masquerade as lower-ability ones simply by earning low incomes. If the only opportunity that these individuals have for market earnings is a relatively low wage with little child care support, and if the welfare system is reasonably generous, then there is a strong incentive to opt for welfare.

Since the government has limited funds for redistribution, an incentive that guides individuals to *self*-select into two groups — the truly needy and those who would otherwise masquerade — must be found. From this point of view, it is understandable that governments do not offer all support in cash. Instead, for example, part of it is offered in the form of public housing. Those tempted to masquerade as needy are less likely to do so if they must move to obtain support. Voluntary workfare is also an effective mechanism for generating self-selection. However, since actual workfare programs are often compulsory, these programs cannot be rationalized as solutions to this moral-hazard problem.

So incomplete information limits the effectiveness of government intervention, just as it causes market failure. In addition, there can be efficiency problems within governments, since they cannot operate on a profit-maximization basis when the whole point of some programs is to provide services free of charge. One topic of active research within economics is the investigation of alternative incentives in non-profit organizations such as government bureaucracies.

An additional problem with the government is that co-ordination must be achieved through the political process — not through market trades — and the political process can operate so that voters have little real choice. To see why, consider a situation in which 100 voters are each given a number, from 0 to 100. A higher number indicates a preference for a bigger government. Assume that there are two political parties that initially offer a real choice for voters. Party A's platform matches the preference of voter 25, while party B's matches that of voter 75. If nothing changes, then each party can expect to receive half the votes, since voters 1 to 50 vote for A and the rest vote for B. But both parties have an incentive to change their platforms. For example, if A offers a platform that matches voter 74, then A will get just under three-quarters of the votes. Since B has an incentive to plan in a similar fashion, both parties can be expected to converge until their platforms are identical — both matching the preferences of voter 50. In a political system involving simple majority voting, then, only the **median voter's** preferences matter. Thus, while the market has flaws, the political process is inflexible. Small minorities are catered to in the market as long as some firm can make a profit serving that niche. However, those with preferences other than those of the median voter do not have such options within a political process involving simple majority voting.

Finally, it often does not pay a voter to expend resources to increase his information concerning the issues. Consider a proposal that the government impose on an industry a regulation that may lead to a cleaner environment. The cost of the regulation is borne by a relatively small number of individuals associated with that industry. The benefits extend to everyone who breathes the cleaner air. But, precisely because the former group is much smaller, much more is at stake on a per-person basis for that group. It has a much higher incentive to be politically active. In a large jurisdiction, each person in the general population sees that his vote will be insignificant, so it does not pay to become informed about the issue. Thus, it is in no single person's interest to resist the lobby group that emerges to represent the special-interest group.

SUMMARY

Here is a brief review of the key concepts covered in this chapter. We have learned that **game theory** can be used to study strategic reactions and that **oligopoly** cartels often break down because participating firms are tempted to cheat on price-setting agreements. Firms can remove this **prisoner's dilemma** only by making credible threats concerning how they will react to such cheating. Even firms that are not in an industry are players since they represent a threat to enter that industry. If that threat leads to **excess capacity** as an **entry deterrent**, then there is waste from society's point of view. If it does not, then the market is **contestable**, and even a monopolist is forced to behave competitively.

Asymmetric information in the labour market leads to another form of co-ordination failure: **unemployment**. Since firms set wages to limit shirking, the wage cannot clear the market. Minimum wage laws can lower unemployment when they are imposed in this **second-best** setting. But there is no ambiguity concerning taxes: equilibrium unemployment rises dramatically with tax rates.

Various institutions have been developed to help us cope with incomplete information. Financial institutions and stock markets permit **diversification**, and **insurance** can be purchased. But problems of **adverse selection** and **moral hazard** limit the effectiveness of these institutions. Governments help as well, but co-ordination failures also develop in this part of our economic system. Transfers in kind, not in cash, can be used to induce individuals to provide more complete information to **welfare** officials. But the **median voter** theorem and the low relevance of any individual's vote limit flexibility within a government compared with the market. Individuals can communicate via markets and via the political process. Neither method of trying for co-ordination is perfect.

SUGGESTIONS FOR FURTHER READING

A. Dixit and B. Nalebuff, *Thinking Strategically: A Competitive Edge in Business, Politics, and Everyday Life* (New York: Norton, 1991) — a witty, insightful, and highly entertaining introduction to game theory.

WEB ACTIVITIES

www.oag-bvg.gc.ca
The Web site of the federal auditor general; annual reports discuss efficiency in government.

CHAPTER EIGHT
Public Goods and Externalities

LEARNING OBJECTIVES

After reading this chapter, you should understand
- why market economies produce too few public goods and goods that generate positive spill-over effects;
- why market economics involve too much pollution and how taxes and tradeable emission permits can help to correct this market failure; and
- why the institution of private property is important for resource conservation.

INTRODUCTION

Thus far, we have spent most of the book discussing how a decentralized market system performs. In the previous two chapters, we saw that the market mechanism can fail to deliver an efficient outcome for society if some individuals or firms are big enough to have market power or to induce others to react strategically. But market power and incomplete information are not the only problems that can develop. Others are incomplete property rights and spill-over effects. An example of the latter problem is second-hand smoke. Neither smokers nor the tobacco companies that create cigarettes have to pay anything for spill-over costs of this sort, so a market system does not take them into account.

Spill-over problems become pervasive when the question of who owns what cannot be answered. To pursue this problem, economists have defined the term **public goods**, which distinguishes the analysis from what we have been studying up to now — the provision of private goods and services.

PUBLIC GOODS

An apple is an example of a private good. It has a feature that economists call *excludability*, which means that it is very easy for an individual to keep the apple for herself. Everyone else can be excluded from having it. This seems to be obvious, but some goods, which we call public goods, do not have this property.

Consider a lighthouse, for example. The fact that one ship has sailed by, seen the lighthouse, and avoided crashing on the rocks does not curtail another ship from deriving the same benefit from the lighthouse. Once the lighthouse is built and operating, no one can exclude passing ships from seeing it and benefiting from the service it provides. The service is not excludable, so a lighthouse is an example of a public good.

It is important to realize that, because users cannot be excluded from enjoying a public good, it is unlikely that individuals, operating in their own self-interests, will offer to pay enough to cover its costs. Everyone hopes that the costs will be paid by others. Because most people try to "free ride" on others, private profit-oriented firms do not find it in their interests to produce public goods. After all, it would cost them something to produce a lighthouse, to return to our example, and once it was built they would get no sales revenue from its operation since there is no mechanism by which they can force consumers of the lighthouse services to pay for them. The only way that such public goods will be produced in our society is to have the government coerce people to pay a share of the costs through the levying of taxes. But this does not mean that the government must actually build and operate the lighthouse. These tasks can be tendered out to competing private firms to see which ones can do these tasks most efficiently.

There are many examples of public goods: national defence, city streets, and our legal system, to name just a few. It is important to recognize that the **actual provision** of public goods is a separate issue from the government **financing** of them. As far as the underlying logic is concerned, the notion of publicness justifies only the government's financing of these services, not the government's provision of them. The institutional arrangement of using tendered bids from private firms is common for the construction of highways and public buildings, and many analysts think that this practice should be expanded to other publicly sponsored activities, such as education.

BENEFICIAL EXTERNALITIES

We now consider goods that are a mixture of public and private goods. Education does not represent a pure public good since each student occupies a spot in the classroom and benefits more from her own education than others do. But there are certainly some positive spill-over effects involved. We all benefit when the level of education at the workplace, and in society in general, is reasonably high.

Education is not unique in this regard. There is a whole range of goods and services that generate favourable spill-over or external effects — for example, garbage collection, good health, and street lighting. A public good is really just a **beneficial externality** in an extreme form — one in which the external beneficiary enjoys the service just as much as the primary "consumer." To analyze the mixed case — a private good with beneficial externalities — we focus on Figure 8.1 and consider an individual's decision to attend university.

There are two benefits from a person's going to university. The first benefit, which we call the *private benefit*, is the higher income and the general intellectual satisfaction received by that individual. As with the consumption of any item, diminishing marginal utility applies, so the private marginal benefit curve is downward sloping in Figure 8.1. The second benefit is that

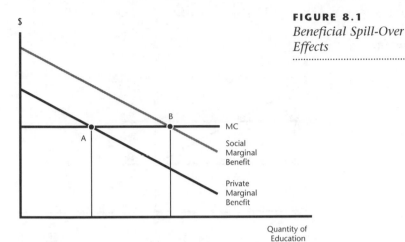

FIGURE 8.1
Beneficial Spill-Over Effects
....

society at large gains from having that more informed and productive person to work and interact with. These extra benefits to society are incorporated within the social marginal benefit curve in Figure 8.1. It includes both the private benefits to the individual being educated and the spill-over benefits to others. (For a purely private good, there is no difference between the private and social marginal benefit curves. Since we focused exclusively on private goods in earlier chapters, we did not distinguish between private and social benefits.)

The third curve shown in Figure 8.1 indicates the marginal cost of educating a person, which must be paid by that individual if there is no public subsidy for education. For simplicity, we assume that this marginal cost is constant. If she is left to her own devices, this individual's private optimum is the intersection of the private marginal benefit curve and the marginal cost curve — that is, point A. But this is not the best outcome from society's point of view since, at this level of education, marginal benefit exceeds marginal cost. From society's point of view, the best point is B, and this outcome involves providing this individual with more education. She stops short of seeking as much education as is in the public interest because she does not receive the benefits that go to society in general, so, acting as a rational maximizer, she attaches little or no weight to them in making her decision.

How can the individual be induced to get more education — that is, to move from the quantity given by point A to that given by point B in Figure 8.1? One solution is to subsidize education. With a subsidy, the cost to the individual would shift down. If the subsidy is the amount shown in Figure 8.2, then there will be a coincidence between what is in this individual's private interest and what is in the public interest. With the subsidy, the individual will choose point C — the intersection of her private marginal benefit curve with the subsidized cost curve. But points C and B involve the same amount of education, so the original problem has been solved. Economists

FIGURE 8.2
*Beneficial Externalities
and Subsidies*
....

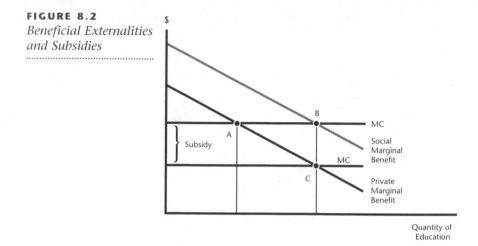

refer to the subsidy as a way of "internalizing the externality" because it causes the private decision-maker to attach weight to what was previously only
an external benefit received by others. This, then, is the ultimate justification
for subsidizing education, health care, and many other activities. There remains much debate, however, since there are many different views concerning the sizes of these beneficial externalities.

Just as with pure public goods, with externalities it is important to stress
the difference between the government's financing of services and the government's provision of these services. Positive externality only justifies government financial support of education; it does not mean that government
employees should actually do the educating. Many policy analysts think that
a system of "education vouchers" could handle this and related cases effectively. We could subsidize the pursuit of education by giving out vouchers and
then letting individuals spend the vouchers at whichever institutions provide
them with the kinds of education they think are best. If the government takes
over the process of actually providing the education, then we lose the effi-
ciencies that come with competition. In that case, we are solving a beneficial
externality problem but introducing a monopoly problem. A voucher system
solves the externality problem without introducing the monopoly problem.

DETRIMENTAL EXTERNALITIES

Spill-over effects can be negative as well as positive, and the classic example
of a negative externality is pollution. In Figure 8.3, there is both the demand
curve for some manufactured good and the constant marginal cost curve involved in producing that good. This supply curve is labelled the private marginal cost curve because it includes only costs that the producers actually
have to pay — such as the costs of labour and raw materials. The private cost
curve does not include the spill-over costs imposed on third parties. For ex-

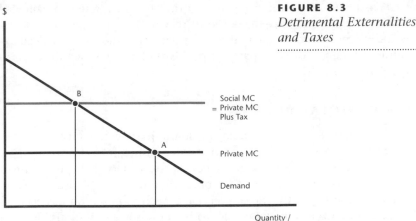

FIGURE 8.3
*Detrimental Externalities
and Taxes*
....

ample, suppose that the production process in this industry generates an effluent that is poured into streams and rivers and that this effluent makes the water unsuitable for drinking or recreational purposes. When these additional costs are included, the overall marginal cost curve is located at a higher position. This all-inclusive cost curve is labelled the social marginal cost curve in Figure 8.3. The vertical distance between the private and the social marginal cost curves represents the magnitude of the negative spill-over effects — the negative externality imposed on the downstream users of the water in the streams and rivers.

The basic problem in situations of this sort is that there is often no mechanism to force private decision-makers to take account of the spill-over costs. The free market outcome is at point A since that is the intersection of the relevant demand and supply curves. But at this rate of output, marginal costs from society's point of view are greater than marginal utility, so the industry has expanded beyond what is socially optimal. If, instead, the negative spill-over effects are included in this decision, then the firms would choose to operate at point B — the intersection of the demand curve and the cost curve that is relevant for all of society.

How can this divergence between the desirable outcome (point B) and what occurs in a decentralized market (point A) be closed? One option is to levy an excise tax on the production or sale of the good whose production is causing the pollution. In this example, a tax per unit imposed on the sellers just equal to the gap between private and social marginal costs would do the trick. It would make the private marginal cost curve (including the tax) coincident with the social marginal cost curve. Thus, just as beneficial externality effects can be "internalized" through a subsidy, detrimental externality effects can be "internalized" with a tax.

An emissions tax forces firms to care about pollution, but not because it makes firms care less about private profits and more about the public interest. Instead, the emissions tax forces firms' private interests to coincide with the public interest since the tax converts what was an external cost that firms could ignore into an internal one. As with subsidies for beneficial externalities, though, the appropriate size of this tax has been the subject of intense debate.

ENVIRONMENTAL POLICY

As we have just seen, the economist's solution to externality problems, whether they are beneficial or detrimental externalities, is to close the gap between private incentives and the overall effects on society through the use of subsidies and taxes. Let us pursue this approach in more detail, using the case of pollution. Until recently, the common approach to pollution has been either to exhort citizens and companies to be more socially responsible or to pass broad legislation imposing specific limits on the quantity of pollution that will be permitted in the future. For example, all firms in a province might be forced to cut pollution emissions by 50 percent within a five-year period.

There is a problem with exhortations to care more about the public interest. This strategy ignores the fact that shareholders generally replace a firm's managers if they are not trying to make the highest profit possible. The problem with direct quantity reductions, such as a 50 percent emissions cut for everyone, is that these rules take no account of the fact that some firms find it fairly easy to lower pollution and others find it very costly to do so. An efficient solution to pollution should exploit these differences rather than pretend they do not exist.

Technological options vary across different industries. Some firms, such as those operating a chemical factory, may legitimately claim that, if they have to reduce their pollution emissions dramatically, they will literally go out of business. They simply do not know how to produce the product any other way, so there will be many job losses as part of the antipollution program. Other firms, such as those operating an electricity generator, can install scrubbers as part of their smokestack system, with the result that significant pollution abatement is possible without any threat to jobs.

Every company has an incentive to tell the government that it is one of the firms that cannot adjust easily. As a result, whenever the government proposes the kind of pollution abatement policy that requires all firms to cut their emissions by the same percentage, it is deluged with requests from firms seeking exemptions. The poor bureaucrats find it costly and difficult to determine the extent of exaggeration, if any, in each appeal. So inevitably the government gets stalled on its time deadlines with this approach. A more efficient system will achieve the aggregate pollution reduction target by encouraging a massive adjustment by firms that find it easy to adjust and little or no adjustment at all for the few firms that cannot adjust and still produce goods profitably.

An emissions tax accomplishes this weeding out automatically. If it really is costly for some firms, such as the chemical factory, to cut pollution, then many of those firms will pay the emissions tax and go on polluting. But if other firms find it easy to change their production methods, perhaps almost totally eliminating pollution, then that strategy will be less costly for them than paying the relatively high tax. In the end, the only firms that actually pay the tax will be those that find it the cheapest thing to do. In other words, they are the ones that would truly generate a lot of job dislocations if the government forced all firms to cut pollution by an equal percentage.

Thus, without any bureaucrat ever having to know anything about any of the industries, we obtain the response to our pollution troubles that respects the technological differences across industries and that imposes the smallest possible cost in terms of forgone manufactured goods and employee dislocations. So the emissions-tax approach is preferable to the equal-percentage-reduction approach that until recently has been the favoured policy of many governments.

Some commentators are so concerned about emissions control that they think it unimportant to argue about more or less efficient approaches to pollution abatement. They think that any policy that makes a positive contribution is good. Most economists disagree. Many share the deep concern for our environment expressed by activists. But they are also concerned that an inefficient approach to pollution will make the trade-off in terms of job losses, and standard of living generally, so expensive that there will be no real action toward pollution control.

Individuals have always demonstrated their reluctance to make sacrifices unless they are convinced that those sacrifices will be effective. Thus, it is important that our pollution-abatement schemes be efficient. This realization leads economists back to the idea of vouchers, in this case for pollution. The basic mechanism is to have the government print a set of tickets known as **tradeable emission permits**. Anyone who owns a permit is allowed to pollute a certain amount each year. Since pollution without a ticket carries a stiff penalty, the aggregate quantity of pollution is controlled simply by limiting the number of permits printed.

One way to distribute the tickets is through an auction. As noted earlier, some firms find it very costly to stop polluting, while others can do so at rather low cost, and these various possibilities are shown in the left-hand panel of Figure 8.4. Since the cost of not polluting is the same as each firm's maximum willingness to pay for a pollution permit, the demand for vouchers in the right-hand panel of Figure 8.4 will be the mirror image of the curve representing the cost of not polluting. The price of a ticket is determined by supply and demand. The firms that really need to keep polluting if they are to produce goods at all, will be prepared to pay a high price for the vouchers. And the firms who find it relatively easy to cut emissions will just ignore the auction and change their production methods. (The benefit to them of continuing is pollute is less than the price of a ticket.) So an emissions permit

FIGURE 8.4
Tradeable Emission Permits

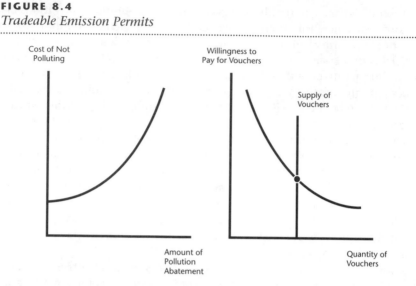

program involves all the efficiency gains of the emissions tax approach. But with a system of tradeable permits, the government does not even have to figure out what level of tax it should set. It just sets an overall quantity limit and lets the auction determine the amount of the emissions tax in the form of the auction price for permits.

Now consider what happens when firms react to this price incentive to find cost-effective methods for reducing pollution. If some firms invest in cleaner technology, then curves representing the cost of not polluting will shift down. This means that, overall, the demand curve for pollution permits shifts down too. As a result, the price of a permit falls. The falling price is a signal to the government that firms are finding it easier to make pollution abatement adjustments. So each year the government can reduce the number of tickets it sells. Over time, by cutting the supply of permits (thereby keeping the price of vouchers high), the government can force more and more firms to use production methods that generate less pollution.

In short, by issuing permits to create a market in pollution rights, we harness all the efficiency aspects of the market mechanism. In this way, market incentives can go a long way toward curing one of the fundamental problems with the market system itself. Unfortunately, pollution permits cannot solve all our problems. On an international scale, deciding which government should have the right to print the tickets is still unresolved. To complicate matters, many of our environmental concerns stem from activities in less developed countries. The residents of these countries obtain farmland by cutting the rainforest, and often the only refrigeration techniques that they can afford are bad for the ozone layer. A permit system must be coupled with other programs (international aid) to tackle these issues.

The idea of tradeable emission permits is not just ivory tower rhetoric. This approach has been used effectively in a number of U.S. states for several years. Indeed, a second-hand market in tickets has developed. Some firms had to buy a ticket for two or three years because initially they had no cost-effective way to stop polluting. But the cost of the ticket was an ongoing incentive to force the firms to invest in new machinery that operated more cleanly. The moment that firms got such a process installed, they had no further need to hold the pollution permit, so they would put an ad in a paper and sell it to somebody else. The more firms that do this, the more they flood the market with tickets, and the price falls. This is an ongoing signal that society can afford more ambitious pollution abatement targets.

Pollution permits have been endorsed at every international conference on the environment in recent years, and various governments are now using such schemes. Economists find this development very encouraging.

RESOURCE CONSERVATION

A decentralized market system works on the basis of mutually agreeable trades between individuals and firms. Such trades cannot be arranged unless private property is well defined and enforced. After all, no one will pay you much for an item if he is not sure it is really yours to sell. Badly defined **property rights** lie behind our resource conservation problems, and to see this we consider deforestation as an example.

Suppose we lease a large tract of forest land to a forestry company for a rather short interval, say, fifteen or twenty years, and stipulate that the land will remain public property after the lease expires. It is then in the private interest of that firm to cut down all the trees and leave. There is no point in putting resources into reforestation because the new trees will not be of benefit until 50 to 70 years after the lease has expired, and perhaps some other firm might then get the new lease. So by keeping the land publicly owned, we have precluded the chance that the firm will act responsibly from society's long-run point of view. But if we lease the land to the firm for a long time, then it is clearly in the firm's interest to undertake reforestation. Otherwise, by just cutting down the trees and not reforesting, it would quickly drive the value of what is then its own asset to near zero.

History provides many examples that this is how people react. For instance, in the frontier west, herds of cows were private property. Nobody killed all his cows; some were always kept alive to keep the herd going year after year. To do otherwise would have deprived the rancher of his livelihood. So it was in his private interest not to squander the resource. But the buffalo were publicly owned; nobody owned particular parts of the herd. So there was no private incentive not to kill nearly all of them, which was precisely what happened. The same thing has been happening with whales despite numerous international treaties. Whether we like to admit it or not, people look after their own private resources, and they tend not to look after something that they do not privately own.

SUMMARY

Many concerned citizens, such as David Suzuki and many religious leaders, worry about whether economic activity can be sustained in a world of finite resources. They have called for a rejection of both the profit motive and the institution of private property. Economists look to history and see that scarce resources have been used wisely only when the force of self-interest has been harnessed effectively. Most economists think that it is better to base social policy on human nature as we know it. This calls for designing our tax system so that private interest and public interest coincide. In this way, the force of self-interest can be used to secure the public interest, and this seems to be more constructive to economists than simply wishing that the force of self-interest would go away.

Here is a review of the key concepts covered in this chapter. We learned that, when **spill-over effects** are dramatic, we encounter the **public good** problem that these items must be **financed, though not necessarily provided, by government**. We saw that, when spill-overs are less extensive, we have **beneficial** and **detrimental externalities**. Pollution — the classic example of a detrimental externality — is most efficiently limited through the use of **effluent charges** and **tradeable emission permits**. For similar reasons, we found that an increase in **private ownership** is one of the most effective ways to foster **resource conservation**.

The main problem with the private ownership of resources is that it can lead to unequal incomes. Thus, we will spend the next chapter investigating the distribution of income that emerges from market economies and exploring how the government can best affect that income distribution.

SUGGESTIONS FOR FURTHER READING

W. Block (ed.), *Economics and the Environment: A Reconciliation* (Vancouver: Fraser Institute, 1990) — essays by economists on David Suzuki's criticism of economics.

S.E. Landsburg, *The Armchair Economist: Economics and Everyday Life* (New York: Free Press, 1993), Chapters 6–9, 24.

WEB ACTIVITIES

www.ec.gc.ca
The Web site of Environment Canada.

CHAPTER NINE

Income Distribution and the Tax System

LEARNING OBJECTIVES

After reading this chapter, you should understand
- how marginal productivity theory explains the distribution of income;
- why a tax on capital hurts workers and how our welfare and personal income tax systems interact to create a poverty trap; and
- how replacing the income tax with a progressive expenditure tax could simultaneously increase average incomes and decrease income inequality.

INTRODUCTION

One thing that many people find unappealing about a decentralized market-oriented economy is that it seems to produce a wide distribution of incomes. Some individuals become extremely wealthy, while other remain very poor. The analysis in this chapter helps to explain why this distribution of incomes occurs. It also explores several features of our tax and welfare systems, with the intention of identifying an efficient way of redistributing income from the rich to the poor.

But before we explore these questions of tax policy, we must understand how the pattern of high and low incomes occurs in the first place. This pattern depends on the productivity of the factors of production owned by each individual, so we start with a review of marginal productivity theory.

MARGINAL PRODUCTIVITY

When developing the law of diminishing marginal returns in Chapter 4, we simplified the analysis by concentrating on just two inputs to the production process: labour and capital. We continue that simplification here. In Chapter 4, we considered the firm hiring increasing amounts of labour while holding its amount of capital fixed. The left-hand panel of Figure 9.1 shows the diminishing marginal productivity of labour. When we first derived this curve, it had an increasing portion for very low quantities of labour, but from now on we deal only with the downward-sloping portion. Recall the rationale for the negative slope: as the labour force gets bigger and the stock of machines does not, each individual worker has a smaller quantity of machines to work with and so is less productive.

FIGURE 9.1

Two Ways of Measuring Total Output

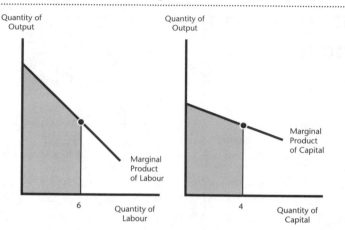

There is a second way of viewing this phenomenon of diminishing marginal returns, and that is to consider the firm hiring more and more capital while holding the size of its labour force fixed. The right-hand panel of Figure 9.1 follows this approach, and it shows the diminishing marginal productivity of capital. As the quantity of capital increases, with the size of the labour force fixed, each additional machine has a smaller quantity of labour to work with, so it adds less to the firm's total output.

It is important to remember that the sum of all the additional outputs yields total output. Thus, the area under a firm's marginal productivity curve measures the total amount that the firm has produced. We can apply this idea to both graphs in Figure 9.1. To have a concrete discussion, we assume that the firm whose operations are shown in the graphs has hired six units of labour and four units of capital. The total output of the firm is shown by the grey area in either panel. (The shaded regions are intended to represent the same area.)

If the firm keeps its machine stock constant but hires one more worker, then its total output would increase. The amount of additional output is shown by the darkly shaded area in the left-hand panel of Figure 9.2. The firm has moved out along the labour input axis by one more unit (from six workers to seven workers), and the extra output is the additional area under the marginal product curve. This extra output is shown in a different way in the right-hand panel of Figure 9.2. Since we are discussing a case in which the firm has not hired any more machines, there is no movement out to the right along the capital input axis. Instead, the four units of capital now have seven instead of six units of labour to work with, so each unit of capital becomes more productive. The entire marginal product of capital curve shifts up, as shown in Figure 9.2. The extra output that results is shown by the additional darkly shaded area under the new higher marginal product of capital curve.

FIGURE 9.2

Two Ways of Measuring Additional Output

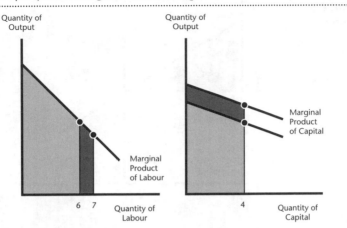

It is worth emphasizing once more that the two panels in Figure 9.2 are just alternative ways of showing the same thing. Thus, the total output of the firm before hiring the seventh worker is the light grey area, and the additional output that follows from the hiring of that seventh worker is the dark grey area — whether we view these areas in the left or the right panel of Figure 9.2. The two light grey regions are the same area, and the two dark grey regions are the same area.

HOW INCOMES ARE DETERMINED

We are now in a position to see how these marginal productivity relationships determine people's incomes. We know from the optimal hiring rule discussed in Chapter 4 that the marginal product curve is the firm's demand curve for that factor. Thus, to find out whether a certain factor, say, labour, receives a high or low payment, we simply add together the marginal product curves for all firms (to get the overall demand curve for labour), and then we see where that demand curve intersects the supply curve for labour.

Equilibrium in the labour market is shown in Figure 9.3. The overall supply curve for labour is shown as completely inelastic. You might find this surprising since you probably know some people who move in and out of the labour force, depending on the wage rate. For example, so-called second earners in families, especially low-income families, tend to respond positively to wage rate changes. Higher wages provide an incentive for second earners to leave the home and enter the work force. However, other individuals, such as some lawyers and other professionals, tend to cut hours of work when their wages go up. Higher wages allow these individuals to achieve all the income they want by working less, so higher wages induce them to opt for more leisure (leading to a smaller labour supply). When we add up everyone's re-

FIGURE 9.3
Income Distribution as Seen from the Labour Market
....

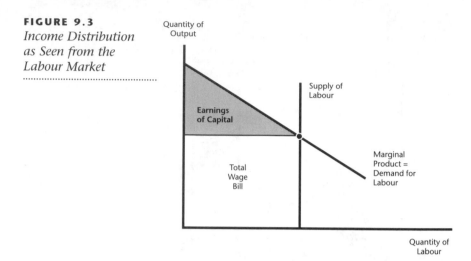

actions, the positive and negative responses to higher wages appear to cancel each other out, so that overall the supply of labour is quite inelastic.

The labour supply and demand curves shown in Figure 9.3 are for the whole economy. As a result, the total income available to all citizens is equal to the value of total goods produced, and graphically this is the area under the marginal product curve (up to the quantity of labour available). The intersection of supply and demand determines the wage rate received by each worker. This rate multiplied by the number of workers gives the total wage bill received by all workers. Geometrically, this total wage earnings is given by the area of the white rectangle in Figure 9.3. (The height of this rectangle is the wage rate, and the width is the number of workers. Total labour income [the area of the rectangle] is the product of these two items.) By subtracting this wage bill from the total value of output (the entire trapezoid under the marginal product curve), we see that the owners of capital receive the shaded triangle. So the graph shows how national income is divided between labourers and the owners of capital.

The second thing that follows from this marginal productivity explanation of income distribution is that the owners of scarce factors of production receive very high incomes, while the owners of abundant factors of production get very low incomes. Let us consider each case in turn. If labour is scarce, the supply curve would be far over to the left in Figure 9.3, indicating that only a few units are available. An example might be star singers or hockey players. The equilibrium wage (which clears the market for such a scarce factor) is very high. Similarly, if labour is abundant, the supply curve would be far over to the right, indicating that there are many units of this factor of production available. An example might be unskilled labourers. The market-clearing wage of such an abundant factor is very low.

These outcomes lead to an efficient use of factors by society. From an efficiency point of view, we want scarce factors to carry very high prices. If it costs firms a lot to use them, then firms will use such scarce items only where they are especially valuable. As a result, society will get the most material welfare possible, given our scarce resources. Thus, the way in which factors get paid in a market economy is efficient, but the outcome can be pretty discouraging for income distribution. For many individuals, especially those who own only a little bit of just one abundant factor of production (unskilled labour), this system of factor pricing leads to poverty.

The distribution of market incomes has become a lot more unequal in the past quarter-century. Many analysts believe that this situation may be due to increased globalization. With open markets, the availability of substitutes for unskilled labour within developed economies such as Canada has increased dramatically. And, as we have just learned, abundant factors earn low incomes. We will assess the role of globalization in Chapter 18.

Economists have considered many extensions to marginal productivity theory — extensions that help to explain certain aspects of income disparity. For example, you may have wondered why company presidents are paid dramatically more than others in their firms — even much more than the person who is second in command. Surely the president's marginal productivity is not that much higher. The answer may be that firms can secure increased efforts (and therefore higher productivity) from *all* their workers if part of each person's reward depends on his or her *relative* performance. For example, if tennis stars are all paid the same amount of money per hour, they would have an incentive to prolong each point and, as a result, offer less exciting games. But with a large prize going only to the winner, every player tries much harder. This principle apparently applies beyond the sporting world, with all employees in the company working harder and more productively as they strive for the "big prize."

Tying each person's pay to results (to marginal productivity) stimulates results. That is why this is an efficient system. Redistribution involves removing part of this payoff, so redistribution can shrink the overall economic "pie." But most people regard *some* cost of this sort worth paying to lessen income inequality.

INCOME REDISTRIBUTION

Once again, we confront the trade-off between efficiency and equity. To many economists, the sensible response to this trade-off is as follows. Let factors be paid their marginal products so that we achieve the efficiency gains that accompany the use of scarce factors carefully; then redistribute some of the resulting incomes from the rich to the poor.

There are three possible ways to redistribute income among individuals. The first is a political solution — we can simply redefine who owns the factors of production. This is the socialist approach, and a common example from poor agrarian economies is to give a piece of farmland to every family.

The second is to leave the ownership of factors as it is but to impose regulations on markets, such as a minimum wage law or a rent control act. These kinds of maximum and minimum price laws are intended to redistribute income; however, as we have seen in earlier chapters, almost every time we consider such a policy, large and undesired side effects occur. As a result, economists have concluded that this second strategy is usually not a good one to follow.

The third is to leave the ownership of factors alone, leave markets working, let factor prices be what they may (so that resources get used efficiently), but then use a general income tax system to redistribute some income from the rich to those with lower incomes.

GENERAL VERSUS SPECIFIC FORMS OF TAXATION

In a general tax system, the same tax rate applies to all forms of income, whatever the source of that income. When there are different taxes for different kinds of income, the government creates incentives for people to change their market behaviour in an attempt to get their incomes into the lower-taxed form. These incentives lead to inefficiency and a frustration of the initial objective of income redistribution. To see the inefficiency of using particular taxes as opposed to general taxes, consider two examples of specific taxes.

The first is a payroll tax imposed on firms for their use of labour but not their use of capital. We have several payroll taxes in Canada; the prime examples are the contributions that we and our employers make to the Canada Pension Plan and to the Employment Insurance fund. Let us examine a version of this type of tax, one in which firms must pay to the government a specified amount of money for each employee. Before the tax is levied, the labour market is as shown in Figure 9.3.

The tax decreases the amounts that firms are willing to pay their employees. After all, firms have to reserve some of what they were paying workers to cover the tax. This decreased willingness to pay employees is shown in Figure 9.4 by the downward shift in the labour demand curve. The vertical distance between the original and the after-tax positions for the labour demand curve is equal to the amount of the payroll tax (measured on a per-worker basis). The intersection of the after-tax demand curve with the labour supply curve gives the new equilibrium. It is clear from Figure 9.4 that the equilibrium wage drops by exactly the amount of the tax. Thus, even though the tax was levied on firms, the employees bear the burden of the tax.

The total revenue collected by the government is equal to the payroll tax per worker times the number of workers, and this amount is shown as the lightly shaded area in Figure 9.4. By comparing Figures 9.3 and 9.4, we can see that this entire revenue rectangle comes out of what used to be labour's earnings. The return to capital is still the same dark grey triangle. Thus, firms have shifted the burden of the tax to employees (through lower wages). Intuitively, firms are able to fully shift the payroll tax burden because (in the aggregate) labour is a "captive" factor of production, as indicated by the inelastic supply curve.

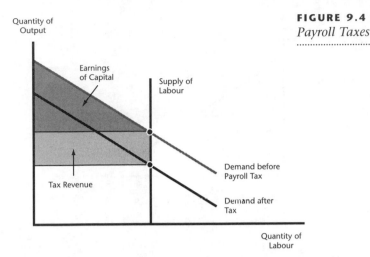

FIGURE 9.4
Payroll Taxes

Quantity of
Output

Earnings
of Capital

Supply of
Labour

Demand before
Payroll Tax

Demand after
Tax

Tax Revenue

Quantity of
Labour

Of course, it is possible that the wage rate is not pushed down by the pay-roll tax. For example, some workers are paid at the legal minimum wage. But in this case, the payroll tax only exacerbates the unemployment problem caused by the minimum wage, because firms reduce the amount of labour they want to hire. In this case, then, labour bears the burden of the tax through job losses instead of through reductions in wages. In either case, firms avoid paying the tax.

As the preceding analysis suggests, labour is opposed to payroll taxes (whether they are nominally levied on the employer or the employee). We have just seen that labour bears the full burden of the tax in either case. Given this result, you might expect that labour would favour a corporate profit tax. But the Canadian corporate profit tax is another specific levy. It taxes only income derived from owning capital that is employed in our country. This is quite different from taxing a Canadian's income, whether that income is labour earnings or a return on capital employed anywhere in the world. Because the corporate profit tax is so different from this general scheme, it does not have the effect that most people expect. Indeed, we will now see that labour is even worse off with the corporate profit tax than it is with a payroll tax!

To examine the effect of a tax on the earnings of domestically owned capital, we focus on a graph depicting the market for capital, as in Figure 9.5. There we see the downward-sloping demand curve for capital and a perfectly elastic supply curve for capital. As usual, the demand curve follows from the hypothesis of diminishing marginal returns and the optimal hiring rule. The supply curve follows from the willingness of foreign owners of capital to let it be employed in Canada, as long as we cover its opportunity cost. Thus, as long as capital can earn in Canada as much as it can in any other country, owners are willing to supply Canada with whatever quantity it wants. We show this availability by drawing the supply

FIGURE 9.5

*Income Distribution
as Seen from the Market
for Capital*

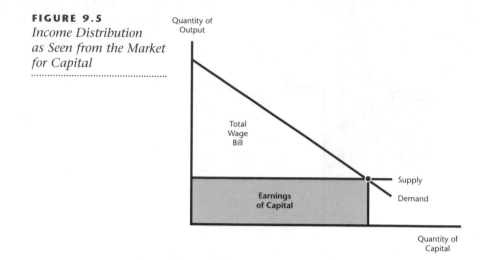

curve of capital as a horizontal line whose height is equal to the yield available to capital in the rest of the world.

Before any tax is levied, capital market equilibrium occurs at the intersection of supply and demand in Figure 9.5. Capital owners receive the internationally competitive yield times the number of units of capital employed within our country, so the total payment to them is the shaded area in Figure 9.5. Labour's income is the residual white triangle.

Suppose a 50 percent tax on the earnings of capital employed in Canada is introduced. Not surprisingly, owners of capital are going to demand double the rate of return on a pre-tax basis — so that on an after-tax basis they will receive what they can still get elsewhere in the world. If capital owners cannot continue to cover their opportunity costs, they simply move their capital to another country. As usual, then, we move the position of the supply curve up by the amount of the tax (on a per-unit basis). The intersection of the new, higher supply curve with the demand curve is shown in Figure 9.6. The arrow along the quantity axis shows how much capital is no longer demanded in Canada. This capital leaves the country. The government receives total revenue equal to the specified tax per unit of capital times the amount of capital that is still employed in Canada. That total tax revenue is indicated by the upper, lightly shaded rectangle in Figure 9.6. Notice that it comes entirely from what used to be labour's triangle of income.

The capital still employed in Canada continues to get the same return per unit as before (on an after-tax basis). The net income involved is shown as the dark grey rectangle in Figure 9.6. Capital owners appear to lose the light grey rectangle on the right-hand portion of the graph, but they do not. That rectangle represents the income earned by the capital that has left the country. This income used to be earned in Canada, but after the tax the same amount is earned elsewhere.

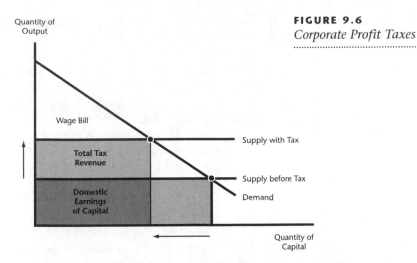

Quantity of
Output

FIGURE 9.6
Corporate Profit Taxes

Wage Bill

Total Tax
Revenue

Supply with Tax

Domestic
Earnings
of Capital

Supply before Tax

Demand

Quantity of
Capital

The tax does generate a loss to the nation as a whole. The total output produced within our country has shrunk by the area of the trapezoid under the labour demand curve formed by the vertical lines drawn down from both the initial and the after-tax equilibrium points. Labour previously earned the white triangular part of this trapezoid. But because labour now has less capital to work with, it is less productive and so it loses this income. Thus, it is labour, not the owners of capital, that suffers an income loss. Indeed, as noted already, the entire tax revenue rectangle comes from what used to be labour's larger triangle. As a result, this tax is worse for labour than the payroll tax, because labour not only pays 100 percent of the tax (as it does with a payroll tax) but also bears the additional loss represented by the small white triangle to the right of the tax revenue rectangle in Figure 9.6. So labour pays more than 100 percent of this tax. If labour has to choose between a payroll tax and this one, it ought to choose the payroll tax.

Labour supporters may find this analysis discouraging. Is there any tax that is at least partially paid by the owners of capital? The answer is "yes" — a tax on Canadians who earn income from capital employed anywhere in the world. The main lesson of this analysis is that unintended outcomes occur when we tax particular forms of income differently. We can avoid problems if we have a **general personal income tax system** in which individuals pay the same tax on all income, whether it happens to be labour income, earnings on capital employed here in Canada, or earnings on capital employed elsewhere in the world.

Unfortunately, even our general personal income tax system causes two problems: it discourages both savings and work. Let us consider each issue in turn.

Critics of our personal income tax system claim that there is "double taxation" of interest income. People pay taxes on their income in the year that it is earned; then, for income that is saved, they have to pay taxes again on the interest earned on it. This second round of tax is avoided if people consume goods and services. But average incomes cannot grow over time if society does not save, and people seem to be less willing to redistribute income to the less fortunate if their own incomes have not been growing. So any disincentive to save is a serious issue. Our tax system recognizes this problem by letting individuals lower taxes on savings through RRSP contributions. Some tax reformers argue that there should be no annual limits on these contributions. If this reform were adopted, then our income tax would become an expenditure tax, and people would be taxed according to what they take out of the economy (what they consume), not according to what they have put into it (what income they create).

The usual worry about consumption-based taxation is that, since the poor spend a higher proportion of income than do the rich, such a system is regressive and unfair. However, when an expenditure tax is not levied as a retail sales tax but is administered as an income tax with unlimited deductions for documented saving, the tax rate structure can be legislated to have the tax-to-income ratio rise with income. Any desired degree of progressivity is possible. Relative to an income tax, then, a **progressive expenditure tax** may increase both efficiency and equity. Greater savings contribute to increasing the size of the overall economic pie, and increased progressivity in the rate structure can increase the sizes of the slices going to the less fortunate members of society. Given these possibilities, we can expect the debate on whether or not our income tax system should move further toward becoming a progressive expenditure tax to continue.

The second problem with our personal income tax system is that, when it is combined with our welfare programs, it creates incentives that discourage many individuals from working at all.

DISINCENTIVES TO WORK AND THE POVERTY TRAP

Figure 9.7 summarizes the tax table that you consult each year when filing your tax return. The table tells you how much tax you have to pay for each level of before-tax income that you have earned. For example, if you have zero income, you don't have to pay any tax. You can earn up to your basic personal exemption (several thousand dollars) before you have to pay any tax. When summarized as a graph, as in Figure 9.7, the tax schedule is coincident with the horizontal axis until you use up your basic exemption. Then, at higher income levels, you move into the lowest tax bracket, and you start paying taxes. In the graph, the tax rate is given by the slope of the tax schedule. As your income continues to increase, your tax payments increase proportionately — with the factor of proportionality being that lowest tax rate. Then, as income increases further, you move into the higher tax brackets, and the tax schedule becomes progressively steeper, as shown in Figure 9.7.

We have another program that is fundamental to income redistribution — the welfare system. It involves giving subsidies to people at the low end of

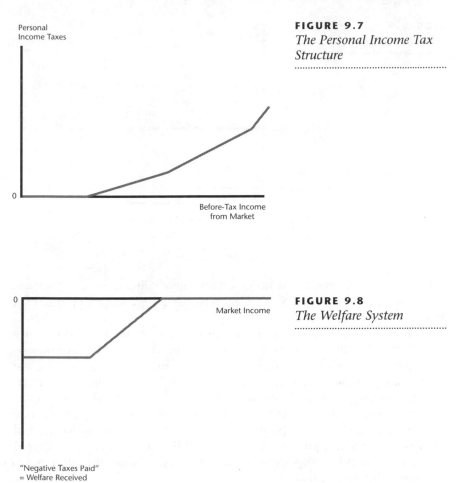

FIGURE 9.7

The Personal Income Tax Structure

FIGURE 9.8

The Welfare System

the income scale. Since our objective is to examine the welfare and personal income tax systems simultaneously, we use the rather unfamiliar language of referring to an individual's receipt of welfare as the payment of negative taxes.

The basic feature of our welfare system is that, if you receive no income from market activities, then you qualify for a certain amount of welfare. This amount of subsidy (i.e., this amount of negative taxes paid) is represented by the vertical intercept of the welfare schedule graphed in Figure 9.8. As individuals start earning market income and move out to the right along the income axis, there is no reduction in welfare payments, at least at the beginning. But after a limit specified by the welfare legislation, welfare dollars start getting withdrawn from individuals as they earn more market income. The amount varies by municipality, but on average individuals lose about

FIGURE 9.9
The Poverty Trap

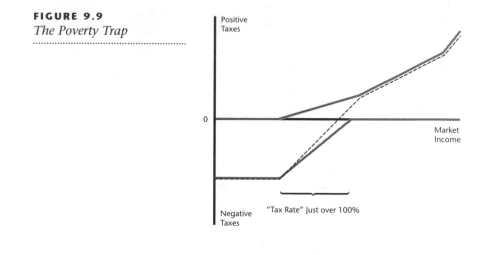

75 cents of welfare every time they earn one more dollar in the marketplace. As a result, people at very low income levels are effectively in a 75 percent tax bracket!

Things are even worse for individuals at these low income levels, as we can see by graphing the personal income tax and welfare systems together as in Figure 9.9. The net implication of the two programs is shown by the dashed line in Figure 9.9. As can be seen, some individuals (those just emerging from being on welfare) face an effective tax schedule that has an even steeper slope than 0.75. These individuals lose welfare at an implicit tax rate of 75 percent, and they pay positive income taxes at a combined federal and provincial rate that is just over 25 percent. All things considered, the overall tax rate is just over 100 percent! Would you work if your discretionary income actually fell as a result?

When combined, then, the income tax system and our welfare programs involve a tremendous disincentive to get a job. This is important since, short of returning to school, the only way that low-income individuals can escape the poverty trap is by acquiring skills while on the job. Only with higher skills will their marginal productivity be higher, and only then will they command a higher wage in the marketplace.

Why do we levy the highest marginal tax rates on such low-income individuals? This outcome was never intended; it is simply a by-product of the different programs devised by different levels of government at different times. Economists have made a suggestion for solving this problem, called the **negative income tax**.

A GUARANTEED ANNUAL INCOME

Another name for negative income tax is **guaranteed annual income**. It is based on the proposition that we must remove the steep section and the

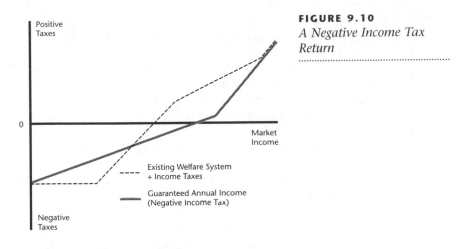

FIGURE 9.10

A Negative Income Tax Return

abrupt kinks in the net tax schedule (the dashed line that incorporates both taxes and welfare) shown in Figure 9.9. The proposal is simply that the kinked line be replaced by a smoother one, such as the solid line in Figure 9.10. The new-policy line must have flatter slope at lower income levels so that we are not taxing punitively that segment of the population that can least afford to pay taxes. A flatter net tax schedule involves a smaller disincentive to work, and the effective tax rate must be less than 100 percent before there is any chance for individuals to escape poverty.

Ardent supporters of the negative income tax have agreed that, from an administrative point of view, there would be significant savings in having one integrated system. No separate welfare department would be needed because all citizens would simply fill out tax forms on a regular basis. Those with higher incomes would pay positive taxes, and those with lower incomes would automatically qualify for negative taxes. With the income tax system extending smoothly into the negative range, there would be no unintended situation in which low-income individuals would face tax rates that make economic activity completely unappealing. The maximum amount of negative taxes would go to an individual who could earn no income. That guaranteed annual income is equal to the vertical intercept in Figure 9.10.

The basic problem with this proposal is affordability. The moment we flatten the net tax line somewhat (to remove work disincentives), we transfer a set of people from the tax-paying group to the welfare-receiving group. One way of appreciating this concern is by noting the break-even level of income that separates subsidy receivers from positive taxpayers. That break-even level under existing programs is given by the point where the dashed line crosses the horizontal axis in Figure 9.10. The break-even level for the negative income tax proposal occurs where the solid line crosses the market income axis in the same figure. Between these two income levels, it appears that individuals might change from being taxpayers to being subsidy receivers if the negative income tax proposal is implemented. The fear is that the government might have higher welfare costs.

One solution to this affordability problem is to shift both the slope and the intercept of the tax-subsidy schedule. That is, as the schedule is flattened to lower the net tax rate for those with low (but positive) incomes, the entire position of that flatter line could be moved up. The flattening lowers the work disincentive problem and the parallel shift up decreases the break-even level of income and thus lessens the affordability problem. But the remaining problem with this suggestion is that it puts a real squeeze on the most destitute — those with no income at all. By shortening the vertical intercept of the net tax schedule, we are shrinking the amount of the guaranteed annual income, perhaps to an unacceptable level.

Defenders of the negative income tax proposal argue that concerns about affordability are based on a misunderstanding. The whole point of this institutional change is to remove the disincentive to work and thus encourage people to move out to the right along the market income axis. Thus, despite the pivoting down of the tax-subsidy schedule, many individuals may increase their market earnings enough to pay more, not less, taxes, and others may qualify for less, not more, welfare.

Critics of the proposal apply the reasoning that we considered back in Chapter 7 (page 86). They argue that many people will not increase work time significantly when the overall tax rate is still high — especially if the stigma of having to report to welfare officials has been removed. Thus, critics argue, there will not be reduced administration costs after all.

During the late 1970s, several communities in Manitoba were chosen by the federal government to try out the negative income tax proposal. Various combinations of slope and intercept were involved in the experiments. The results of these and related experiments in the United States suggested two things. The first finding was that the cost of supporting those already receiving payments under a traditional welfare program did not increase. Individuals either worked more or found a job that was better paying enough that the cost to the government was no higher — even though welfare was "taxed back" at much lower rates. But the second finding confirmed the affordability worry. A significant number of individuals who were not previously receiving welfare were pulled into the subsidy-receiving group.

Overall, then, the negative income tax proposal involves more redistribution, so it is a more expensive program. This fact has made governments hesitant to adopt this reform. But many analysts have concluded that the removal of the fundamental reason for the poverty trap (the 100 percent effective marginal tax rate for the poor) is worth an increase in cost. The negative income tax plan has been endorsed by every royal commission that has investigated poverty in recent years.

SUMMARY

Here is a review of the key concepts covered in this chapter. We learned that people's incomes are limited by the willingness of firms to pay them for using the factors of production they own. This is the essence of the **marginal productivity theory** of **income distribution**. Incomes can be redistributed by using either **general** or **specific taxes**, and we learned that the general approach can avoid many unintended outcomes. For example, when their effects are combined, our welfare and income tax programs lead to large **disincentives to work**. We learned that a **guaranteed annual income** plan, otherwise known as a **negative income tax** system, may reduce this problem.

By accomplishing redistribution through a general income tax, we can avoid relying on strategies such as minimum wage laws and import tariffs to protect people's incomes. We saw in Chapter 1 the inefficiencies involved with minimum wage laws, and we will appreciate the costs of import tariffs after studying free trade in the next chapter. Taken as a group, these chapters make a strong case for focusing on a reformed income tax system as a most effective mechanism for helping those with lower incomes.

SUGGESTIONS FOR FURTHER READING

W. Block (ed.), *Morality of the Market: Religious and Economic Perspectives* (Vancouver: Fraser Institute, 1985) — essays discussing the relationship between economic analysis and religious principles.

R. Freeman, *The New Inequality* (Boston: Beacon Press, 1999), and R. Solow, *Work and Welfare* (Princeton, NJ: Princeton University Press, 1998) — two essays on how we can combine government initiatives for income support and job creation.

WEB ACTIVITIES

www.caledoninst.org
The Web site of the Caledon Institute of Social Policy in Ottawa, a group dedicated to monitoring Canada's performance regarding income inequality and poverty.

www.ncwcnbes.net
The Web site of the National Council of Welfare in Ottawa; many publications that focus on the plight of those on low incomes or government support.

www.ucobserver.org/archives/jan99_cv.htm
The Web site of the United Church of Canada's monthly magazine; this article takes aim at the market system.

Free Trade

INTRODUCTION

The preceding four chapters have focused on some of the shortcomings of the market mechanism. The implicit assumption has been that government intervention is recommended. But we must remember that well-intentioned policies can and do cause harm as well as good. The imposition of trade barriers provides an excellent example. Thus, to reintroduce balance, we end the microeconomics half of the book with an analysis of free trade.

Free trade involves dropping all import tariffs and quotas so that our companies (and those operating in other countries) compete directly with each other. Many people are suspicious of free trade because they are worried about layoffs in industries previously protected from foreign competition by tariffs. But economic analysis suggests that we should not reject free trade if what concerns us are layoffs and unfair income distributions. It indicates that the layoffs are most often temporary and that other policies can be much more effective than a permanent rejection of free trade for redistributing income and for ending recessions.

THE BENEFITS OF FREE TRADE

There are three main benefits of free trade. First, the competition provided by foreign firms forces domestic monopolists to behave more competitively. As consumers, we get more goods at lower prices since free trade is a substitute for what many people think has been an ineffective competition policy. Second, free trade opens up markets that are much larger than Canada's, so our firms can achieve large-scale economies of production and can therefore produce more goods at a lower cost per unit. Over the years, much of Canadian industry has operated at a size that simply has not allowed it to achieve full economies of scale. Third, when we trade with other countries, people in each country benefit from the fact that worker productivity varies from industry to industry and country to country.

Most of this chapter's analysis is focused on this third benefit. We investigate what economists call the principle of **comparative advantage**. This principle is perhaps most easily explained with an example used by David Ricardo, a famous economist who wrote nearly 200 years ago. He was advising the British government as to whether it should embark on a free-trade arrangement with other countries. The example concerns potential trade between England and Portugal. To keep his numerical example simple, Ricardo made several assumptions that we will follow.

To simplify, we assume that each country has just 100 workers in its labour force. There are no diminishing returns or economies of large scale no matter how big or small each industry is. And, to simplify the graphing, we consider just two industries: cloth and wine.

Table 10.1 shows how much labour is needed to produce one unit of each good in our example. To produce one barrel of wine, it takes ten of the workers in England but only two of the 100 workers in Portugal. So Portugal is better than England at producing wine in Ricardo's example. In the cloth industry, producing one bolt of cloth takes two workers in England and only one worker in Portugal. So once again the Portuguese get more output per worker than the English.

In Ricardo's example, Portugal is better at everything in absolute terms. This is the kind of situation in which people doubt that there will be benefits from free trade. How could Portugal get anything beneficial from trading with England as it is portrayed in this example? When a country is less efficient at producing everything, it has lower living standards. One would think that Portugal would fear having free trade with a country that has such "cheap wages." Similarly, one would expect the English to be very suspicious of free trade. Since they are uncompetitive in both industries, they would fear that they could not sell anything to Portugal, and they would fear mass unemployment if tariff protection were dropped. We shall see that these fears are unfounded since they are based on a confusion between a country's **absolute advantage** and its **comparative advantage**.

TABLE 10.1 *Ricardo's Free-Trade Analysis: Labour Requirement*

**Number of Workers
Needed to Produce**

	Portugal	England
One Barrel of Wine	2	10
One Bolt of Cloth	1	2

COMPARATIVE ADVANTAGE

We say that England is at an absolute disadvantage in the production of both commodities because English workers are less efficient at everything. But since they are only half as efficient in cloth production and two-tenths, or one-fifth, as efficient in the wine industry, we say that they actually have a comparative advantage in the production of cloth because that is the activity in which the workers are least bad. And Portugal has a comparative advantage in wine because, while Portuguese workers are more efficient in absolute terms at producing both wine and cloth, the margin of their extra efficiency is greater in the wine industry. As a result of these differences, both countries can benefit if each specializes in that area in which it has a comparative advantage and then trades with the other.

Most readers will be able to think of a similar example from their personal lives. Perhaps you have a neighbour who is an excellent auto mechanic, but she finds it more valuable to practise law. She trades with other people and hires someone else to work on her car. She has an absolute advantage in both providing legal services and repairing automobiles, but she specializes in the activity for which she has a comparative advantage — practising law.

Returning to Ricardo's example, we define comparative advantage according to which country's industry involves the lowest opportunity costs. As summarized in Table 10.2, in Portugal it takes two workers to produce one barrel of wine. The same two workers could also be producing two bolts of cloth, so the opportunity cost of using the two workers to produce a barrel of wine is that they are not available to produce two bolts of cloth. And since one worker in Portugal can produce half of a barrel of wine, this means that the opportunity cost of producing one bolt of cloth is half of a barrel of wine.

Now we proceed through similar reasoning for England. In that country, it takes ten workers to produce one barrel of wine, but the same workers could also be producing five bolts of cloth, so the opportunity cost of a barrel of wine in England is five bolts of cloth. Similarly, since the two workers that it takes to produce a bolt of cloth could also produce one-fifth of a bar-

TABLE 10.2 *Ricardo's Free-Trade Analysis: Opportunity Costs*

	Portugal	England
One Barrel of Wine	2 Bolts of Cloth	5 Bolts of Cloth
One Bolt of Cloth	1/2 Barrel of Wine	1/5 Barrel of Wine

rel of wine, the opportunity cost of a bolt of cloth in England is one-fifth of a barrel of wine. All these calculations are summarized in Table 10.2.

Which country has the lowest opportunity cost in each industry? Clearly, the opportunity cost of producing wine is lower in Portugal, so we say that Portugal has a comparative advantage in wine. Also, the opportunity cost of cloth is lower in England, so it has a comparative advantage in the production of cloth. It is cheaper to buy wine in Portugal, but it is cheaper (in terms of the amount of wine that must be given up) to buy cloth in England.

Suppose that without free trade England uses its 100 workers to produce 25 bolts of cloth and 5 barrels of wine, while Portugal uses its 100 workers to produce 10 bolts of cloth and 45 barrels of wine. In that case, world production is 25 + 10 = 35 bolts of cloth and 5 + 45 = 50 barrels of wine.

World Production with No Trade
cloth = 25 + 10 = 35 bolts
wine = 5 + 45 = 50 barrels

Now let us see what would happen if these countries specialized in the industry in which each has a comparative advantage and then traded that product. If the English produce nothing but cloth, then they will create 50 bolts of cloth. They can then trade some of the cloth to Portugal for wine. If the Portuguese specialize in wine, they will produce 50 barrels of wine and no cloth. They can trade some of the wine to England to get cloth in exchange. In that case, world production is as follows.

World Production with Free Trade
cloth = 50 + 0 = 50 bolts
wine = 0 + 50 = 50 barrels

After specialization, there are still 50 barrels of wine in total, but now they are all being produced in Portugal. And now there are 50 bolts of cloth, not just 35. So there are fifteen more bolts of cloth in this example — that is a 43 percent increase in the availability of one of the two goods with no loss of the other good. Thus, overall, there is an unambiguous gain to the citizens in both countries.

This gain follows from specialization. International trade does not represent a win–lose situation. One country does not gain because the other loses. Both countries can share the benefits of using their scarce resources in the most efficient way by having each economy concentrate on producing what it is, comparatively speaking, better at producing.

Economists consider it a shame when countries cannot get together to enjoy these benefits. This lack of co-ordination often happens for two reasons. For one thing, there is a lack of knowledge concerning the principle of comparative advantage. Another problem is that usually, at the individual level, there are both winners and losers. There is an overall net gain. But some individuals in both countries must switch jobs, and doing so can be very disruptive.

To look at how gains and losses are distributed, we turn to supply and demand, and we focus on the wine industry as our example. We proceed in three stages. First we examine how market equilibrium is determined when international trade is involved.

SUPPLY AND DEMAND WITH FREE TRADE

Figure 10.1 shows the demand and supply curves for wine in both Portugal and England. As a base for comparison, we first consider the equilibrium in each country that would exist with no foreign trade. Because wine production is costly in England, the price of wine would be high in the right-hand panel of Figure 10.1. Portugal has a relatively low price because the opportunity costs of producing wine there are lower.

Now consider free trade. For simplicity, we abstract from transportation costs and assume them to be negligible. Given this assumption, a free-trade equilibrium will emerge with just one world price, and at that price the world quantity demanded must equal the world quantity supplied. Put another way, at the world price the excess quantity of wine demanded in the importing country must equal the excess quantity supplied in the exporting country.

The equilibrium price is given by the height of the horizontal line running across both panels in Figure 10.1. At this price, consumers in England demand more wine than is produced domestically, so there is a shortage that is just covered by what they receive from Portugal as imports. Portugal is willing to export this amount since at this higher price (than obtained before trade), Portuguese producers want to sell more than Portuguese consumers

FIGURE 10.1
Supply and Demand with Free Trade

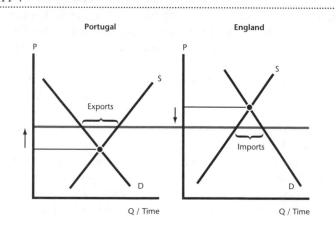

want to buy. An equilibrium exists because there is a common price ruling in both countries, with the excess supply in Portugal (its exports) just balancing the excess demand in England (its imports).

In reality, of course, the transportation costs involved in taking goods from one country to another affect these conclusions somewhat. But even with transportation costs, free trade provides competition that forces the prices of traded items to differ across two locations only by precise amounts. To return to Ricardo's example, as long as the gap in prices is greater than the transportation costs, it pays for someone to buy more wine in the low-price location (Portugal) and sell it in the high-price location (England). Just as before, this process makes wine more scarce in Portugal, so wine prices rise there, and it makes wine more plentiful in England, so wine prices fall there. Thus, the price differential is narrowed by these competitive forces until it just equals transportation costs. By ignoring transportation costs, then, our analysis of free trade will overstate slightly how much convergence to a common price takes place. But to understand who are the winners and who are the losers following a move to free trade, it is convenient for us to simplify by ignoring transportation costs.

THE EFFECTS OF FREE TRADE IN THE IMPORTING COUNTRY

We can now use the supply and demand graphs for the wine industry to analyze who gains and who loses, and what are the net benefits for both countries, following a move to free trade. First we consider which individuals in England gain and lose from a policy of free trade.

We assess free trade by comparing the no-trade outcome with what occurs after a free-trade equilibrium is reached and by focusing on a particular range of output at each stage of the analysis. We begin in England, the importing country. With the falling price of wine there, households slide down their demand curve and consume a greater quantity — an amount given by the width of the shaded area in the right-hand panel of Figure 10.2. The extra satisfaction that these English wine drinkers receive from this extra consumption is given by this area under their demand curve over this range of output — the shaded trapezoid in Figure 10.2. To get that extra satisfaction, the English just have to pay Portugal the going world price times the number of units consumed — in other words, the lightly shaded rectangle in Figure 10.2. So the surplus — the excess of additional benefits over what must be paid — is the small dark triangle in Figure 10.2. This is the net benefit to wine drinkers in England. It is a gain for wine drinkers and not a loss to anyone else in England.

The next range of output that we consider is indicated by the shaded trapezoid in Figure 10.3. This range is the amount produced by wine producers in England before free trade. This domestic wine has been replaced by imports from Portugal. Domestic producers have reacted to the falling price

FIGURE 10.2

Free Trade in the Importing Country

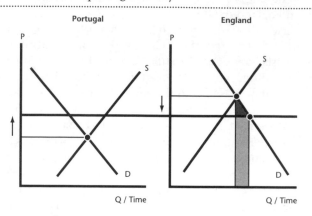

FIGURE 10.3

Free Trade in the Importing Country: Efficiency Effects

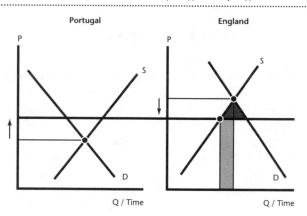

by sliding down their supply curves. Before free trade, the cost to England of producing this wine domestically was the area under the supply curve — the shaded trapezoid in Figure 10.3. But, after free trade is established, the cost to England of getting that wine from Portugal is just the lightly shaded rectangle (since this area is defined by world per-unit price times this number of units). So the cost with free trade is less than the cost that the English used to incur by getting this amount of wine from domestic producers. The cost saving is the difference in area between the trapezoid and the rectangle, so the darkly shaded triangle is another part of the net gain to the English that follows from free trade. Resources previously used to produce wine at a high cost have been freed up to produce cloth.

The final range of output that we discuss is indicated by the width of the shaded rectangle in Figure 10.4. This quantity of wine is the amount that the

FIGURE 10.4

Free Trade in the Importing Country: Equity Effects

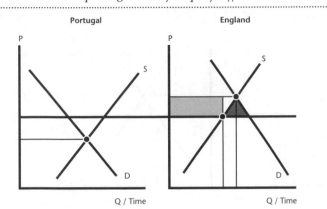

English produce domestically and consume both before and after free trade. For this range of output, the only change is that English wine drinkers used to pay a high price per unit, and now they have to pay only the lower world price. The per-unit saving is given by the height of the shaded rectangle in Figure 10.4, and the total saving for consumers is the area of the rectangle. But this saving is a straight transfer from wine producers to wine drinkers. What consumers gain, domestic producers lose. So this area is not a net gain or loss for the country as a whole.

This transfer from domestic producers to domestic consumers can certainly explain why the producers of wine in England would lobby hard to keep their government from allowing this move to free trade, even though there is a net gain to England as a whole (given by the area of the two darkly shaded triangles in Figure 10.4).

All moves to free trade create gains and losses like those of the English consumers and producers in our example because free trade changes prices, and buyers like price decreases, while suppliers do not. The distribution of gains and losses (between buyers and sellers) displays the opposite pattern in the exporting country, as we will see in the next section. But it is important to remember that the gains outweigh the losses by an amount equal to the dark grey triangles. Furthermore, the graph represents what goes on every period, so the total value of a move to free trade is a whole series of net benefits, with each item in this sum equal to the area of the shaded triangles in Figure 10.4.

THE EFFECTS OF FREE TRADE IN THE EXPORTING COUNTRY

The output of wine in Portugal increases with free trade by an amount equal to the width of the shaded trapezoid in Figure 10.5. The value of resources

FIGURE 10.5
Free Trade in the Exporting Country

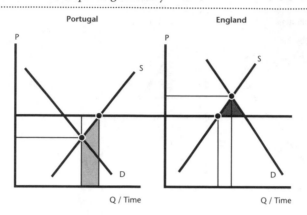

FIGURE 10.6
Free Trade in the Exporting Country: Efficiency Effects

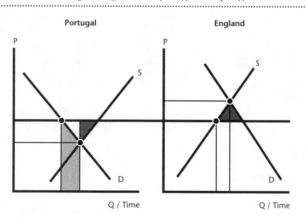

involved in producing this much extra wine is equal to the area under the marginal cost curve over this range of expanded output — that is, the area of the shaded trapezoid. But the English are paying the Portuguese a larger amount than this for that extra wine — a rectangle with the same width as the trapezoid and a height given by the world price line. (The world price times that many barrels of wine is what the English have to pay.) So the payment from England exceeds the amount that Portugal incurred in terms of actual resources used to get the payment by an amount equal to the darkly shaded triangle shown in the left-hand panel of Figure 10.6. This area represents a net gain for Portugal.

The next range of output that we analyze is defined by the width of the shaded trapezoid in Figure 10.6. This amount was, and still is, produced within Portugal. It used to be consumed by Portuguese wine drinkers, and their

FIGURE 10.7
Free Trade in the Exporting Country: Equity Effects

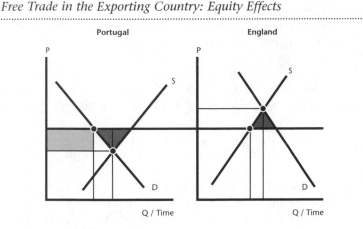

benefits equalled the corresponding area under their demand curve — the shaded trapezoid. With free trade, Portuguese consumers lose that benefit, but Portuguese producers receive the entire rectangle indicated by the world price times this many barrels of wine that they are now exporting to England. So total compensation to the Portuguese for the loss of that amount of wine is the entire rectangle, and this compensation is bigger than what they had to give up to get it (just the trapezoid portion of the rectangle). So there is another triangle of net gain for Portugal, and it is shaded in dark grey in Figure 10.7.

The rest of the wine production is the amount indicated by the width of the lightly shaded rectangle in Figure 10.7. This rectangle represents a redistribution within Portugal. Domestic wine drinkers have lost at the expense of the wine producers since they must pay the higher world price on each unit purchased. But, as in the case of England, where the transfer went in the opposite direction, it is important to remember that this transfer does not represent any net gain or loss for Portugal. Transfer payments cancel each other from the nation's point of view. Overall, gains exceed losses in Portugal by the sum of the two darkly shaded triangles in the left-hand panel of Figure 10.7 and this net gain is received every period.

COMPARING THE BENEFITS AND COSTS OF FREE TRADE

Economists have estimated the elasticities of supply and demand for all the major commodities that are traded, so they have estimated the size of the shaded triangles in Figure 10.7. In the Canada–U.S. case, economists estimated that the total benefits to Canada from the Free Trade Agreement in 1989 amounted to an annual flow of increased Canadian income roughly equal to 3 percent of the total output of the Canadian economy. This increase in income exists for every year into the indefinite future, now that the expansion of our exporting industries and the contraction of our import-competing industries has been completed.

In Chapter 20, we will see how to calculate the present discounted value of this entire stream of benefits. The result is that the benefits stemming from the Canada–U.S. Free Trade Agreement are estimated to be equivalent to a once-and-for-all increase in the material welfare of Canadians equal to five-sixths of the entire output of the Canadian economy. So the overall gains from free trade can be large. The problem is that these benefits do not come immediately; they come in relatively small amounts over many years. And the dislocation costs of moving to free trade do come immediately. The question that Canada faced in the late 1980s was "Should we give up five-sixths of an entire year's output of our economy to avoid the costs that are imposed on the subset of the population that must relocate and retrain when previously protected industries are exposed to foreign competition?"

One way of answering that question is to ask another. We could ask those individuals who would be forced to relocate and retrain, "How much would you need to receive to feel fully compensated for this income loss and dislocation?" Economists have considered the amount of compensation that might be required, and in Chapter 20 we see how those calculations are made. Even when pessimistic assumptions are made concerning how many people are adversely affected in the short run, the costs of free trade are dominated by the benefits. Those who gain from trade receive far more than enough to compensate those who lose from it. For this reason, economists favour free trade.

Many Canadians were less than impressed with the actual free-trade agreement achieved with the United States, and later with Mexico. Economists can understand this reaction because these agreements are just one part of the suggested two-part package advocated by economists. The FTA and NAFTA deals embraced free trade but offered little **adjustment assistance** beyond policies already in place to people hurt by the need to retrain and relocate.

We can all benefit by gearing our trade policy decisions to providing higher incomes over the longer term (i.e., by embracing free trade) if we use our other policy instruments to redistribute income and cushion the blows from big changes in the economy. The cost of failure to use these other policies is limited political acceptance of free trade. Over the longer run, then, living standards will be noticeably lower if we do a poor job of managing economic change through adjustment assistance.

They key word here is *managing* change, which is very different from resisting change. The whole point of removing tariffs is to force people to move out of industries in which Canada does not have a comparative advantage and to get jobs in industries in which we do have a comparative advantage. In the long run, once that adjustment is complete, people receive higher wages because they are employed in an industry in which they are truly productive. So it is an issue of long-term gain with short-term pain. This change can be managed if tariff reductions are accomplished gradually, with a clear schedule that is well announced and adhered to over the years. When this strategy is adopted, workers can plan their careers sensibly. As long as young people enter a declining industry at a slower rate than older workers retire, the work force can contract gradually without any layoffs. By following a gradual plan of this sort, we can achieve the longer-term benefits of free trade while limiting the government's need to offer adjustment assistance.

The inequitable income distribution effects that follow from free trade do not indicate that free trade is bad on balance. Instead, these problems indicate that our distribution policy, not our trade policy, deserves attention.

Economists have a similar reaction to people's concerns about layoffs in industries protected by tariffs before a free-trade arrangement is put in place. Many of the remaining chapters of this book are devoted to a detailed discussion of what is called **stabilization policy**. If used properly, the tools of stabilization policy can limit the size and duration of a recession.

ASSIGNING POLICY INSTRUMENTS TO ECONOMIC GOALS

We have several objectives in conducting economic policy, and the government has several instruments with which to pursue those goals. There is more than one way to allocate the policy instruments across the various objectives, and experience suggests that there is a preferred assignment. Economic policy has three broad goals:

A) efficiency;
B) equity; and
C) stabilization

We face many trade-offs if we do not consider at least three independent tools of economic policy, such as

1) market regulations (e.g., tariffs);
2) the tax system; and
3) monetary, fiscal, and exchange rate policy.

Economists generally favour the following assignment of instruments to goals. Market regulations such as tariffs should be phased out to maximize efficiency and thereby raise the standard of living for the average person. Then, the progressivity of a general income tax (perhaps including generous exemptions for saving and a negative income tax component) should be adjusted to ensure that this higher standard of living is distributed fairly. Finally, monetary, fiscal, and exchange rate policy should be set so that the severity of recessions and inflationary episodes is lessened. In short, economists favour pairing policy instrument 1 with policy goal A, instrument 2 with goal B, and instrument 3 with goal C. Any other assignment fails to exploit the comparative advantage of each policy instrument.

SUMMARY

Here is a review of the key concepts covered in this chapter. We have learned that **free trade** brings several benefits: it forces domestic monopolists to behave **more competitively**; it allows firms to operate at a scale that is larger than the domestic market (and thus to achieve the lower unit costs that stem from **scale economies**); and it permits all countries to exploit **comparative advantage**.

Every country must have a comparative advantage in something, since there must be some industry in which the extent of its low-productivity problem is the least. A country's standard of living depends on its **absolute advantage**, but no matter how low that standard is it can be raised because of comparative advantage.

There are individual winners and losers when a country enters a free-trade agreement, but the present value of the net benefits exceeds the short-run costs by a wide margin. Also, the costs can be spread more evenly by embracing free trade gradually (as Canada has done over the postwar period) and by offering **adjustment assistance**. Finally, short-run adjustment costs can be lessened if recessions can be limited by **stabilization policy** — an issue that we will pursue in the next several chapters.

SUGGESTIONS FOR FURTHER READING

T.G. Bucholtz, *New Ideas from Dead Economists* (New York: Penguin, 1990), Chapter 10.

S.E. Landsburg, *The Armchair Economist: Economics and Everyday Life* (New York: Free Press, 1993), Chapter 21.

WEB ACTIVITIES

www.irpp.org
Policy Options June 1999 is devoted to "Free Trade at 10."

www.strategis.ic.gc.ca/engdoc/main.html
The Web site of Industry Canada; click on "Economic Analysis and Statistics." The spring 1999 issue of the *Micro-Economic Monitor* contains "A Report Card on Canada's Trade and Investment Record." The autumn 1999 issue of the *Micro-Economic Monitor* contains "Canada in the 21st Century." The *Micro-Economic Monitor* can be accessed at www.strategis.ic.gc.ca/sc_ecnmy/engdoc/homepage.html.

CHAPTER ELEVEN

Unemployment, Inflation, and National Output

LEARNING OBJECTIVES

After reading this chapter, you should understand
- how unemployment, inflation, and national output are measured;
- how inflation interacts with our tax system to discourage saving and investment, thereby reducing living standards in the long run; and

- how the tools of supply and demand are used to understand why business cycles occur in the short run and why governments sometimes try to stabilize these fluctuations in employment, thereby refusing to rely entirely on the economy's self-correction mechanism.

INTRODUCTION

Over the years, the total output of the Canadian economy grows. For example, by the end of the twentieth century, output per person was more than two and a half times its 1950 value. But this large increase in material living standards has not been steady; the economy has gone through a series of cycles. Sometimes we have a recession — a period during which total output of the economy shrinks and unemployment rises. At other times, our economy is "overheated" — and the level of total output is beyond the economy's long-run capacity. Inflation occurs in this case. In the next several chapters, we will work toward understanding how these cycles in our economy develop. In the final chapters of the book, we will focus on the determinants of the long-run trend. We will consider these issues from a country-wide point of view, often examining the question as if we were the federal minister of finance or the governor of the Bank of Canada. Economists call this part of their subject, which deals with the whole economy at once, **macroeconomics**.

UNEMPLOYMENT

We measure unemployment by interviewing a representative survey of the population each month. Those interviewed fall into one of the following three categories:

1) employed
2) unemployed
3) not in the labour force

People are listed as employed if they have a job or are working in a family business such as a farm. If people do not have a job but want one, then they are listed as unemployed. The sum of the people in these two categories is called the labour force. Not everyone is in the labour force — some people are happy without a job. Retired people and full-time students are among those classified in the third group.

The **unemployment rate** is the total number of unemployed as a proportion of the labour force. In terms of people in the groups just listed, the unemployment rate is $[2/(1 + 2)]$ x 100%. As we have already noted, the unemployment rate goes up during recessions, but the amount that it goes up is understated because of what is known as the **discouraged worker effect**. Consider a recession. The fall in demand for firms' products means that firms lay off some workers. Some people thus move from group 1 to group 2. But at the same time, with the chance of getting a job so much reduced, a number of people stop looking for work. These discouraged workers are then listed as not in the labour force. Surveys show that sometimes almost as many people move from group 2 to group 3 as move from group 1 to group 2, so the measured unemployment rate understates economic hardship. It does not rise as much as it should during a recession. We can check the magnitude of this measurement problem by watching how much the **participation rate** falls below trend during recessions. The participation rate is the ratio of the labour force to the population (i.e., in terms of numbers in the labour force survey groups, $[(1 + 2)(1 + 2 + 3)$ x 100%].

INFLATION

As with unemployment, we measure inflation by conducting a survey. About every five years, the government surveys people and uses this information to decide the basket of goods and services intended to represent the typical purchases of a Canadian household. Then the government traces the changing cost of that fixed base of items for the next several years. As time passes, people change their expenditure patterns, so the longer we focus on a particular basket of items, the less relevant it is to know how much that set of items costs. Many therefore regard the resulting index, the **consumer price index**, or **CPI**, as somewhat arbitrary. For example, we know that people shift to less expensive items (at least partially) when prices increase, thereby decreasing to some extent the increase in their cost of living. Since the CPI traces the cost of living without allowing for this substitution for more costly items, its increase tends to overstate the true escalation in the cost of living by about half a percentage point per year. In any event, the inflation rate is simply the percentage change in this surveyed price index from one period to the next.

The CPI traces the prices of goods in terms of the amount of Canadian money it takes to buy them. So inflation means that domestic money loses some of its purchasing power. If Canada experiences inflation while our trading partners do not, our currency loses international purchasing power as well. In such a case, the Canadian dollar falls in international value — that is, our exchange rate falls. Overall, there are three variables that measure one aspect of the value of money: its domestic purchasing power is measured by the CPI; its international purchasing power is measured by the exchange rate; and the price of borrowing money is measured by the interest rate. In this chapter, we focus on the CPI and domestic inflation; consideration of interest rates and exchange rates is left for later chapters.

WHY UNEMPLOYMENT AND INFLATION ARE UNDESIRABLE

Everyone has read about some of the hardships of the Great Depression in the 1930s, a period in which our unemployment rate reached 25 percent. It seems obvious that high levels of unemployment are undesirable. Material living standards fall when our available resources are not used, and people's sense of self-worth suffers when they are not wanted. There is much evidence that physical and mental health problems and criminal activities rise with unemployment

But the costs of inflation are less apparent. What is so bad about just a few percentage points of inflation each year? One problem is that inflation redistributes income in an arbitrary way. At 6 percent inflation, it takes only twelve years for prices to double. A pensioner who saves all through her working life is fundamentally hurt by an inflation that occurs after she retires. When prices double and her income is fixed in dollar terms after her retirement, her real welfare is much reduced. Indeed, the real value of her pension is cut in half after twelve years.

Inflation also affects the amount that society is willing to invest in new equipment that workers can use to make themselves more productive and earn higher incomes. A society will not have any newly produced output to be used in this investment process if its citizens are not willing to save — that is, to abstain from current consumption so that the new machines can be built. In short, lower household saving makes less investment by firms possible, and inflation reduces the incentive to save.

Suppose you save by lending money to someone during a period in which prices double. Suppose that person buys a house. When she repays you the money, you receive an amount that will buy only half a house. So inflation makes saving less appealing, unless inflation makes the interest you earn on your savings go up enough to compensate.

Savings depend on what economists call the **real after-tax rate of interest**. We can calculate this yield by using this formula:

real after-tax yield on savings = $r(1 - t) - p$.

To calculate the true yield on savings, we first take the market rate of interest, denoted by r, and scale it down by the factor $(1 - t)$, which is one minus the saver's income tax rate, denoted by t. The proportion of interest that the lender gets to keep is (1 – t). But even that amount overstates the lender's real yield. We also have to subtract the inflation rate over the lending period, denoted by p, to find out what her after-tax return is in terms of real purchasing power.

Let us substitute some representative numbers into this real-yield formula so that we can realize the implications of inflation. Consider a lender who faces a 50 percent marginal tax rate, and assume that initially the market interest rate is 6 percent and that there is no inflation. The lender's after-tax nominal return is 3 percent. With no inflation, the real rate of return is also 3 percent. Now suppose inflation rises to 6 percent. Let us assume that the market interest rate rises by the same 6 percentage points (to 12 percent) so that, without considering taxes, the lender would be fully compensated for the decreased purchasing power of money that occurs while her money is lent out. The lender is left with a 6 percent nominal return on an after-tax basis. But then she still has to subtract the inflation rate of 6 percent to get her real yield, and this is now down to zero. So in this instance, *even* when the market rate of interest rises by the full amount of the inflation, the real return to lending has fallen from 3 percent to zero.

This example makes clear that, when inflation interacts with a tax system designed for no inflation, the return to saving is decreased. As noted earlier, only when a society saves does it make available some of its newly produced output in the form of new machines and factories. So, with lower levels of saving, there is less new equipment for the future labour force to use. As a result, we have lower standards of living in the future, compared with what we could have with no inflation. So even mild inflation interacting with our tax system means significant income losses in the future.

Since both unemployment and inflation are costly, many individuals expect their government to "do something" to solve these problems. But we cannot assess the potential of government policies to be effective in preventing unemployment and inflation unless we have a detailed idea of what causes them to vary. It will take us several chapters to develop this understanding fully, but we begin that task here. We now focus our attention on what determines the country's total output, what economists call the **gross domestic product**, or **GDP**. We proceed with three tasks: we see how the GDP is measured, how it has varied, and how economists analyze those movements.

GROSS DOMESTIC PRODUCT

What we are trying to measure with the GDP is job-creating activity. The gross domestic product is the sum of all currently produced final goods and services created in the country in a particular period, say, one year. Some sales do not involve current production. For example, if Brian sells David his old car, that transaction would not enter this year's GDP calculation. Brian's old car is a pre-existing object; no production activity takes place in the swapping of existing assets such as dollars for the car. So workers at Statistics Canada cannot simply add up all transactions.

Statisticians must also take care when calculating GDP to avoid counting the same economic activity more than once. For instance, wheat production gets counted when statisticians add in the sales of wheat farmers. Then, when they include the sales of bread, wheat production gets counted again since the price of bread includes what bakers have to pay to farmers for the wheat. One way of avoiding this double-counting problem is to include only final goods and services. One problem with this approach, however, is that it is hard to know when something is a final good. For example, natural gas sold to heat a private home is a final good, but that sold to heat a factory represents an intermediate product.

Luckily, there are several methods of calculating GDP. When all measures give similar totals, our confidence in the data increases. Here we consider just one of the other methods. It does not involve looking at the financial records of firms (as does tallying up sales figures of the producers of final goods). Instead, this method involves adding up all the pre-tax incomes earned by households (not including capital gains or losses on pre-existing assets). This method works because every time some value is created in the production process, some income is earned — either paid out as wages, rents, or interest payments or kept as profits for the owners of the firms. Thus, the sum of all income (including profits) must equal the GDP.

Of course, some of the income generated by economic activity within Canada does not represent income for Canadians. To the extent that foreigners own some of the capital equipment employed in Canada, and to the extent that Canadians are in debt to foreigners, the income of domestic nationals is less than domestic production. Thus, what is known as the **gross national product**, or **GNP**, is less that the gross domestic product. Since the cyclical swings in GDP and GNP are almost identical, we ignore the difference between them in our analysis.

As noted earlier, with more than one method to calculate GDP, statisticians can develop some confidence that they are measuring variations in the overall level of job-creating activity with a fair degree of accuracy. But we cannot forget something we all learned in school — that we cannot add apples and oranges. Instead of adding up baskets of apples and crates of oranges, statisticians add up the dollar amounts of sales in each industry. They measure everything in dollar amounts, not in physical quantities.

However, there is a problem with this method — the measure can stretch with inflation. Suppose that from one year to the next the price of every product doubles and that no new jobs are created. In this case, our GDP measure will say that the level of overall production has doubled. But of course no more real goods and services were produced in this case. The only thing that doubled was the set of entries on all the price tags.

So measuring the GDP by using the current market values for all newly produced final goods and services each year is not such a good idea after all. But this total, called **nominal GDP**, serves as a useful stepping stone to a better statistic. Statisticians take the appropriate price index and divide nominal GDP by this average level of prices to get what we call **real GDP**. If all prices double, then both nominal GDP and the price index double, and this general increase in prices cancels out in the calculation of real GDP, so this measure is unaffected.

Thus, real GDP is the sum of all currently produced final goods and services measured in constant prices, and it is what we should focus on when we hear news reports about the economy. It is the variation in this measure that indicates swings in the overall amount of job-creating activity. Economists call these swings **business cycles**.

BUSINESS CYCLES

Figure 11.1 illustrates Canadian real GDP for the last four decades: 1960 until 2000. You can see the typical pattern for essentially all economies. GDP follows a rather wavy line. Analysts refer to this wavy line as a series of business cycles. The periods involving a downswing, when real GDP is falling, are referred to as **recessions**. The upswings are often called periods in which the economy is becoming **overheated**. We can appreciate why this term is used by focusing on the other line in Figure 11.1, which shows the country's potential GDP. Potential GDP refers to level of overall output that the economy could have produced in each year if all the available resources — machines, factories, and workers — were utilized.

Two facts are evident in the graph. First, the potential GDP path has few wiggles because, in short periods of time, there are few drastic changes in the size of the population or in the quantity of capital equipment and technical knowledge available. Second, the actual GDP line has often been below the potential GDP, indicating periods involving excess capacity, and the actual GDP line is sometimes above potential.

FIGURE 11.1
Canada's GDP Gap for Recent Years

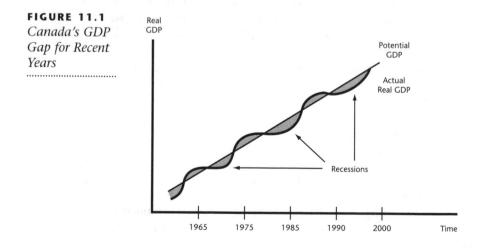

You might well wonder how we sometimes did better than our potential. It is because we define potential not as the maximum output possible in the short run but as that possible on a sustainable basis — assuming that workers are receiving adequate time to rest and that machines are being properly maintained. With heavy doses of overtime labour and by running machines without adequate downtime for proper repair, we can produce more than is possible on a longer-run sustainable basis. This is reflected at several points in Figure 11.1, when actual GDP exceeds potential GDP.

The shading in Figure 11.1 highlights periods when actual GDP fell significantly short of potential GDP — the recessions when our unemployment rate was much higher than at other times. If we add up all the areas between the actual GDP time path and the potential line, then we get some idea of the total value of goods and services that we could have produced had Canada not had any business cycles. For the period shown in Figure 11.1, when this calculation is done, the total is equal to about 70 percent of the final year's GDP, so there's a lot of material welfare lost when we have recessions and high unemployment.

AGGREGATE SUPPLY AND DEMAND CURVES

Several of the remaining chapters are devoted to developing a detailed understanding of why these cycles in overall economic activity occur. With this understanding, we will have a mechanism through which we can evaluate the government's ability to limit unemployment and inflation. The remainder of this chapter introduces the basic tools of business cycle analysis: **aggregate supply and demand curves**.

The overall demand for goods produced within our economy depends on many things, and several of the more important influences are listed in Table 11.1. The first three items affect aggregate demand in a positive way; for example, as people's incomes rise, government expenditures rise, and as export sales increase, demand for our products increases. Other things affect aggregate demand in a negative way; for example, as the prices of products increase, people pay more in taxes, and as interest rates for borrowing increase,

TABLE 11.1 *Some Determinants of Aggregate Demand*

People's Incomes Government Expenditures Amount of Exports	} Positive Influences
Price of Goods Level of Taxes Borrowing Costs	} Negative Influences

FIGURE 11.2
The Aggregate Demand Curve
....

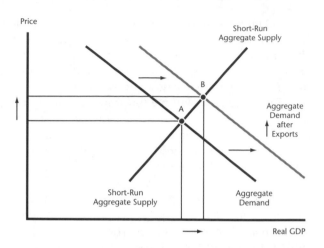

demand for our products decreases. The aggregate demand curve shows the effect on the quantity demanded of just one of these many influences. The inverse dependence of demand on the price of goods is shown by the negative slope of the aggregate demand curves in Figure 11.2.

The way that we show the influence of all the other determinants of demand is to shift the entire position of the demand curve. For instance, to pick just one of the influences listed in the table, an increase in export sales would stimulate spending and thus be shown as a move to the right of the demand curve, as shown in Figure 11.2. While not shown in the graph, a cut in government spending, an increase in taxes, or an increase in borrowing costs would decrease spending and thus shift the demand curve to the left. So variations in price involve a movement along the aggregate demand curve, while variations in the other determinants of demand cause a shift of that curve.

On the supply side, there are many influences as well (as indicated in Table 11.2). Again, the price of goods matters, but this time a higher price makes it possible for firms to profitably produce more output, so price is one of the positive influences. Another is technical knowledge. The higher the level of worker productivity, the more goods and services we can produce at any price. Negative influences on the quantity supplied are things such as higher input prices; for example, the higher the wages firms must pay for labour and the more expensive the foreign currencies needed to pay for imported raw materials and other intermediate products, the less the quantity supplied.

The dependence of aggregate supply on the price of the product itself is shown as a positively sloped line in both Figures 11.2 and 11.3. The entire position of this aggregate supply curve moves whenever we consider a change in any of those other determinants of the supply of goods. For instance, an increase in productivity, a cut in sales taxes, a decrease in wage rates, a decrease in the world price of oil — all shift the supply curve out to

TABLE 11.2 *Some Determinants of Aggregate Supply*

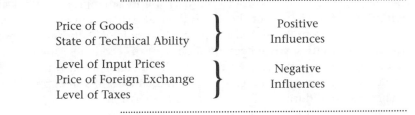

| Price of Goods | } | Positive |
| State of Technical Ability | | Influences |

Level of Input Prices	}	Negative
Price of Foreign Exchange		Influences
Level of Taxes		

the right (to show an increased ability or willingness of firms to produce goods) or down (to show a decrease in costs). The opposite case is shown in Figure 11.3. An increase in the price of raw materials, such as oil, raises firms' unit costs, so it shifts up the short-run aggregate supply curve. As with the demand curve, variations in the price involve a movement along the supply curve, while variations in the other determinants of aggregate supply cause a shift of that curve.

Armed with these basic tools, we can understand how real GDP is determined and why variations in its level occur. Real GDP is determined by the intersection of the aggregate demand and supply curves, so let us think of the economy as being initially at point A in either Figure 11.2 or Figure 11.3 before a shock hits the economy. Business cycles are caused by either demand shifts or supply shifts. For example, suppose that other countries drop their tariffs and that, as a result, we manage to sell many more exports to the rest of the world. That increase in demand for our products is shown by the shift to the right of the aggregate demand curve in Figure 11.2, and the new outcome is point B. Projecting the location of points A and B onto both axes to show the results of this shift, we see that one is rising prices, which is inflation,

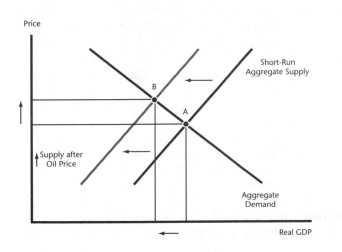

FIGURE 11.3
The Short-Run Aggregate Supply Curve

and the other is rising levels of real output. With more goods being produced, more workers get jobs (so there is a decrease in unemployment associated with the increase in output shown on the real GDP axis in Figure 11.2).

So we see from Figure 11.2 that there is a **trade-off between unemployment and inflation** when demand shocks hit the economy. Unemployment goes down when inflation goes up. But this outcome occurs only with shifts in demand. Business cycles can also be caused by shifts in supply. One instance occurred during the 1970s, when the Organization of Petroleum Exporting Countries (OPEC) formed a cartel and quadrupled the world price of oil. This increase in input prices meant a major shift to the left in Canada's aggregate supply curve, so we moved from an initial observation point A in Figure 11.3 to the new outcome point B. Again, projections onto the axes show the effects of that development — higher prices but lower levels of real goods and services produced. Of course, with less production, fewer jobs are available. So in the case of shifts in the position of the short-run aggregate supply curve, there is not a trade-off between unemployment and inflation. We see in Figure 11.3 that we experience rising inflation and rising unemployment at the same time.

A SELF-CORRECTION MECHANISM

At several points in this chapter, we have acknowledged that many people expect the government to "do something" about unemployment or inflation. But in the earlier chapters on microeconomics, we focused on the existence of the invisible hand and noted that often intervention by the government is not needed. Is there an analogue to the invisible hand in macroeconomics? The answer is "yes." While it sometimes works very slowly, a self-correction mechanism can eliminate unemployment and inflation automatically. We now use aggregate supply and demand curves to explain how this self-correction mechanism operates.

We have been using the term *short-run aggregate supply curve*. It is now time to clarify the difference between the short-run and the long-run capacity of the economy, which is our potential GDP. We impose a long-run capacity constraint in our graphs by drawing in a vertical line, positioned along the real GDP axis at the level of potential GDP, as in Figure 11.4. Recall that by potential we mean the level of production that can be sustained over a long period. When the aggregate demand and short-run supply curves intersect to the left of the long-run potential line, we know that we have a level of output too small to generate jobs for everyone. On the other hand, if the intersection of the demand and short-run supply curves occurs to the right of the long-run potential line, then it means that we are producing more than we can maintain on a sustainable basis.

This situation is shown in Figure 11.5. There we see that the economy is experiencing what economists call an **inflationary gap** — with actual GDP exceeding its long-run potential. In this situation, factors of produc-

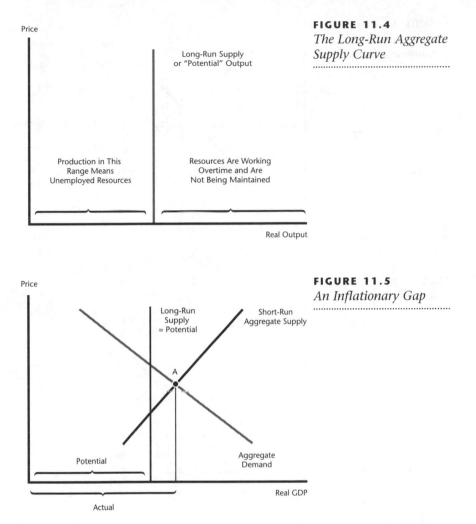

FIGURE 11.4
The Long-Run Aggregate Supply Curve

FIGURE 11.5
An Inflationary Gap

tion are scarce. Everyone is working overtime, so the wages that people are able to command will rise. Firms are competing with one another to acquire these scarce factors. As wages and other input prices rise, firms' unit costs rise. Since the short-run aggregate supply curve is the entire economy's marginal cost curve, it shifts up (as shown in Figure 11.6) as wages and other input prices rise. So we gradually move from the starting point A to the final point B.

To summarize, whenever the economy starts off at a point that is beyond its long-run supply potential, the process of wage and price inflation pulls it back to the long-run sustainable level of output. In short, a bout of inflation will cure an inflationary gap. As already emphasized, this happens automatically. We do not need a policy-maker to fix an inflationary gap.

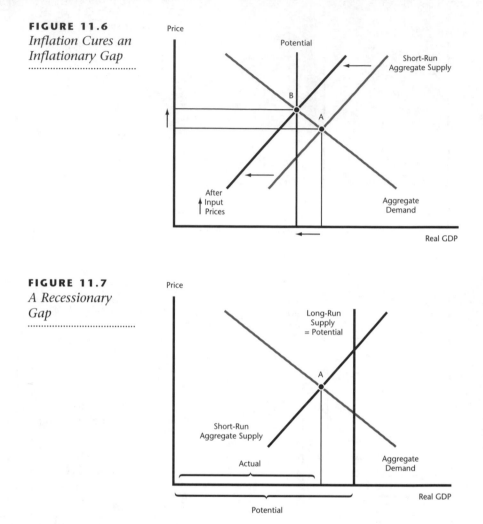

FIGURE 11.6
Inflation Cures an
Inflationary Gap
....

FIGURE 11.7
A Recessionary
Gap
....

Now let us consider the other kind of imbalance with which we could start. The aggregate demand and short-run supply curves could intersect to the left of the long-run potential line. This situation, called a **recessionary gap**, is shown in Figure 11.7. In this case, men and women want jobs but cannot find them, and machines are idle. We do not observe large wage increases in this case; indeed, in trying to get jobs, workers typically accept concessions, and there are lower input prices. Lower input prices mean a shift down and to the right of the short-run supply curve. So gradually, without any policy-maker doing anything, the short-run supply curve drifts out to the right, causing the economy to move from initial point A to final point B, as shown in Figure 11.8. Prices fall as competition among firms forces them to pass on part of the decrease in input prices, and as a result output increases. So a recessionary gap can be automatically cured

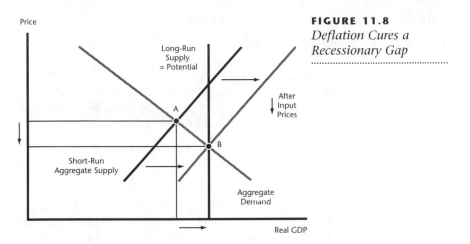

FIGURE 11.8

Deflation Cures a Recessionary Gap

through a process of deflation — that is, falling wages and prices. As before, economists describe this process as the economy's self-correction mechanism.

Some economists believe that the self-correction mechanism works too slowly, especially in the case of recessionary gaps when workers resist wage cuts. These economists want the government to step in by shifting the position of the aggregate demand curve whenever actual and potential values of GDP do not coincide rather than waiting for the position of the aggregate supply curve to adjust on its own. But other economists believe that the self-correction mechanism works fine as long as individuals do not expect the government to intervene. They argue that the main reason why workers resist wage cuts during a recession is that they expect the government to solve the unemployment problem for them. In the next several chapters, we will examine how successful these job-creation initiatives can be expected to be.

SUMMARY

Here is a review of the key concepts covered in this chapter. We have learned how **unemployment, inflation**, and **GDP** are measured and why they are important. The tools of **aggregate supply** and **demand** have been introduced to explain why **business cycles** occur and how those swings in real output, which cause **inflationary and recessionary gaps**, can be eliminated automatically through the **self-correction mechanism**. Finally, we acknowledged that there is controversy concerning the speed with which the self-correction mechanism works. Should the government be engaged in an ongoing attempt to stabilize the economy? The analysis in the next several chapters is designed to help you develop your own opinion on this central question.

SUGGESTIONS FOR FURTHER READING

Government Spending Facts and *Taxation Facts* — annual publications of the Fraser Institute in Vancouver that summarize the involvement of government in the Canada economy.

G. Mankiw, R. Kneebone, K. McKenzie, and N. Rowe, *Principles of Macroeconomics*, First Canadian Edition (Toronto: Dryden Press, 1999) — Chapters 10 and 11 discuss the details of the data of macroeconomics.

WEB ACTIVITIES

www.statcan.ca

The Web site of Statistics Canada; click on "Canadian Statistics," then, under "The Economy," to access data on all topics; also given are full background details of the labour force survey and the calculation of the CPI.

CHAPTER TWELVE

GDP and the Multiplier Process

LEARNING OBJECTIVES

After reading this chapter, you should understand
- why economic fluctuations can develop from the temporary mismatch between saving by households and investment spending by firms;

- how the expenditure multiplier can magnify the economy's reaction to both foreign shocks and domestic policy initiatives; and
- what determines the size of the expenditure multiplier.

INTRODUCTION

Each year, the government tables a budget in Parliament. The budget is a detailed statement of what the government will spend money on and how it will raise tax revenue. Sometimes the government adjusts its overall level of spending or taxation with a view to lowering unemployment or inflation. For example, the government might increase expenditures in an attempt to create jobs, or it might lower expenditures to lessen the overall demand for goods and services, so that firms are less likely to increase prices. This range of policies — the varying of government spending and taxes to stabilize the economy — is called **fiscal policy**. The purpose of this and the next chapter is to understand fiscal policy. This is accomplished by taking a major "behind the scenes" look at the aggregate demand curve.

A SIMPLE SCALE-MODEL ECONOMY

To examine the logic behind aggregate demand, we consider a simplified model economy whose main features are highlighted in Figure 12.1. Notice that there are only households and firms in this flowchart. Nowhere in the chart is there any reference to the government, the rest of the world, or a financial sector, since we ignore all these complications for now.

Production takes place where firms are located in the flowchart. Firms use the labour time and the machines owned by households to produce goods and services. We have learned that the value of all these goods produced (i.e., firms' total sales of final goods and services) equals the value of all the income earned by all households. After all, what do firms do with all the revenue they collect when they sell their commodities? They pay some of it as wages, some as rent payments, and some as interest on borrowed items. The amount left over is profit. In this simple economy, we assume no retained earnings, so all the profits are distributed as dividend income to shareholders. The arrow at

FIGURE 12.1

The Circular Flow of Income and Spending

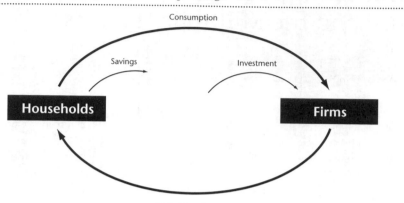

the bottom of the flowchart indicates that all income earned in the production process is sent to households to do with as they wish.

Households can either spend the income (an amount we call **consumption**) or save it, and the two arrows indicating funds leaving households in the flowchart show these two possibilities. The funds that are spent travel directly back to the firms. If savings were zero, then the total amount of consumption expenditures by households would just equal their income. Since this total also represents the value of goods produced, there could be no problem of accumulating inventory for firms in this case. But since households do save, consumption is less than the total value of production. So, if there is not some other component of demand (in addition to consumption spending by households), then there will not be enough purchases to justify the level of production that the firms undertook to create the income in the first place.

There is a second component of demand, since (as a group) firms buy some of their own output. Some of the currently produced output is new machines and new factories. We call this category of expenditures on new plant and equipment **investment** spending. The system will be in equilibrium (i.e., firms will go on producing whatever level of output they have been producing) if the sum of household consumption purchases plus firms' investment expenditures equals the amount of goods produced in that period. In other words, demand equals supply.

EQUILIBRIUM IN THE CIRCULAR FLOW OF INCOME AND SPENDING

As just noted, equilibrium exists when supply equals demand. Since supply is the value of GDP and demand is the sum of the intended consumption spending by households (abbreviated as C) and the intended investment spending by firms (abbreviated as I), the equilibrium condition is

GDP = C + I.

There is another way of stating the equilibrium condition for this simple economy, and it follows from the fact that household saving is all income that is not consumed. Saving (abbreviated as S) equals GDP – C. Combining this definition with the equilibrium condition given above (to eliminate GDP by substitution) yields

I = S.

This alternative statement of the equilibrium condition says that the injection of funds by firms' **investment** spending has to be the same magnitude as the amount of funds withdrawn from the circular flow of income and spending by households' **saving**. Only if there is this balance will overall demand equal supply.

We are using the term "investment" differently from its everyday interpretation. When an individual household buys a Canada Savings Bond, most people refer to that as an investment in government bonds. Economists call it an act of saving, not investment. The term "investment" is reserved for purchases of new capital equipment by firms. Economists use terms in this way to stress the fact that households' saving decisions and firms' investment decisions are separate. As a result, there is no reason to assume that intended saving and intended investment will automatically equal each other. After all, households make decisions about how much to save without having any knowledge of what firms may need in terms of new plant and equipment. Similarly, firms make investment decisions without any reference to whether households want to do much saving that period.

Let us examine what happens when households become worried about the future, perhaps fearing the loss of jobs. In this situation, households decrease consumption and increase saving. Doing so throws the initial equilibrium out of balance. With decreased household spending, there is not enough demand to justify the pre-existing level of production, so firms will have to lay some people off. And these job losses do not constitute the whole story. Those laid off will earn less, so there will be a smaller amount of income flowing to households along the bottom arrow in Figure 12.1. The result is yet another decrease in household consumption expenditures, and firms will have to lay off even more people.

When households react to their fears of layoffs, they set in motion a chain of events that causes the very layoffs they feared. The anticipation of a recession can cause a recession. Many people find this fact discouraging. They become even more concerned when they realize that the recession can feed on itself, with each round of layoffs leading to less household spending and thus to still more layoffs. Does this vicious circle of lower incomes and lost jobs keep feeding on itself forever?

FIGURE 12.2
*The Consumption
Function*
....

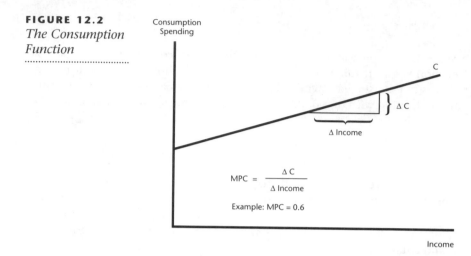

To answer this question, we have to make more specific assumptions about how households behave. Let us assume that household spending depends on household income as summarized in Figure 12.2. We see from this graph that consumption spending goes up when income goes up. When we take annual data for any country, data on total consumption and total income, and plot it, the result is a set of observations that looks like this straight line. Economists call this relationship the **consumption function**, and they call the slope of this line the **marginal propensity to consume**, or **MPC**. The marginal propensity to consume is positive, but it has a value that is less than one. The consumption function has this slope because, when people get an extra dollar of income, the increase in consumption is always some fraction of that dollar — such as 90 cents, with the remainder, 10 cents in this example, being saved.

We can emphasize the fact that the marginal propensity to consume is a fraction by adding a 45° line to the graph, as in Figure 12.3. A 45° line shows all those points at which consumption would be equal to income (i.e., where saving is zero). When people's incomes vary, they spend more than current income during low-income periods (perhaps by drawing down bank balances), and they spend less than current income during high-income periods (using leftover funds to build up bank balances). Saving is negative in the first case and positive in the second. The second case is shown in Figure 12.3.

What we wish to show graphically is that level of total income and production that will just be bought by households and firms, assuming that households make their spending decisions according to this consumption relationship. We simplify at this stage by assuming that firms have fixed investment plans. We assume that firms want to spend an amount on new equipment equal to the height of the line labelled I in Figure 12.4.

Figure 12.4 involves two schedules of spending intentions, one for each of the two groups in our model economy: households and firms. It contains

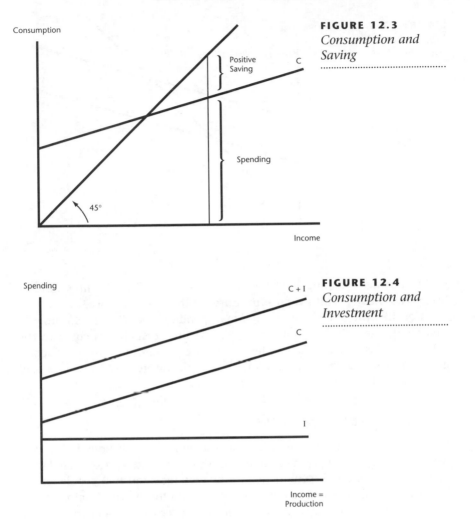

FIGURE 12.3
Consumption and Saving
....

FIGURE 12.4
Consumption and Investment
....

the upward-sloping consumption line (the households' decision rule show-ing that spending increases with income) and the horizontal investment line (the firms' decision rule showing their fixed investment plans). Figure 12.4 also shows these two plans combined (labelled as the C + I line). By adding the C and I lines together vertically, we get an overall intentions-to-buy schedule that shows how much total spending will be at all possible levels of national income.

We can use Figure 12.4 to illustrate the equilibrium level of GDP. For any level of total output measured along the horizontal axis, we can read off the corresponding height of the total spending line to determine total demand for goods. Equilibrium occurs where supply (the distance along the produc-tion axis) is just equal to demand (the height up to the C + I line). But it is difficult to compare a horizontal distance to a vertical one. We solve this

FIGURE 12.5
Equilibrium GDP
....

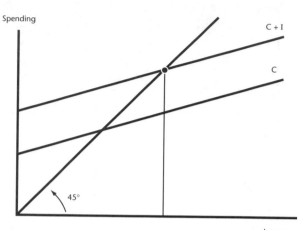

problem by again adding a 45° line, as in Figure 12.5. The 45° line transfers horizontal measures into vertical measures of the same distance.

Consider the intersection of the total spending line with the 45° line. At this point, the height of the total spending line (demand) is equal to the value of goods and services produced and the income that this production generates (supply) since the right-angled triangle in Figure 12.5 involves sides of equal length. This point determines equilibrium.

THE MULTIPLIER PROCESS

Earlier in this chapter, we considered a situation in which households were worried about job loss. That concern led to caution, and they increased their savings. This decreased spending led to the very recession that people feared. We now have the tools that allow us to understand this process in more detail.

A multiplier process is set in motion whenever there is a change in any component of total spending, and the same process unfolds whichever direction the change in spending pushes the economy. Let us consider an increase in investment spending by firms, and you can consider a decrease in spending by households on your own for review.

Suppose firms spend an additional $1 billion on new equipment. We are interested in determining how much this event will change the nation's GDP. It turns out that the resulting change in GDP is a multiple of the original $1- billion change in investment spending. We call this ratio of changes the **multiplier**: writing this ratio of changes in compact form, we have

multiplier = $\Delta GDP/\Delta I$.

We now derive a formula for this multiplier. When producers respond to the extra investment demand of $1 billion by creating that additional amount of new machines and equipment, they will employ additional workers, and an additional $1 billion of income will be created. This fact is shown in Figure 12.6 by the "plus 1" entry by the investment and production components of the flowchart. Once this extra income reaches the households, they do some additional spending. To have a specific numerical example, we take the marginal propensity to consume to be 0.6. In other words, 60 cents of every additional dollar gets spent, and 40 cents is saved. Given this assumption, there is an induced increase in consumption demand because of the additional $1 billion of income earned. Thus, there is a second round of increased expenditure equal to $600 million. This fact is indicated by the "plus 0.6" entry by the consumption component of the flowchart.

Firms have to increase the level of production again. They have met the new investment demand, but they have not yet met the $600 million of extra demand by households. So once firms create more jobs for that demand, they will have created $600 million more income, so six-tenths of that $600 million will get spent by the next group of people who get hired. This fact is indicated by the "plus $(0.6)^2$" entry by the production and consumption components of the flowchart.

We can see that, when all these amounts of extra income are added together, the overall increase in production is

($1 billion) times $(1 + 0.6 + (0.6)^2 + ...)$.

Thus, the multiplier, $\Delta GDP/\Delta I$ is $(1 + 0.6 + (0.6)^2 + ...)$. This infinite sum has a finite total equal to $1/(1 - 0.6)$, or 2.5. For this numerical example, then, the expenditure multiplier is 2.5.

The easiest way to see that the multiplier is 2.5 is to multiply both sides of the multiplier equation by 0.6:

multiplier = $(1 + 0.6 + (0.6)^2 + ...)$
(0.6)(multiplier) = $(0.6 + (0.6)^2 + ...)$.

FIGURE 12.6
The Multiplier Process

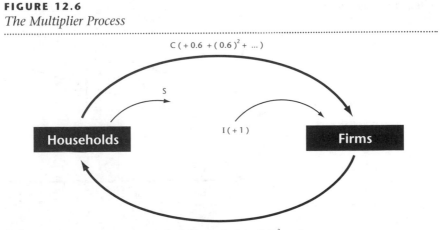

Subtracting the second line from the first yields

(1 – 0.6)(multiplier) = 1, or
multiplier = 1/(1 – 0.6).

We should remember, of course, that we picked the marginal propensity to consume value of 0.6 as an arbitrary example. We should also remember that each additional dollar of income must be either consumed or saved. Thus, if we define the marginal propensity to save (MPS) as the change in saving divided by the change in income, then we have

MPC + MPS = 1, and
multiplier = 1/(1 – MPC) = 1/MPS.

Do not let all these formal expressions for calculating the multiplier distract you from the basic intuition behind why there is a multiplier in the first place. You can think of the multiplier working like a ripple effect — what happens when you throw a pebble into a pond. The ripples spread across the pond. In the same way, getting a new job means you have more income to spend. That creates another job and so on, but in ever smaller amounts. In like fashion, the ripples across the pond eventually die down.

We now illustrate the multiplier in terms of an income–expenditure diagram in Figure 12.7. The initial equilibrium is point A. Now assume that investment increases by an amount equal to ΔI. The higher level of investment spending raises the I line, and therefore the position of the C + I line, by ΔI. The new equilibrium point is where the now relevant C + I line intersects the 45° line — point B. Figure 12.7 makes clear that the overall increase in GDP exceeds the initial change in investment spending that causes the expansion,

FIGURE 12.7
The Multiplier Process
....

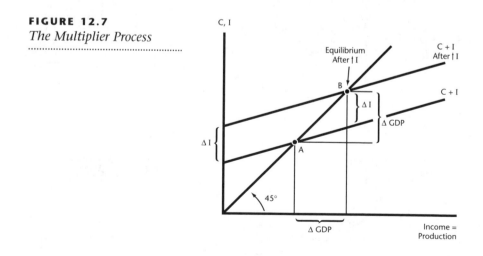

so a multiplier effect does exist. The multiplier is the ratio of the GDP change distance to the investment change distance.

A MORE REALISTIC MODEL ECONOMY

Now that we understand the basic principles, let us make our model economy more realistic by adding a government and a foreign sector. These additional features are included in Figure 12.8. As before, we start our discussion of how the economy works with firms. Production takes place there, and the total value of production creates the nation's pre-tax income (GDP), which starts on its way over to households near the bottom of the flowchart. But the government takes some of this income in the form of taxes (abbreviated as T), so there is a withdrawal of funds at that point. What is left to make it all the way over to the households is called **disposable income**; it is that part of pre-tax income that households can dispose of as they wish. Thus, the existence of government means an additional withdrawal of funds (taxes) from the circular flow.

As before, more funds are withdrawn at the household stage for savings. Consumption is noticeably smaller than total production in this case since households consume only a fraction of their disposable income, and disposable income is only a fraction of pre-tax income. It is pre-tax income that equals the value of production. Furthermore, some of the household expenditures are not for our products at all. They are for imports (abbreviated as **IM** — products coming from the rest of the world), so yet another withdrawal of funds from the circular flow occurs at the top of the flowchart. Funds come the other way too — the rest of the world buys some of our products, and those incoming funds are shown in Figure 12.8 by the arrow indicating

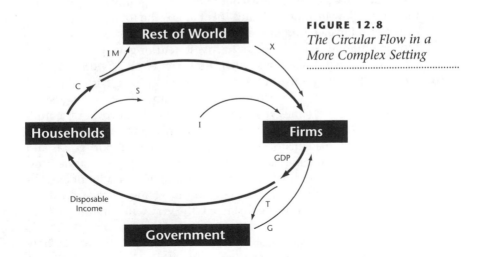

FIGURE 12.8
The Circular Flow in a More Complex Setting

exports, labelled **X**. Firms still do some investment spending on new machines and equipment, and the government buys some goods and services (government spending is abbreviated as **G**). All these arrows pointing toward the firms in Figure 12.8 show that there are many more components to aggregate demand in this more complicated and realistic model economy.

But despite this extra detail, the reasoning that we used before still applies. The equilibrium level of national product is reached when the sum of all the demands is just balanced by the level of production — that is, GDP. Things are a bit more complicated here solely because total demand is no longer just consumption plus investment. In this more general setting, total demand is

consumption + investment + government spending + net exports, or
total demand = C + I + G + (X – IM).

This fact means that, when we draw an income–expenditure diagram to show the determination of equilibrium graphically, we do not just add up the C line and the I line. We now have to draw in three more lines: an export line, a government expenditure line, and an import line. And we must do some adding and subtracting to derive the total spending line. Nonetheless, the economic reasoning is the same. Equilibrium occurs where the total spending line intersects the 45° line.

Two points are worth emphasizing. First, since both taxes and imports rise when people's incomes are higher, the subtraction of these components makes the slope of the total spending line (labelled C + I + G + X – IM from now on) much flatter than in our previous discussion. Remember that the taxes levied on high-income individuals are greater than those levied on low-income individuals. As a result, when the consumption line gets pulled down because of taxes, it gets pulled down more at the high-income end of the graph than at the low-income end, and this flattens the total spending line.

This flatter total spending line means that, when we consider a change in total expenditure, such as a change in investment or government expenditure or exports, it will involve a smaller multiplier effect. Try drawing two income–expenditure diagrams on your own — one with a fairly flat total spending line, and one with a steep total spending line. A change in government spending shifts both lines vertically by the same distance, but the multiplied change along the GDP axis is much smaller when the total spending line is flatter. Since Canadians have a high propensity to import goods and services and we face high marginal tax rates, Canada's multiplier has been estimated to be less than two. It is therefore misleading to give a lot of emphasis to the multiplied effects that follow expenditure changes. Once a realistic slope for the total spending line is considered, the very term "multiplier" has a misleading connotation.

This fact means that we must have modest expectations about how much fiscal policy can do to reduce a recession. With a small multiplier, it

takes a large increase in government spending or a large tax cut to significantly raise GDP. Since it is difficult for governments to contemplate large
spending increases or big tax cuts when they are trying to avoid a budget
deficit, the small expenditure multiplier makes it difficult for the government
to create many jobs.

INFLATION AND THE MULTIPLIER

We started our study of business cycles by noting that we would focus on the
twin problems of unemployment and inflation. But so far in this chapter, we
have simplified the analysis by assuming that all increases in demand lead to
more workers being hired. There has been no mention of firms raising prices
in response to the higher demand for their products. We now fill in this gap.

Variations in domestic prices affect our country's international competitive position. The more expensive our products are, the less successful we are
in selling goods to the rest of the world. Also, the higher our prices are, the
less our holdings of money and other financial assets are worth. To allow for
these facts, we must draw a whole family of total spending lines, one for
every possible level of domestic prices. In Figure 12.9, we see two members of
this family of total spending lines. The lower one is the total spending line
for price level P_1, which stands for a high price level. Expensive domestic
goods mean low export demand and a high level of imports, so the result is
a low position for the total spending line in the graph. We also see a higher

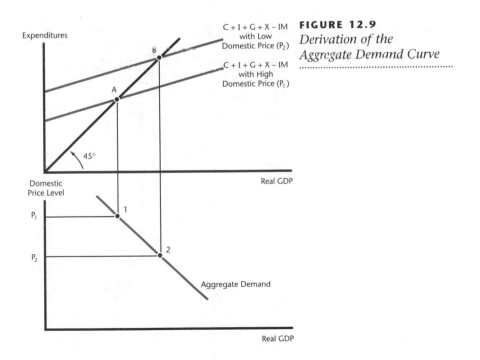

FIGURE 12.9

*Derivation of the
Aggregate Demand Curve*

total spending line in Figure 12.9 corresponding to price level P_2, which stands for a lower level of domestic prices. These lower prices lead to high export sales, a smaller amount of imports, and a higher real value of financial assets. The result is a higher position for the total spending line.

The lower quadrant in Figure 12.9 summarizes this relationship. If the price level is high, at P_1, then the lower spending line is relevant, and GDP is given by point A. This combination of values for price and real GDP is recorded in the lower quadrant by point 1. If the price level is lower, at P_2, then there is higher spending, and GDP is given by point B. This second combination of values for price and real GDP is recorded in the lower panel of Figure 12.9 by point 2. So we have two points in the summary quadrant of the graph that show combinations of domestic price and output for which firms just manage to sell all their current output. We join all such dots and call the resulting summary line the aggregate demand curve.

In the preceding chapter, the aggregate demand curve was introduced and, in this chapter, the details behind it have been provided. Now we can understand more precisely how government policy changes affect the position of the aggregate demand curve.

The effect of an increase in government spending is shown in Figure 12.10. Higher government expenditures shift up the entire family of total spending lines, so this policy moves the position of the summary line, the aggregate demand curve, to the right. Now that we are summarizing the whole multiplier process in terms of the position of the aggregate demand curve, we

FIGURE 12.10
Shifts in the Aggregate Demand Curve
....

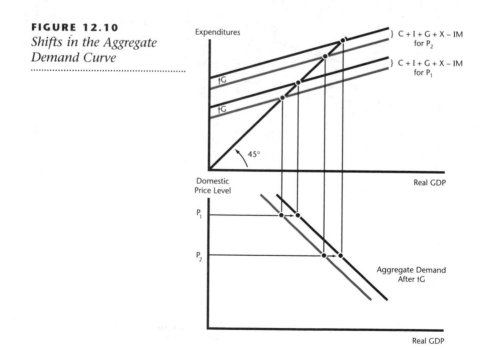

see that the expenditure multiplier represents how much the aggregate demand curve moves horizontally per unit of vertical shift in the family of total spending lines.

So the expenditure multiplier summarizes what would happen if prices stayed constant. As illustrated in Figure 12.11, prices would stay constant only if the aggregate supply curve were horizontal. In that case, an expansion in government spending, for example, would shift the economy from point A to point B. However, the aggregate supply curve is not horizontal. It has a positive slope. Thus, the actual intersection point that the economy moves to following a policy intended to create jobs is not point B. The basic multiplier formula yields an overestimate of the true outcome. In fact, we obtain a smaller increase in real output, such as that given by point C. Some of the effect of the policy is dissipated in the form of higher prices.

Thus, there are two broad categories of reasons why government demand-management policy does not work as well as some would like. First, when the government raises its expenditures, it cannot move the aggregate demand curve very far to the right. With high tax rates and a high propensity to import goods and services as our incomes increase, the expenditure multiplier is simply too small. Thus, the first stumbling block is that it takes a major policy initiative to move the demand curve very far to the right. Second, even if the government does engineer a noticeable movement of the demand curve to the right, it has to confront the fact that the aggregate supply curve can be fairly steep. This forces the increase in demand to result mostly in inflation, with the policy having only limited effect on real output and therefore on job creation. Putting these two considerations together, we are justified in having modest expectations about how well the government can create jobs. Fiscal policy can be used to ward off a major collapse in aggregate demand, but the government cannot fine-tune the economy.

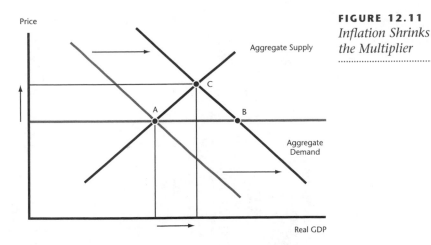

Price

Aggregate Supply

C

A

B

Aggregate
Demand

Real GDP

FIGURE 12.11

*Inflation Shrinks
the Multiplier*

SUMMARY

Here is a review of the key concepts covered in this chapter. We have understood how **equilibrium GDP** gets determined, and we have used this understanding to follow through the **expenditure multiplier** process. By deriving both the multiplier formula and how the position of the aggregate demand curve depends on the multiplier, we were able to appreciate why Canada's multiplier is small. In the next chapter, we will use this set of tools to examine the government's **fiscal policy** in more detail and to determine the effect of this policy on the government's deficit and on our national debt.

SUGGESTIONS FOR FURTHER READING

T. Courchene, *Social Canada in the Millennium: Reform Imperatives and Restructuring Principles* (Toronto: C.D. Howe Institute, 1994) — fiscal policy involves attempts to stabilize the economy through the multiplier process while adjusting government spending and taxes, but getting the timing right is a challenge when there are so many fiscal agreements between Ottawa and the provinces; Courchene's book is a landmark evaluation of these sharing arrangements.

WEB ACTIVITIES

www.fin.gc.ca
The Web site of the federal Department of Finance; click on "About the Department," then, under "Frequently Asked Questions," to learn the department's views on macroeconomics and numerous topical items, such as why the Canadian unemployment rate is so much higher than the U.S. rate; click on "Hotlinks" to gain access to all provincial ministries of finance.

CHAPTER THIRTEEN
Fiscal Policy and the National Debt

LEARNING OBJECTIVES

After reading this chapter, you should understand

- why the budget deficit is an incomplete indicator of the stance of fiscal policy;
- which taxes are best for stabilization policy; and

- what caused the national debt to explode during the 1970s and 1980s and what caused the debt-to-GDP ratio to begin falling again in the 1990s.

INTRODUCTION

In the previous chapter, we learned how the overall level of economic activity is determined and how a change in one component of the demand for goods and services — such as a change in the level of government expenditure — can have a multiplier effect on the level of total output. **Fiscal policy** refers to the government's attempts to vary its expenditures and taxes to promote stability. The purpose of this chapter is to use that analysis to assess the effectiveness of fiscal policy. One problem that confronts an active government policy is that the budget deficit can get out of control. If the government tries to both raise its expenditures and cut its taxes to stimulate spending and create jobs, then it will go ever more into debt. One task of this chapter is to assess whether, and to what extent, this national debt represents a problem.

THE BASIC RATIONALE OF FISCAL POLICY

In the previous chapter, we focused on the total spending line. Recall that there are four components of total spending: purchases by households, called consumption spending; purchases by firms, called investment spending on new plant and equipment; purchases by government, called government spending on goods and services; and net purchases by foreigners — that is, exports minus imports. We saw that equilibrium GDP occurred where the total spending line crossed the 45° line. That level of output creates just enough income to buy that quantity of goods, with no unintended inventory accumulation or decumulation. Thus, the income–expenditure diagram determines equilibrium only from the point of view that the output is willingly purchased.

But this amount of output does not mean that the economy's labour markets are in equilibrium. We saw in Chapter 11 that the equilibrium GDP can be less than the economy's potential, and in that case the level of economic activity is not enough to create full employment. If the government believes that the self-correction mechanism is too slow and weak to eliminate recessionary gaps, then what can it do? In an attempt to create jobs, the government can try to alter the position of the total spending line. One way in which the government can stimulate spending is to raise its component of aggregate demand — government expenditure. Clearly, if the government builds new highways or does anything of that sort, it can move the entire position of the total spending line up. One of the results is a higher level of economic activity.

Other government policies can have the same result. For example, the government can cut taxes. We do not see taxes in the definition of aggregate demand (C + I + G + X − IM), but taxes are in the background. For instance, if the government cuts personal income taxes or offers more transfer payments to those on welfare, then it leaves households with a higher level of disposable income so that they can afford to raise consumption spending. So by this method of fiscal policy, the government raises GDP indirectly, by raising the consumption component rather than the government expenditure component of the total spending line. (By taxes, we mean *net* taxes — that is, taxes less transfer payments.)

Other taxes can be used as well. For example, the government can cut corporate profit taxes and leave firms with more income to spend (so the investment component of aggregate demand can go up). Foreign developments also affect the position of our total spending line. A lower value of the Canadian dollar makes our exports cheaper for foreigners to buy. Thus, a cheaper domestic currency raises the net exports component of the total spending line and creates a higher level of economic activity and more jobs. Similarly, foreign tariffs reduce our net exports and thus lead to a lower level of economic activity.

At the most general level, there are three possible strategies that the government can use to try to stimulate total spending and therefore job creation. Using our abbreviations (G for government spending and T for [net] taxes), these options are

1) raise G while leaving T constant;
2) cut T while leaving G constant; or
3) raise G and T by the same amount.

Option 1 raises the total spending line by working on the government spending component. Higher economic activity comes with a larger government sector. Option 2 shifts the total spending line up by raising either the consumption or the investment component. Higher economic activity comes with a larger private sector. If you are like most students of economics, you will be puzzled that option 3 is included in the list. It seems that, if the government raises its own spending and takes away dollars from households and firms by the same amount, these two initiatives would nullify each other's effect on total spending. Why would the increase in the government's injection of funds not simply cancel the increase in the government's withdrawal of funds from the circular flow? We can use our theoretical tools to answer this question and to understand why this third policy is, in fact, expansionary.

It is instructive to break the third policy option down into its two component parts. First, an increase in government spending of $1 billion raises the total spending line by precisely $1 billion. This is because government spending is a direct component of total spending. An increase in personal taxes of $1 billion lowers the total spending line because it lowers the disposable income that households have to spend. But households pay for some of the extra taxes by cutting savings, so they pay for only a fraction of the taxes by cutting consumption. In the previous chapter, we used the term "marginal propensity to consume" to indicate the fraction of changes in income that households take out of consumption as opposed to saving. Thus, if households lose $1 billion of income through higher taxes, they will cut their consumption by the MPC times $1 billion. So higher taxes lower the total spending line, but by just a fraction of that increase in taxes.

Taking the increase in government spending and taxes together, we have competing effects on the position of the total spending line. It goes up by $1 billion, and it goes down by a fraction, MPC times $1 billion. On balance, the total spending line moves up by (1 – MPC) times $1 billion. The resulting equilibrium point is farther out to the right, so more economic activity and more jobs are created.

Many people think that the government must either raise expenditures or cut taxes to create jobs, so the government must increase its deficit to reduce unemployment. The analysis that we have just discussed is a counterexample to this view. A balanced increase in spending and taxes provides some job creation without any increase in the deficit. The intuition behind this counterexample is that it involves a shift in some of the economy's spending power away from the private sector and toward the government sector. The private sector has a marginal propensity to consume that is less than 100 percent, while under this policy the government spends every dollar of new tax revenue (so it has a marginal propensity to spend of one). So it is not surprising that a redistribution of income away from the private sector and toward the government sector raises total spending.

THE BUDGET DEFICIT AS AN INDICATOR OF FISCAL POLICY

The budget deficit is the excess of the government's spending over its tax revenue. Most commentators interpret an increase or decrease in the deficit as an indicator of whether the government has been trying to expand or contract the economy. One dramatic way to see that this assumption can be

FIGURE 13.1
*The Budget and the
Economy: Automatic
Stabilizers*
···

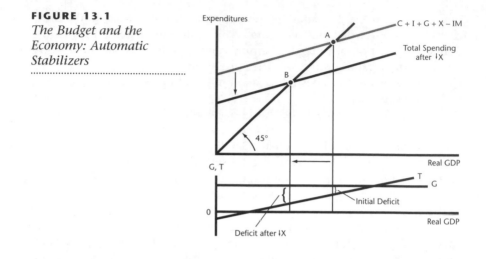

wrong is to consider a recession in which the government makes no change in its policies — a situation that we examine in Figure 13.1.

Before the recession occurs, equilibrium GDP is determined at point A in the top part of Figure 13.1. The implications for the deficit are seen in the lower part of the graph. The positively sloped tax function reflects the fact that people must pay higher taxes at higher income levels. The horizontal government spending line indicates that the government has fixed expenditure commitments. The budget deficit equals the amount by which the height of the government spending line exceeds the height up to the tax function, at the equilibrium level of national income — as labelled in Figure 13.1. Now suppose that we lose a major part of our export sales. That loss in demand causes a drop in the total spending line, so the equilibrium point moves from point A to point B. A recession (a leftward move along the real GDP axis) occurs. Suppose the government does nothing to try to counteract this recession. This lack of action is made evident in the graph by the fact that the heights of both the government spending line and the tax function are unaltered. Despite this lack of action, however, because GDP has shrunk, the government collects less in taxes. The height up to the spending line is still the same, but the height up to the tax line is much shorter. With people losing their jobs, they are earning lower incomes and paying less in taxes. Since the tax base has shrunk, the budget deficit has increased.

So a recession has occurred, and the deficit has increased. On the surface, the bigger deficit makes it appear that the government has tried to counteract the recession. But that is an incorrect interpretation since by assumption the government has done nothing. The key point is that the deficit is affected both by government policy (which determines government spending and the tax rates) and by everything else that determines GDP (because that overall level of income is the tax base to which the government's tax rates apply). Thus, when you read about the annual budget, do not focus just on the deficit. Consider also the announced changes in both government spending and taxes separately.

You may hear commentators talk about the government budget providing our economy with an **automatic stabilizer**. This concept is also illustrated in Figure 13.1. Since the budget *automatically* moves more into deficit during a recession, the government automatically cushions the fall in demand — even when no discretionary action is taken.

THE SCOPE FOR FISCAL POLICY IN QUANTITATIVE TERMS

To form an independent opinion about the government's fiscal policy, we must have some idea concerning what can be reasonably expected in terms of job creation (when policy is expansionary) and job losses (when policy is contractionary). To establish that benchmark, we must understand the magnitude of the connection between the instrument that the government controls (the level of its own expenditure) and the items that people care about, such as the unemployment rate. Knowledge of the muliplier process lets us make part of this connection — that between the government's instrument and overall GDP. But to predict the effects of policy on the number of jobs, we need to know the precise link between overall output and labour input in the production process in quantitative terms. We now discuss each of these connections.

The multiplier is a small number — even ignoring inflation, about 1.67. To see why, consider our basic equilibrium condition: supply equals demand. Supply is the real GDP of the country, and demand is the (by now) familiar sum of expenditures by households, firms, the government, and foreigners. As I stressed earlier, GDP is not just the value of production. Since the production process is what creates income, real GDP is also total income earned. That income must go into one of three places: taxes, savings, or consumption.

We can recast our equilibrium condition by simply substituting this definition of the uses of income into the supply equals demand condition as shown in Table 13.1. Since the left-hand sides of the first two lines in the table equal real GDP, we can equate the right-hand sides. The result is an alternative version of the equilibrium condition (the bottom row in the table), which stipulates that the injection of funds into the circular flow (investment spending, government spending, and exports) must be just big enough to make up for the withdrawal of funds (savings, taxes, and imports).

It is important to realize that the magnitude of all these withdrawals depends on the overall amount of income earned in the country. The higher our incomes, the more saving we do, the more importing we do from the rest of the world, and the more tax revenue the government collects from us. The numbers involved are roughly as follows. We tend to save about one-tenth of any increase in income. The tax rate relevant for the average citizen is about

TABLE 13.1 *Derivation of the Multiplier*

Equilibrium:

$$\underbrace{\text{Real GDP}}_{\text{Supply}} = \underbrace{C + I + G + X - IM}_{\text{Demand}}$$

Definition:

$$\underbrace{\text{Real GDP}}_{\text{Income}} = T + S + C$$

Equilibrium:

$$\underbrace{S + T + IM}_{\text{Withdrawals}} = \underbrace{I + G + X}_{\text{Injections}}$$

$$(0.6) (\Delta\,GDP) = \Delta\,\text{Withdrawals}$$

Equilibrium:

$$\Delta\,\text{Withdrawals} = \Delta\,\text{Injections}$$

$$(0.6) (\Delta\,GDP) = \Delta\,\text{Injections}$$

Multiplier:

$$\frac{\Delta\,GDP}{\Delta\,\text{Injections}} = \frac{1}{0.6} = 1.67$$

25 percent. And as a society, whenever we get a dollar of extra income, we seem to import about 25 cents more. So if we add up these three propensities to have funds withdrawn from the circular flow of income and expenditure, we get 0.6. We can conclude that the change in withdrawals in Canada equals roughly 0.6 times any change in GDP.

To maintain equilibrium both before and after an expenditure change, the change in withdrawals must equal the change in injections. Both this equilibrium requirement and the rate at which withdrawals respond to national income are summarized in Table 13.1. If we combine the two expressions by substitution, then we obtain the relationship between changes in GDP and injections. After cross-dividing, we see that the multiplier is indeed 1.67.

As noted in the previous chapter, however, these calculations ignore the fact that part of any shift in aggregate demand ends up affecting the price level, not real GDP. On average, this fact means that the multiplier formula overstates the true effect on real output by about a factor of two. Thus, a more relevant multiplier coefficient is 1.67/2, or 0.83.

We must now focus on the link between output (GDP) and input (labour). This link can be summarized by simply comparing the percentage increases in real GDP over the years with the corresponding changes in the unemployment rate. The typical pattern for most Western countries, including Canada, is that an increase of one percentage point in the level of real economic activity translates into only about half a percentage point decrease in the unemployment rate.

There are two reasons for this lack of a one-for-one response. One is the discouraged worker effect that we discussed in Chapter 11, and the other is the fact that firms can vary their labour inputs by adjusting hours per worker without making any variations in the number of people hired.

Now we can complete our quantitative analysis of a typical budget. When the Liberal government took power, it faced a large budget deficit. Its response, in its second budget, was to introduce expenditure cuts of $10 billion in an attempt to reduce the deficit. With a multiplier of 0.83, this contractionary policy reduced real GDP by about $8.3 billion — that is, by about 1.2 percent below what it otherwise would have been. Since the unemployment rate responds only with a coefficient of one-half to any GDP change, the budget pushed the unemployment rate above what it otherwise would have been by about six-tenths of one percentage point.

When the purpose of fiscal contraction is to lower the budget deficit (as in this case), government officials are pleased that the unemployment effects that follow policy changes are not too large. At other times, however, when the government is trying to create jobs with an expansionary fiscal policy, many people are discouraged by how impotent policy appears to be. We must remember, too, that six-tenths of 1 percent of Canada's labour force represented 84 000 jobs in the mid-1990s, and these individuals and their families did not regard fiscal policy as unimportant. Perhaps a balanced view is that we should have only modest expectations about how fiscal policy can contribute to stabilizing the economy.

WHICH TAXES ARE BEST FOR STABILIZATION?

Thus far in discussion of fiscal policy, we have focused primarily on changes in government expenditure. Now we analyze tax changes to determine which taxes represent effective instruments for short-run stabilization policy.

For many years, the Canadian government has favoured using the corporate profit tax for stabilization purposes. The idea is that, when the corporate profit tax is cut, firms have more income and can use it to buy new plant and equipment. Doing so raises the investment component of total spending. But what is often overlooked is that many of the firms operating in Canada are foreign-owned. They are subsidiaries of multinationals. A parent company gets credit for taxes already paid in Canada when calculating the taxes it owes to its home government. Thus, a tax cut by the Canadian government is nothing but a reduction in that foreign tax credit, so it is a straight transfer from the Canadian government to the foreign government. Since the firm gets no more disposable income, it does not increase investment spending. The Canadian government suffers a large revenue loss, and we obtain no stimulation of aggregate demand. So corporate tax concessions are not recommended.

A favourite instrument for stabilization policy in the United States has been variations in personal income tax rates. Sometimes these tax cuts stimulated the economy; sometimes they did not. When the tax cuts were announced to be very temporary, say, just lasting for the worst part of a recession, they did not stimulate spending significantly. But when they were permanent tax cuts, and announced to be so, consumption spending by households increased significantly. Economists were not surprised by this mixed record since basic theory has long suggested that the more frequent personal income tax changes are, the less effective they are for stabilizing aggregate demand.

People do not make their consumption–savings decisions solely on the basis of *current* disposable income. Many people gear consumption spending to the longer-run average level of income that they expect to receive. When they have short-run variations in income, especially those caused by tax changes that are known (by announcement) to be temporary, they let their savings be the buffer so that consumption can remain insulated from these temporary disturbances. The more frequently the government tries using tax changes for stabilization purposes, the more certain people can become that the increases and decreases in their taxes are temporary. Thus, the more ineffective this stabilization strategy becomes.

Is there any tax for which the more temporary the change, the bigger the impact? The answer is "yes" — the more temporary a sales tax change, the more it causes people to change the timing of their expenditures on big-ticket items. Suppose your refrigerator is wearing out, and you want to replace it fairly soon anyway. Suppose the government offers a temporary reduction in sales tax. You know that you can get a major price decrease by buying the new refrigerator now rather than waiting until next year (since the temporary sales tax cut will be a matter of history by then). Many people choose to bring forward their replacement purchases in this situation. And the more temporary the sales tax change, the better an instrument it is for getting people to shift the timing of their expenditures to the period when the economy most needs stimulation.

Until the late 1980s, our federal government did not have a general retail sales tax. Whatever else you may think of the GST, it does give the federal government access to the one tax that it could use to conduct a sensible short-run fiscal policy.

THE NATIONAL DEBT

The national debt is the sum of all the annual deficits run by the federal government for the entire history of our country. By the end of the twentieth century, the federal debt was not far short of the $600-billion mark. In 1967, the debt was about $25 billion. So the debt increased 22 times more during the first 30 years or so of Canada's second century than it did in the entire first century following Confederation.

Government debt would not have accumulated if the government had taken the advice that follows from our theory of fiscal policy. That advice is to run a deficit (by raising expenditures and/or cutting taxes) during the recessionary phase of each business cycle and to run a surplus (by cutting expenditures and/or raising taxes) during the boom half of each business cycle. This policy would help to balance the economy over the cycle, and it would balance the budget over the interval of each full cycle. This would be sufficient to keep the debt from increasing over the long term.

Governments have followed this advice during recessions — indeed, they have appreciated the fact that economists condone deficit spending during these periods. But governments have chosen to disregard the other half of the advice from economists, for they have not run surplus budgets half the time. Indeed, the federal government never ran a surplus between the early 1970s and the late 1990s, and for much of the 1980s and 1990s the deficit in any one year (which is the annual increase in the debt) exceeded the entire national debt incurred during the country's first century. By the 1990s, our governments had become so preoccupied with stopping the growth in debt by balancing their budgets that they could no longer give any attention to trying to help balance the economy.

Governments pay for each annual deficit by selling a large quantity of government bonds each year. When those bonds are sold domestically, they compete for the limited quantity of household savings. That competition makes it harder for firms to obtain funds to finance their investment expenditures in new plant and equipment. Canadian workers are left with less equipment (and outdated equipment) to work with, so our standard of living does not rise as much in the future as it would have without the government's borrowing "crowding out" the firms' attempts to obtain funds. Thus, the buildup of debt has meant a major transfer across generations. Current generations have "spent beyond their means" and bequeathed a lower standard of living to future generations.

Many individuals are concerned that many government bonds are sold to foreigners. By relying on foreign lenders, governments have not competed so much with domestic firms for domestic savings. As a result, investment spending by firms is not reduced as much. But our children and grandchildren are stuck with high taxes just to make interest payments to the rest of the world. Since foreign debt pushes GNP below GDP, future living standards are lowered just the same. As of 1999, foreign interest payments alone lowered each four-person Canadian family's income by $3000 every year.

Such figures convinced many Canadians that it was important that the deficit be eliminated in the late 1990s. After all, getting the deficit to zero stops the accumulated debt from continuing to rise. Many years with budget surpluses are needed to bring the debt down and therefore to start reversing the intergenerational transfer.

So there is a substantial long-term gain to be had from deficit and debt reduction. But the short-term pain is significant. Contractionary policy raises unemployment, and the more our tax dollars go to cover interest payment obligations, the less they can be used on social policies and other programs that have come to be regarded as part of the Canadian identity.

Confronted by such large up-front costs involved with deficit reduction, many politicians had hoped that we could simply grow our way out of our debt problem. This hope is based on the proposition that, if the debt becomes an ever smaller proportion of our income, it will represent an ever smaller burden. According to this view, then, we should be concerned only with the ratio of the debt to our GNP. While it is not quite as appropriate, many commentators (and government documents) focus on the ratio of the debt to our GDP.

It is easy to appreciate why it was not possible for growth to eliminate our debt problem during the ten years that the Conservatives were in power (1983–93). Let G, T, D, B, and r stand for the government's program spending, taxes, deficit, bonds outstanding, and the interest rate. The deficit is defined as the excess of program spending, G, and interest payments on the debt, rB, over taxation, T:

$$D = G + rB - T.$$

The national debt increases by the size of the deficit each year:

$$\Delta B = D.$$

The primary deficit excludes the interest payments, so it is defined as $(G - T)$. During the Conservatives' ten years in power, they averaged a zero primary deficit. During that period, then, $D = rB$, so

$$\Delta B/B = r.$$

To see what this implied for the debt-to-GDP ratio, we define it as $b = B/GDP$. This definition implies that the debt ratio increases whenever the numerator rises by a larger proportion than does the denominator. Thus,

$$\frac{\Delta b}{b} = \frac{\Delta B}{B} - \frac{\Delta Y}{Y}$$

Let the GDP growth rate be n. Thus, the Conservative policy implies:

$$\Delta b/b = r - n,$$

or (since Δb is the change in the debt ratio between time periods t and t + 1: $\Delta b = b_{t + 1} - b_t$),

$$b_{t + 1} = (1 + r - n)b_t.$$

Given that the interest rate exceeded the growth rate, this last equation implies that the debt ratio had to keep rising forever. Thus, it was impossible to grow our way out of the problem. The intuition behind this formal result is straightforward. If the government covers each year's interest payment obligations by issuing that many more government bonds, then the debt must grow at an annual rate equal to the rate of interest. Thus, the numerator of the debt-to-GDP ratio must grow faster than the denominator as long as the rate of interest exceeds the economy's growth rate. Since this has been true for many years, it was simply unreasonable to expect an "automatic" cure to the debt crisis. Direct government action was needed over a prolonged period.

When the Liberals took power in 1993, they set annual targets for the overall deficit ratio, not the primary deficit ratio. They cut program spending and raised taxes by whatever it took to hit the annual target for d. Once a balanced budget was achieved, D and ΔB were both zero, so the Δb equation became $\Delta b/b = -n$, or

$$b_{t+1} = (1 - n)b_t,$$

which states that the debt ratio must fall indefinitely as long as the long-run average GDP growth rate is positive. With this policy, we *can* grow our way out of the debt problem. But this more appealing outcome required much pain initially since getting the overall deficit to zero was much tougher than eliminating the primary deficit. Either painful budget cuts in the short run or lower living standards in the long run were the legacies of our imprudent fiscal policies of the past.

By the end of the 1990s, the focus was on a much rosier scenario. People were speaking of the "fiscal dividend," which referred to the extra room in the budget created by the shrinking interest payment obligations. With the prospect of the debt ratio falling from its peak of about 75 percent to 15 percent (a bit below the minimum achieved in the postwar period), there are significant interest payment savings. A drop in the debt ratio of 0.6 times an interest rate of 0.05 means a saving of 3 percent of GDP *every* year. There has been no shortage of people ready to advise the government about how to spend this fiscal dividend — some arguing for increased programs and others advocating tax cuts. To have some idea of the magnitudes involved in this debate, we should note that 3 percent of GDP permits either a *permanent* 25 percent increase in government spending or a *permanent* elimination of three-eighths of personal income tax. With so much at stake, it is no wonder that the fiscal dividend has been, and will continue to be, a hot topic.

SUMMARY

Here is a review of the key concepts covered in this chapter. Aggregate demand is affected by any of its components, so **fiscal policy** can work through several channels: changes in **income** or **sales taxes** to alter consumption, changes in **corporate profit taxes** to alter firms' investment spending, or changes in **government spending**. Furthermore, government policy can change tariffs or our foreign exchange rate to alter net exports.

The government's **budget deficit** is the excess of its expenditure over its tax revenue. A well-designed fiscal policy involves stimulating aggregate demand during recessions by running a deficit and contracting aggregate demand when the economy is overheated by running a surplus. For a full quarter-century beginning in the early 1970s, however, many Western governments ran deficits through all phases of each business cycle, forcing high taxes, painful government cutbacks, and high levels of **debt** for many years.

By the late 1990s, the Canadian government was finally running budget surpluses, and the debt-to-GDP ratio was beginning to come down. New optimism concerning how to spend the resulting **fiscal dividend** became the order of the day. Nevertheless, servicing high debt levels will continue to constrain fiscal policy for some time yet, so some commentators argue that increased emphasis should be given to another instrument that they believe can be used to help regulate the business cycle. This other instrument is monetary policy, and it is the subject of the next several chapters.

SUGGESTIONS FOR FURTHER READING

R. Boadway, P. Kuhn, W. Robson, and W. Scarth, "The Fiscal Dividend: How to Get It and What to Do with It" *Canadian Public Policy* 24 (1995) — this round table presents estimates of the benefits that accompany debt reduction and recommendations regarding how best to "spend" these gains.

P. Fortin, "Slow Growth, Unemployment, and Debt: What Happened? What Can We Do?" in *Stabilization, Growth, and Distribution: Linkages in the Knowledge Era*, ed. T. Courchene (Kingston: John Deutsch Institute for the Study of Economic Policy, 1994) — an account of how mistakes in macropolicy contributed to recent difficulties.

WEB ACTIVITIES

www.fin.gc.ca
The annual economic update (each fall) and budget documents (each spring) are available under "Publications;" the summary charts on macrodevelopments — comparing Canada with other countries on matters such as taxes and debt — are easy to read and informative.

www.irpp.org
Policy Options 1998; the January issue has a set of articles on the fiscal dividend, and the December issue discusses which taxes to cut (as falling debt service costs permit new government initiatives).

CHAPTER FOURTEEN
Money and Banking

LEARNING OBJECTIVES

After reading this chapter, you should understand

- why banking crises occur and which institutions can limit these problems;
- how the private banking system creates and destroys money; and

- which actions the Bank of Canada uses to adjust the money supply and why the Bank Rate and the Monetary Conditions Index are useful summaries of the Bank's actions.

INTRODUCTION

In the previous two chapters, we discussed fiscal policy — the attempt by government to vary its expenditures and taxes to try to influence the overall level of economic activity. In this chapter, we continue our focus on the government's attempts to stabilize the economy, but we turn our attention to what is called monetary policy.

Most of us have borrowed money to finance some purchase such as a new car or our university education. We know that the interest rate on that loan is an important determinant of how much money we can spend. **Monetary policy** concerns how the government tries to affect the level of interest rates, and to understand this process we must become acquainted with Canada's financial system.

In the circular flowchart back on page 142, there was no mention of the financial system. The households, saving arrow just went off to an unspecified area on the flowchart, and no details were offered concerning how firms finance their investment spending. We fill in those details now.

There are four ways in which firms can finance investment expenditures. They can simply retain some earnings and not pay out all the profits as dividends. They can sell shares on the stock market. They can borrow money by selling a bond. Or they can take out loans from banks. Whichever financing method firms rely on, they acquire cash that can be used to pay for investment expenditures. The macroeconomic implications are the same whichever option is chosen. Thus, to keep things simple and to avoid repetition, we focus on just one of the financing options. We assume that the firms take out bank loans. But before we talk about money and banking in detail, consider Table 14.1. It highlights the role of money in our economy.

The Bank of Canada is the institution through which the government prints money. Suppose the Bank prints more money. What is that going to do? Since most individuals deposit the bulk of their money in a chartered bank

TABLE 14.1 *How Money Affects Economic Activity*

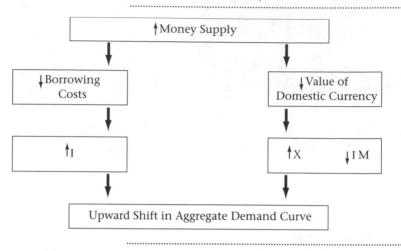

or trust company, most of the new currency will find its way into what we call the *reserves* of the chartered banks. Banks earn no interest on reserves since they are just units of currency held in the vault. Since banks want to make profits, they try to hold no more reserves than are necessary to facilitate the withdrawals made by their customers. Banks lend out the rest of these funds, and they make money when borrowers pay interest on these loans. Thus, when the Bank of Canada prints more currency, chartered banks get extra reserves, and this means an increased capacity to make loans.

But the only way that banks can get more people to take out those loans is to have lower interest rates. When they charge lower interest rates, more people can afford to buy large items, and more firms can afford to expand plant and equipment. So the consumption and investment components of total spending increase, and aggregate demand expands. Thus, jobs can be created and prices are increased when there is a significant increase in the nation's money supply. This chain reaction is summarized on the left-hand side of Table 14.1.

We have already discussed the latter stages of the chain reaction (how higher investment spending has a multiplied effect on aggregate demand). The job for this chapter is to develop the details of the early part of the causal sequence.

What we have just sketched is the domestic route showing what happens following an increase in the money supply. If some of the extra money is used in foreign transactions, then the avenue of effect is a little different, but the net result is the same. An increased supply of Canadian dollars in the world's currency markets causes a fall in the international value of our currency. This makes it cheaper for foreigners to buy our goods and more expensive for us to buy imports. In this case, then, it is the net export component of aggregate demand that increases to create jobs and inflate prices. This transmission mechanism for changes in money supply is summarized on the right-hand side of Table 14.1.

Whether changes in money supply affect interest rates or the exchange rate, the result is the same. It will be helpful to keep this flowchart in mind (as a general "road map") while we delve into the details of the financial system.

HISTORICAL BACKGROUND

We have just seen how monetary policy works. But to discuss this policy in more detail, we must also talk about institutions. Sometimes banks and trust companies go bankrupt, and there are crises of confidence in the financial community. To appreciate the origin of these problems, we must understand the history of money.

Money was invented many centuries ago as a mechanism for people to avoid what economists call "the double coincidence of wants." This difficulty in finding trading partners is necessarily involved when people simply barter one good for another. All kinds of commodities have served as money, but a commodity needs to satisfy several criteria before it can last as useful money. It must be storable, it has to be easy to carry around, and it has to be hard to counterfeit. Precious metal coins satisfied these needs and thus were widely used. But coins can still be stolen, so many years ago enterprising individuals set up warehouses where people could deposit their gold coins. They were given receipts for their gold deposits. These receipts were IOU slips that depositors could use to retrieve their gold whenever they wanted to make an expenditure.

After a while, people realized that they could just trade the IOU slips. If Brian wanted to buy something from David, then he crossed out his own name on the slip and wrote in David's name. As a result, the warehouse then owed David the gold instead of Brian. So with this practice of financing trades by exchanging the warehouse receipts, societies moved away from using commodity money (which had its own intrinsic usefulness) to paper money (a system in which the medium of exchange, paper currency, had no intrinsic value). Despite having no real value on the used-paper market, this kind of money was accepted because it was regarded "as good as gold." After all, if people started to lose confidence in the paper currency, they could cash it in for gold at the warehouse.

After a while, the gold warehouse managers realized that they were hardly ever asked for the gold. They realized that a profit could be made by lending out the gold. Every time they lent some of the gold, someone would receive it as payment for the goods and services that someone sold to the borrower. That someone then deposited the gold in her warehouse, receiving another IOU slip as a receipt. Considering the entire group of gold warehouses, there soon came to be many more IOU slips than there was gold in storage. When depositors realized this fact, some feared that when they took in their IOU slips there might not be any gold left. In that case, the warehouse company would go bankrupt, and the depositors would lose their wealth.

As you have probably guessed, the warehouses eventually became banks and trust companies, and government regulations were introduced. The regulations were designed to avoid crises of public confidence by keeping these institutions solvent. One arrangement that we now have is **deposit insurance**. Even if a financial institution goes bankrupt, as long as your deposit is less than $60 000, the government will pay you back out of general tax revenue. So now there's no reason to have a run against a bank (unless your account is large).

What serves as most of our money today, then, is not even paper currency. Since we often pay by cheque, it is mostly the passbook entries in our deposit accounts at banks that represent the nation's money supply. If we are to understand how the quantity of money varies, then we have to understand chartered banking.

CHARTERED BANKS AND THE MONEY MULTIPLIER

The easiest way to understand banking is by considering the balance sheet of a typical bank, as shown in Table 14.2. The balance sheet keeps a record of all the **assets** and **liabilities** of the bank. An asset is anything that an individual or an institution owns, and a liability is anything that that individual or institution owes to someone else.

As can be seen in Table 14.2, one thing that a chartered bank owns is its reserves (currency kept in the vault), and the second important asset is the stock of loans that the bank extends to its customers. Loans allow households and firms to buy many items, such as houses and factories. From the bank's point of view, each loan is an asset because it represents an income stream of interest payments coming into the bank. The loan is a liability from the household's or the firm's point of view, but it is the bank's balance that we are considering here. Finally, there are other assets, such as the bank building, but they do not figure into our discussion of monetary policy.

TABLE 14.2 *Balance Sheet for a Private Bank*

Assets	*Liabilities & Net Worth*
Reserves	Deposits
Loans	
Buildings	Net Worth

On the liabilities side, the main entry is deposits. These deposits are the customers' assets; however, since the deposits represent an obligation to its customers, they are liabilities from the bank's point of view. Banks make money by charging a higher rate of interest on loans than they pay on deposits, and the accumulation of profits is reflected in the fact that the company's assets exceed its liabilities. Accountants call the amount by which assets exceed liabilities the company's *net worth*. They record net worth on the liabilities side of the balance sheet so that the sum on each side reaches the same number.

The most common definition of the nation's money supply (called M1) is the total of the public's chequing deposits at chartered banks plus any currency circulating outside banks. Other definitions include all deposits in banks and some deposits in trust companies and caisses populaires. However, since it is not necessary to consider this wider set of deposits to understand monetary policy, we focus on just the chartered banks and M1.

Since most of the money supply is at the level of bank deposits, we must understand how much the total quantity of deposits rises when any given amount of new currency is printed. We now consider a specific example to illustrate what economists call the **money multiplier**.

For simplicity, we consider a situation in which no one holds any money in the form of currency. Thus, initially we assume that everyone who receives money puts it all on deposit at banks. Also, we assume that banks choose to hold on reserve an amount equal to 10 percent of their deposit obligations. Actually, banks hold a much lower reserves-to-deposit ratio since very little is needed to satisfy the withdrawal habits of the banks' customers. But we just want a simple numerical example to illustrate the principles involved.

Suppose a new $100 bill is sent to you as part of your student loan. Given our first assumption, you will either deposit it in your bank or use it to pay for something — say, the services of a typist for your economics essay. In that case, the typist is the one who puts the $100 into his bank, say, Bank Number 1 (see Table 14.3). After this initial deposit, there is $100 more in that chartered bank vault (because the $100 bill is now there), and that bank will record an additional $100 obligation to the typist for having deposited the money there.

TABLE 14.3 *Balance Sheet for Bank 1: After Initial Deposit*

Assets	Liabilities
Reserves + 100 Loans	Deposits + 100

TABLE 14.4 *Balance Sheet for Bank 1: After Making New Loan*

Assets	Liabilities
Reserves + 10 Loans + 90	Deposits + 100

TABLE 14.5 *Balance Sheet for Bank 2: After Making New Loan*

Assets	Liabilities
Reserves + 9 Loans + 81	Deposits + 90

But Bank Number 1 will not be comfortable with this outcome because it is holding reserves on a one-for-one basis for this new deposit of $100. The bank cannot make a profit by paying interest on the deposit while earning none on the reserves. We have assumed that banks want to hold reserves on a one-for-ten ratio compared with deposit obligations. Thus, the bank will lend out $90 of that $100.

The second step in this process is that Bank Number 1 shuffles its portfolio of assets, drawing the new reserves down to just $10 and lending out $90 to some other customer (see Table 14.4). That person buys something with the funds. Whoever receives that payment deposits it in her bank, say, Bank Number 2. So in Bank Number 2, there will be $90 more in both reserves and deposits. But just like Bank Number 1, this bank cannot make money by holding a full dollar more of reserves for every new dollar on deposit. Given the one-for-ten desired reserve-to-deposit ratio, Bank Number 2 will pull its extra reserves down to just $9, and it will make an additional loan equal to $81 (see Table 14.5).

Of course, just as before, that new loan will get spent, and somebody else will deposit $81 in yet another bank. You can see what is happening — it is another multiplier process.

Our goal is to determine the total quantity of bank deposits created as a result of the extra $100 of new currency introduced into the system. To determine this total, we add up all the extra deposits created round after round:

$100 + $90 + $81 + ...

A more fruitful way of writing this sum is

$100 x $(1 + 0.9 + (0.9)^2 + ...)$.

This sum is similar to the expenditure multiplier formula that we calculated in Chapter 12. The sum equals

$100 x (1/(1 – 0.9)) = $100 x (1/0.1) = $1000.

Thus, there is a money multiplier as well as an expenditure multiplier, and in this numerical example, because the reserve-to-deposit ratio of the banks is one-tenth, the money multiplier is the inverse of that, or ten.

How does the actual value of the money multiplier compare to this example value of ten? In fact, our simplifications involve both an upward and a downward bias. For one thing, people do not hold all their money as deposits; they hold some of it as cash. To that extent, banks do not get to lend out as much as they did in our example, so the actual money multiplier is smaller. But more important is the fact that there is no longer any legal minimum reserve ratio imposed on financial institutions, and modern banks can satisfy the day-to-day needs of their depositors with a reserve-to-deposit ratio of much less than one-tenth. Since a tiny stock of reserves (relative to deposits) is sufficient, the nation's money supply is a large multiple of the quantity of currency that the government prints. As a result, it is important that the government not print an inappropriate quantity of currency.

BANK OF CANADA OPERATIONS

The last step in understanding the mechanics of money and banking is to appreciate how the initial $100 of new currency gets introduced in the first place. To facilitate this understanding, we must learn a few things about Canada's central bank, the Bank of Canada.

The Bank of Canada came into existence with the passage of an act of Parliament in 1935. Some of the provisions in this act put regulations on our chartered banks to make sure that they do not take part in such risky ventures that people lose confidence in the stability of the financial system. The act established the Bank of Canada as a kind of **lender of last resort** that can lend out reserves to any chartered bank that is running short in any particular period, again to provide stability to the financial system.

The governor of the Bank of Canada is appointed for seven years, and, while he or she normally works closely with the federal minister of finance, the governor is able to be somewhat independent. Central bankers take it as one of their fundamental purposes to preserve the purchasing power of money, and that means keeping inflation under control. Since ultimately inflation results from "too much money chasing too few goods," central bankers often find themselves serving as independent checks on a government's temptation to print a lot of new currency as a method of financing government expenditures in excess of the government's willingness to raise taxes.

TABLE 14.6 *Bank of Canada's Balance Sheet*

Assets	Liabilities & Net Worth
Gold	Currency in Existence
Foreign Exchange	Deposits
Government Bonds	of Chartered Banks
	of Federal Government

We can better understand the Bank of Canada if we focus on a simplified version of its balance sheet (Table 14.6). The main items that our central bank owns, or controls, are gold, the country's foreign exchange reserves, and government bonds. Gold used to be the international medium of exchange, and that is why it appears in the list of things that the Bank of Canada has purchased over the years. On the liabilities side of the Bank of Canada balance sheet, the major item is the total number of dollar bills that have been issued — the currency in existence. Paper currency is a unique liability; it is an IOU slip from an accountant's point of view, but of course you cannot get anything if you present your $10 bill to the Bank of Canada (other than a crisp new $10 bill in exchange). The other liabilities are the deposit obligations of the Bank of Canada. The general public is not allowed to hold deposit accounts there. The only institutions that do are the chartered banks (and similar institutions) and the Government of Canada.

We can now see the main way in which the Bank of Canada changes the overall reserves of the chartered banking system. At the intuitive level, it is simple. To increase the supply of currency, all the central bank has to do is buy something and pay for it with the new currency. Since the Bank of Canada usually does so through a purchase of government bonds on the open market, called **open market operations**, we follow through the recording of that transaction in the balance sheets. Refer now to Table 14.7, which contains both the Bank of Canada's balance sheet and a balance sheet for the chartered banks.

Table 14.7 contains numbered arrows, 1 through 4, that summarize the Bank of Canada's purchase of some government bonds. As the Bank of Canada buys the bond (previously held by some member of the public), we show the central bank's acquisition of the bonds by arrow 1 in Table 14.7. The Bank of Canada pays for these additional bond holdings by writing a cheque to the member of the public who sold the government bond. That individual deposits the cheque in her account, at whichever chartered bank she does her banking, and that is why arrow 2 is included in Table 14.7. This individual now has a larger bank deposit.

But this is not the end of the story because the cheque has to be cleared through the banking system. After all, why should the chartered bank go

TABLE 14.7 *Open Market Operations by the Bank of Canada*

Bank of Canada		Chartered Banks	
Assets	*Liabilities*	*Assets*	*Liabilities*
Gold	Currency	Reserves:	Deposits:
For. Exchange	Deposits:	Deposits at	Gov't
Gov't Bonds ↑1	Gov't	B. of Can. ↑4	Public ↑2
	Banks ↑3	Loans	

more in debt to this individual? It is compensated (for honouring the cheque on behalf of the Bank of Canada) by sending the cheque back to the Bank of Canada, which credits the chartered bank's account there by the same amount. This final settling of the transaction is recorded in Table 14.7 by arrows 3 and 4.

So the chartered bank's deposit at the Bank of Canada goes up by the same amount as the original purchase of bonds. That fact represents both an increase in the Bank of Canada's liabilities (arrow 3) and an increase in the chartered bank's assets (arrow 4). The complete set of four arrows is needed to fully record the open market operation. However, while the description of that transaction is now complete, what follows from it is just about to begin.

The chartered banks are just at the first stage of the money multiplier process described earlier. The reserves of the chartered banks can be held either as cash in their vaults or as funds on deposit at the central bank. So, as a result of the open market purchase of bonds by the Bank of Canada, chartered bank reserves have gone up dollar for dollar with their deposit obligations. Banks want to hold only a tiny fraction of this amount as additional reserves. We have already seen how new loans and further deposits get created when the banks have excess reserves. The point of this discussion was to explain how the additional reserves are created in the first place.

There is one additional point worth emphasizing. We could move arrow 1 from the government bonds entry to the foreign exchange entry (among the list of Bank of Canada assets) and the other three arrows would stay the same. This implies that, as far as what happens to the reserves of the chartered banks is concerned, it does not matter what the central bank buys. Central bank purchases of foreign exchange have the same effect on the nation's money supply as do purchases of government bonds. Either action is referred to as an "expansionary" monetary policy.

The Bank of Canada often buys or sells foreign exchange, hoping to affect the international value of the Canadian dollar (i.e., our exchange rate).

What the balance sheet analysis makes clear is that an exchange rate policy of this sort and monetary policy are the same thing. Our central bank can try to control the international value of our currency by standing ready to buy or sell large quantities of foreign exchange. For example, to keep the value of the Canadian dollar from rising, the Bank of Canada must make more Canadian dollars available by buying foreign exchange (an expansionary monetary policy). Because of this promise to control the exchange rate, then, monetary policy is dictated by whatever develops in the foreign markets. The central bank gives up its freedom to have an independent monetary policy if it fixes the value of our exchange rate.

In addition to conducting open market operations involving bonds and foreign exchange, the Bank of Canada is involved in **deposit switching**. On a day-to-day basis, there is a great of shuffling deposits from one chartered bank to another (as people and firms settle their accounts). This can cause short-run variations in the overall quantity of reserves and thus lead to some instability in financial markets. The central bank can iron out these fluctuations. All the Bank of Canada has to do is write a cheque from the government to the government. Doing so may seem to be pointless, but by consulting the balance sheets we see that it does matter for the nation's money supply.

For instance, suppose the Bank of Canada writes a cheque against the Government of Canada's deposits held at the central bank. This action draws down that account, as shown by arrow 1 in Table 14.8. The cheque is made payable to the Government of Canada, so the cheque is deposited in one of the government's accounts at a chartered bank (raising the balance in that account by the same amount — arrow 2). The government neither gains nor loses, but it is important to see what happens when the cheque clears. The chartered bank sends the cheque back to the Bank of Canada and, for honouring the cheque, gets compensated by having its deposit account at the Bank of Canada (i.e., its reserves) credited by that amount (arrows 3 and 4). Once again, chartered bank reserves and deposits have gone up one for one. But in a fractional reserve system, banks do not need or want reserves to go

TABLE 14.8 *Open Market Operations by the Bank of Canada*

Bank of Canada				Chartered Banks			
Assets		*Liabilities*		*Assets*		*Liabilities*	
Gold		Currency		Reserves:		Deposits:	
For. Exchange		Deposits:		Deposits at		Gov't	
Gov't Bonds	↑1	Gov't	↓1	B. of Can.	↑4	Public	↑2
		Banks	↑3	Loans			

up this much. So once again, by this simple shuffling of government funds, the Bank of Canada has arranged it so that the chartered banks can start a multiple expansion of loans and deposits.

So the day-to-day operations of monetary policy are deposit switching and open market operations in bond or foreign exchange markets. Deposit switches toward chartered banks and open market purchases are "expansionary" monetary policies, while deposit switches toward the central bank and open market sales are "contractionary" monetary policies. But these sorts of transactions are fairly hard for people to understand. What we need, and luckily what we have, are two simple indicators to see whether the central bank is trying to expand or contract the country's money supply. The first indicator is the Bank Rate.

THE BANK RATE

The overnight lending rate is the rate at which chartered banks and other participants in the money market borrow and lend one-day funds to each other. Such loans can become necessary if one bank needs funds to cover net withdrawals at the end of the day, while another bank may have acquired more reserves than it wants. The bank that is short of reserves has a second option: it can borrow from the Bank of Canada at the Bank Rate.

The Bank of Canada establishes a range — called the operating band — in which the overnight lending rate can move up or down. The **Bank Rate** is set at the upper limit of this band, which is half a percentage point wide. The Bank of Canada stands ready to lend out reserves at a rate given by the upper limit of the band, and it stands ready to borrow funds from financial institutions at the lower limit of the band. These commitments ensure that the overnight rate stays within the band.

By changing the operating band and thus the Bank Rate, the central bank sends a clear signal about the direction in which interest rates will move. On the one hand, Bank Rate changes are "trend-setting" since it is the Bank that has announced any change in the operating band. On the other hand, Bank Rate changes follow the market. The Bank changes the operating band only when it has been conducting behind-the-scenes transactions — deposit switching and open market operations — and these determine the change in both market yields and the Bank Rate.

THE MONETARY CONDITIONS INDEX

The other summary indicator that the Bank of Canada publishes in its semi-annual *Monetary Policy Report* is the **monetary conditions index (MCI)**. It is a weighted average of the interest rate and the exchange rate (the international value of the Canadian dollar). As clarified in Table 14.1 (page 168), monetary policy affects aggregate demand through two channels: it affects firms' investment spending through interest rates, and it affects net exports through the exchange rate. Researchers at the central bank have estimated that it takes roughly a 3 percent change in the exchange rate to affect aggregate demand by the same amount as a 1 percentage point change in the interest rate. This three-to-one factor is what Bank officials use in calculating the weighted average. Suppose, from one quarter to the next, the Canadian dollar appreciates by 2 percent while the level of Canadian interest rates falls by 1 percentage point. Without the MCI, it would be difficult to know whether monetary conditions became easier or tighter. The more expensive Canadian dollar reduces net exports, while the lower borrowing costs stimulate investment. But the MCI provides a unique signal; it falls because its change equals (one times the interest rate change) plus (one-third times the exchange rate change), or $(1)(-1) + (1/3)(2) = -1/3$. As long as the Bank's target for the MCI has not changed, the lower value for the actual MCI in the short run means that, overall, monetary policy has moved in an expansionary direction.

SUMMARY

Here is a review of the key concepts covered in this chapter. We learned how our system of **fractional reserve banking** evolved. The total quantity of the public's deposits at chartered banks is a major component of the country's **money supply**, and that total is equal to the **money multiplier** times the quantity of bank reserves. In a simplified setting, the money multiplier is the inverse of the chartered banks' reserves-to-deposits ratio. Chartered bank reserves can be increased by **open market purchases of bonds or foreign exchange** and by **switching government deposits** into chartered banks. Expansionary monetary policies of this sort put downward pressure on interest rates, which we can monitor by observing changes in the **Bank Rate**. The Bank of Canada also publishes a more general summary indicator of monetary policy — a weighted average of interest rates and the exchange rate called the **Monetary Conditions Index**.

Throughout this chapter, we have discussed Bank of Canada operations as if the Bank knows the "appropriate" value of the money supply. We have focused on how the central bank regulates the reserves available to the private banking system, but we have not explored in detail why this is necessary. Our job in the next chapter is to determine the "appropriate" level for the money supply. We will switch our attention from the mechanics of monetary policy to the purposes of monetary policy.

SUGGESTIONS FOR FURTHER READING

B. Montador, "The Implementation of Monetary Policy in Canada," *Canadian Public Policy* 21 (1995) — much detail on how the Bank of Canada operates.

J. Carr, F. Mathewson, and N. Quigley, *Ensuring Failure: Financial System Stability and Deposit Insurance in Canada* (Toronto: C.D. Howe Institute, 1994) — an evaluation of reform proposals for the deposit insurance system.

WEB ACTIVITIES

www.bank-banque-canada.ca
The Web site of the Bank of Canada; good source of historical information on the financial sector; click on "Publications & Research," then on "Backgrounders," for helpful one-page summaries on central topics.

www.bank-banque-canada.ca/english/dollar_book/full_text-e.htm
The Web site of the Bank of Canada gives a detailed account of the history of money in Canada.

CHAPTER FIFTEEN

Interest Rates and Exchange Rates

LEARNING OBJECTIVES

After reading this chapter, you should understand
- how the tools of supply and demand are used to explain the determination of interest rates and exchange rates in the short run;

- how the balance of international payments is measured and why the trade balance correlates with the budget balance; and
- why speculation is a serious problem in a fixed exchange rate setting.

INTRODUCTION

In the previous chapter, we discussed the history of money, the basic tools that the Bank of Canada can use to control the reserves of the banking system, and how the central bank signals its use of these tools by adjusting the Bank Rate. This chapter's task is to connect these developments in money and banking to the earlier analysis of aggregate supply and demand. Understanding this connection involves learning how both interest rates and exchange rates are determined. Once these analyses are complete, we will understand how developments in the financial markets affect the rest of the economy and how changes in output and the price level affect financial markets.

First we review the basic logic behind monetary policy, at least how it operates through domestic financial markets. You may wish to refer back to the left side of Table 14.1 (page 168). Suppose the central bank increases the reserves of the banking system. The result is an increase in the money supply. With extra reserves available, chartered banks try to earn more profits by making more loans. To find the additional customers to take these loans, banks must lower interest rates. Lower borrowing rates lead to more spending, particularly the investment component of aggregate demand, and that means a shift to the right in the aggregate demand curve. The result is higher real output, higher prices, or both.

The only stage of this chain of reasoning that we have not discussed fully in earlier chapters is the connection between changes in the money supply and interest rates. To make this connection clear, we develop a supply and demand analysis of the nation's money market.

THE MONEY MARKET

On the quantity axis of our money market graph (see Figure 15.1), we measure the quantity of money, denoted by M, and on the price axis we measure

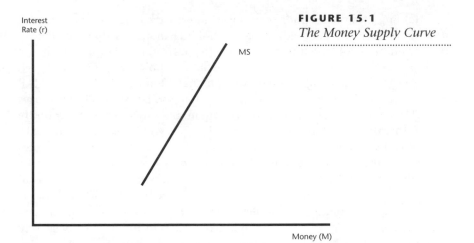

FIGURE 15.1

The Money Supply Curve

the rate of interest, denoted by r. By the interest rate, we mean the rate of re-turn that can be earned on assets other than money — that is, the yield avail-able on bonds and stocks. First we consider the money supply curve, for which we use the label MS. The higher the interest rate that people can earn on their deposits at banks, the more they forgo the convenience of carrying a lot of currency, and they deposit their funds at their banks. The result is that the banks acquire more reserves, so they can make more loans. The money multiplier then applies to a bigger quantity of reserves. The result is a larger money supply when interest rates are high, as shown in Figure 15.1 by the positive slope of the money supply curve.

If the central bank purchases treasury bills on the open market, then this action increases chartered bank reserves and moves the entire position of the money supply curve to the right. But before we can explain what will hap-pen to the interest rate, we must derive a money demand curve. Thus, we em-bark on an extended consideration of the decisions that households face in their financial affairs.

Broadly speaking, households have two decisions to make. First, they have to decide the rate at which they want to add to their accumulated wealth. So there is an *additions-to-wealth decision*, another name for the con-sumption–savings choice. Whenever we save, our wealth goes up by that amount. The consumption line that we drew in the income–expenditure graph is the decision rule that households in our model of the economy use to solve their additions-to-wealth decisions.

But households also have to decide the form in which they want to hold the wealth that they already have. So they must make an *allocation-of-wealth decision* as well. Assume that households have only two ways to hold wealth. Either they can hold money, in the form of cash or on deposit at a bank, or they can hold what we call "bonds" — all assets that earn higher interest rates than bank deposits, such as government bonds and corporate stocks.

Holding money has both advantages and disadvantages compared with holding bonds. The main advantage of holding money is that it is convenient; you can easily use it to buy things. In contrast, if your wealth is in the form of a bond, then you have to incur delays and brokerage charges to sell your bond before making payment for a purchase. But people do not hold all their wealth in the form of money, because doing so has some disadvantages too. The main disadvantage is that holding money involves an opportunity cost — the forgone interest that you could earn if you hold a bond instead.

We can summarize how households react to these good and bad features of money and bonds as follows. The more transactions people make, the more they need to hold their wealth in the form of money to facilitate all those purchases. One convenient measure of the total value of purchases is the nominal value of the gross domestic product. Thus, we summarize by saying that the amount of money people would like to hold varies positively with nominal GDP. It will be convenient to use abbreviations in our graphs, so we use MD to stand for money demand and Y and P to stand for real GDP and the price level, respectively. Given these definitions, we denote nominal GDP as the product PY, and the summary just given can be abbreviated as MD increases when PY increases. Remember that, by the amount of money demanded, we mean the amount of people's wealth that they want to hold in the form of money, not bonds.

The second determinant of the amount of money that people demand is the rate of interest that can be earned on the alternative — bonds. The higher that interest rate, the less people want to hold their wealth as money. Overall, then, the amount of money demanded depends on two things; it increases when nominal GDP is higher, and it decreases when interest rates are higher. As usual with two-dimensional graphs, we show the dependence of money demand on one influence as the slope of a curve, and we show its dependence on the other influence as a shift in the entire position of that curve. The money demand curve is shown in Figure 15.2; the negative slope

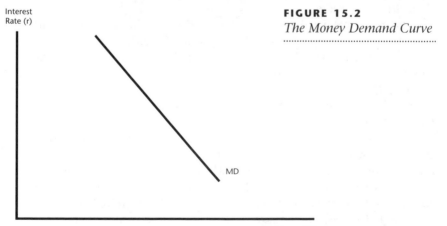

Interest
Rate (r)

FIGURE 15.2
The Money Demand Curve

MD

Money (M)

TABLE 15.1 *Determinants of Money Demand*

MD	Money Demand		P	Price Level
Y	Real GDP			↑P Is Inflation
P	Price Level		Y	Real GDP
PY	Nominal GDP			↑Y Means More Jobs
MD ↑	when PY ↑		PY	Nominal GDP
MD ↓	when r ↑			↑PY Means MD Curve Shifts to the Right

indicates that the lower the interest rate that can be earned on bonds, the more money people will want to hold. The other determinant of money demand is the level of transactions. We show that influence by shifting the curve; for instance, the money demand curve shifts to the right when there is a higher level of transactions in the country (i.e., when PY is higher).

A summary of our abbreviations is provided in Table 15.1. P stands for the price level, and we care about it because a rising P is inflation. Y stands for the level of real GDP, and one reason we care about it is that an increase in Y means job creation. The product P times Y stands for the level of nominal GDP, and we care about it because changes in that measure cause shifts in the position of the money demand curve. We can now understand the determination of interest rates by putting the supply and demand curves for money together in the same graph, as shown in Figure 15.3.

Equilibrium in the money market is determined by the intersection of supply and demand. But to fully understand why, we should consider what happens if the market is not at this point. Thus, to see how the money market operates, suppose the interest rate happens to be 10 percent, as in Figure 15.3. At this high rate, bonds are appealing, so people do not want much of

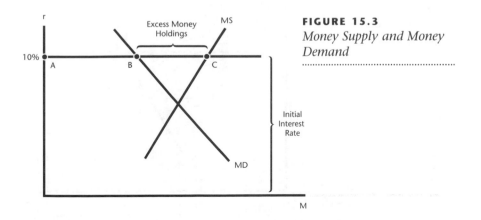

FIGURE 15.3
Money Supply and Money Demand

their wealth in the form of money. The amount of money demanded is given by distance AB, and it is much smaller than the available money supply, given by distance AC. So there is more money available than people want to hold. Consequently, they use these excess money holdings to start buying bonds. As individuals begin switching over their portfolios toward more bonds, they bid up the price of bonds.

What does a higher bond price mean for the yield that can be earned on bonds? We must remember that a bond is simply a piece of paper saying that whoever owns it will receive the payments stipulated on the contract. For example, consider a bond stipulating that the owner will receive $10 a year for five years, and then she will get $100 when the bond matures (i.e., when the contract expires). If you pay precisely $100 to buy this bond, then you will receive a 10 percent annual interest yield. You receive $10 every year on an investment of $100. If you have to pay $110 for the bond, however, then your percentage yield is lower. You still receive $10 a year, but that return would be for a larger initial investment of $110. Dividing 10 by 110 yields less than 10 percent. Thus, the more we have to pay for bonds, the lower the effective interest rate we earn on those bonds.

Now that we understand that effective bond yields vary inversely with bond prices, we can return to Figure 15.3. At a bond yield of 10 percent, individuals start off with too much money in their portfolios, so they try to buy bonds with their excess money holdings. This activity bids up the bond price, and we now know that this is just another way of saying that it will bid down the effective bond yield — what we are measuring as r on the vertical axis in the graph. This process of falling interest rates continues until the money supply and demand imbalance is completely eliminated. The equilibrium is given by point E in Figure 15.4, and in this example the interest rate settles at 6 percent.

FIGURE 15.4
Equilibrium in the Money Market
....

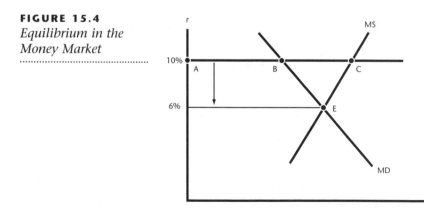

Now we can understand precisely how central bank policy affects interest rates in the short run. If the central bank buys some government bonds and pays for them by issuing some new currency, then the position of the money supply curve shifts to the right, as shown in Figure 15.5. As a result, the equilibrium point moves down from E to F, interest rates decline, and a reduction in the Bank Rate is announced to ensure that it is consistent with developments in the money market. Contractionary monetary policy works in the same way — just in reverse. By shifting the money supply curve to the left, the contractionary policy makes loans more scarce, so both market interest rates and the Bank Rate rise.

In the next two chapters, we will use this analysis of interest rate determination in two ways. First, it is all that we need to know to discuss interest rates in a large economy, such as the United States, whose financial markets represent a significant part of the world's financial system. Economic developments in Canada depend very much on those in the United States; after all, we export about one-third of our GDP, and 80 percent of that goes to the United States. As a result, this large-country analysis has an indirect, though important, relevance for Canada. Second, this analysis serves as a stepping stone for understanding small economies, such as Canada's, whose financial markets are only a tiny fraction of world markets.

Financial markets are highly integrated throughout the world. No one will hold a Canadian-issued bond if the yield is not as high as can be obtained elsewhere. Since competition in world markets forces Canadian interest rates to settle at levels roughly equal to foreign yields, Canadian policies can affect interest rates only temporarily. As a result, the lasting effects of Canadian monetary policy come from our ability to change our exchange rate, not our interest rate. But to appreciate how exchange rates are determined, we must understand temporary interest rate changes, and that is the second reason we must understand the domestic money market analysis that we have just completed.

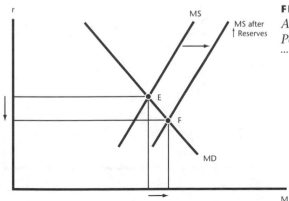

FIGURE 15.5

An Expansionary Monetary Policy

NOMINAL VERSUS REAL INTEREST RATES

You may have noticed that "short run" has been mentioned many times in preceding paragraphs. This is because monetary policy has both a **liquidity effect** and an **inflationary expectations effect**. Since it takes time for forecasts of inflation to be revised, the liquidity effect occurs first, and only later does the inflationary expectations effect come into play. This chapter has focused only on the liquidity effect — that increased money growth makes banks more liquid and thus leads to *lower* interest rates. But in the long run, the resulting increase in aggregate demand eliminates the excess liquidity and creates an inflationary gap. Once the resulting inflation causes lenders to revise upward their inflationary expectations, lenders demand an "inflation premium" in market interest rates. This is the inflationary expectations effect — considered by itself, it implies that higher money growth *raises* market interest rates. So in the short run, only the liquidity effect operates, while in the long run only the inflationary expectations effect matters.

FOREIGN EXCHANGE RATES

By foreign exchange, we mean the currencies of other countries, such as U.S. dollars, German marks, and Japanese yen. To simplify our discussion, we refer just to U.S. dollars. We now develop a supply and demand analysis that can determine how much a U.S. dollar is worth in terms of Canadian dollars.

On the quantity axis in Figure 15.6, we measure the quantity of foreign exchange (U.S. dollars) traded each period. On the price axis, we measure the Canadian price of a U.S. dollar. The exchange rate can be measured in either of two ways. It can be defined as the number of Canadian dollars needed to buy one U.S. dollar, as in Figure 15.6, or it can be defined the other way around — the number of U.S. dollars needed to buy one Canadian dollar.

FIGURE 15.6
The Foreign Exchange Market

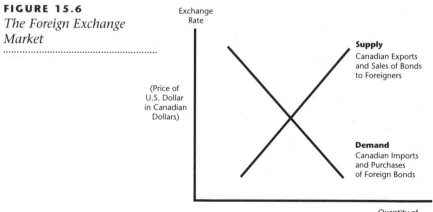

One definition is simply the inverse of the other. To say that the Canadian dollar is worth 70 cents U.S. is the same as saying that the U.S. dollar is worth $1.47 Canadian (since 1/0.7 = 1.47).

Supply and demand curves for foreign exchange are shown in Figure 15.6. Among the suppliers of foreign exchange is anyone who sells goods or financial assets to the rest of the world. Consider Canadian farmers selling wheat on the world market as an example. The contracts are typically in U.S. dollars. When farmers bring their sales proceeds home, these U.S. dollars must be converted into Canadian dollars since the farmers have to pay labour and other costs in Canadian dollars. These individuals must then enter the foreign exchange market as suppliers to turn their sales proceeds into domestic currency.

Among the demanders of foreign exchange is anyone who buys goods or financial assets from the rest of the world. For example, Canadian importers of Florida oranges need U.S. dollars to pay for the oranges. The importers collect Canadian dollars from Canadian customers and must convert them into U.S. dollars. The importers must enter the foreign exchange market as demanders of U.S. dollars to turn their sales proceeds into the foreign currency needed to pay for the imports.

The higher the Canadian price of the U.S. dollar, the more profitable it is for Canadians to export goods and services, because the U.S. dollars earned through export sales can be converted into more Canadian dollars. So the higher the Canadian price of a U.S. dollar, the more exporting we do, and that is why the supply curve of foreign exchange has a positive slope. For Canadian imports, though, a higher Canadian price for the U.S. dollar means that imports are more expensive. Thus, we demand fewer imports and less foreign exchange to buy these imports when the price of foreign exchange is high. This relationship is shown by the negative slope of the demand curve in Figure 15.6.

The Canadian–U.S. dollar exchange rate was not allowed to vary during the late 1940s and during the 1960s, but authorities have allowed it to vary for the rest of the postwar period. The government's exchange rate policy is conducted by the Bank of Canada. We can now use supply and demand analysis to explain how both fixed and flexible exchange rate regimes operate. Before we do so, however, we indicate how international transactions are recorded.

Each country keeps what are called its **balance of payments accounts**. In principle, every transaction that crosses the border is recorded; those that bring in foreign exchange (e.g., exports and sales of our financial assets to foreigners) enter with a plus sign, while those that use up foreign exchange (e.g., imports and purchases of foreign financial assets) enter with a minus sign. The accounts are divided into two parts: the current account (which records the purchases and sales of goods and services such as wheat, oranges, and interest payments on foreign debts) and the capital account (which records that period's purchases and sales of financial assets). For many years, Canada has had a deficit on the current account since, while exporting more than we import, our foreign debt service obligations have been large. Canadians have paid for this "overspending" by increasing our foreign indebtedness — that is, by running a surplus on the capital account.

The news media often refer to countries as having a **"twin deficits"** problem. When a country's government runs a budget deficit, either the government sells the corresponding new bonds to foreigners or its increased presence in the domestic bond market pushes other borrowers overseas. Thus, the budget deficit creates a surplus on the capital account. Without the country's central bank intervening, though, all private participants in the foreign exchange market must find a private sector partner, so the capital account and the current account *must* sum to zero. Thus, a capital account surplus means a current account deficit, so budget deficits and current account deficits go up and down together. Countries with large current account deficits (i.e., those importing much more than they are exporting) often blame their trading partners, arguing that they are suffering from unfair trade restrictions. As often as not, however, as the twin deficits phenomenon implies, their trade deficits simply reflect the overspending by their own governments.

FIXED AND FLEXIBLE EXCHANGE RATES

With a flexible exchange rate, the Bank of Canada simply takes no action and lets the foreign exchange market operate by free market forces. The exchange rate is determined by the intersection of supply and demand, such as at point E in Figure 15.7, where in this example it takes $1.50 Canada to buy one U.S. dollar.

But central bankers sometimes take the view that short-term fluctuations in the exchange rate can be disruptive to international trade decisions. Thus,

FIGURE 15.7
A Flexible Exchange Rate

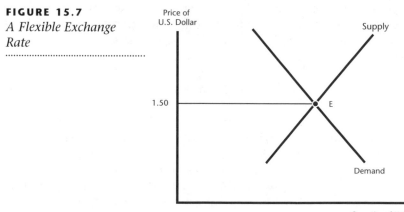

they sometimes enter the foreign exchange market and try to keep the price from fluctuating much. The extreme form of this approach is called a **fixed exchange rate policy**. In the situation shown in Figure 15.8, the Bank of Canada has decided to keep the Canadian price of a U.S. dollar at $1.60, and thus to keep it from falling to the equilibrium value given by point E.

At this high price of foreign exchange, the quantity of U.S. dollars demanded is much smaller than the quantity supplied. Thus, to fix the exchange rate, the Bank of Canada has to act as a residual buyer of the otherwise unwanted foreign exchange entering the country (the amount labelled as excess supply in Figure 15.8). By adding that additional demand for foreign exchange to the amount demanded by private traders, the total demand is just balanced by supply at the $1.60 price. This policy requires that the Bank of Canada buy precisely the amount of U.S. dollars shown as the private excess supply every period. This amount of "official" foreign exchange purchases is called the **balance of payments surplus**. To pay for these foreign exchange purchases, the central bank must issue Canadian dollars. All the Bank does in this case is print the necessary Canadian dollars.

While fixing the exchange rate is therefore feasible, it is not clear that doing so is desirable. If the policy is maintained period after period, then the Bank will have to keep printing new domestic currency every period. A large expansion of chartered bank loans and deposits will result. So the real check on fixing the exchange rate in this range is that the resulting expansion in the money supply causes inflation. Central bankers usually try to avoid inflation by abandoning a fixed exchange rate policy in this situation.

What about a fixed exchange rate policy in which the central bank tries to maintain an exchange rate on the other side of the free market equilibrium? Suppose the Bank of Canada tries to fix a low Canadian price for the U.S. dollar, such as $1.35 as shown in Figure 15.9. With a cheap U.S. dollar, Canadians want to do a lot of importing, so we demand a large quantity of U.S.

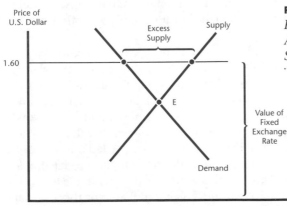

FIGURE 15.8
Fixed Exchange Rates: A Balance of Payments Surplus

FIGURE 15.9
*Fixed Exchange Rates:
A Balance of Payments
Deficit*
....

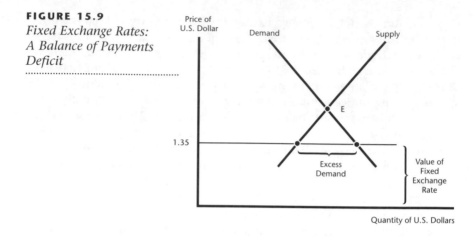

dollars to finance this importing. But at a low Canadian price for the U.S. dollar, the revenues of Canadian exporters are low. As a result, less exporting is done, and this small quantity of foreign exchange is supplied to the market. The excess amount demanded is shown in Figure 15.9, and it is called the **balance of payments deficit**. With a fixed exchange rate policy, the central bank does not allow this excess demand (which is the sum of the current account and the capital account balances) to be eliminated through a bidding up of the price of foreign exchange.

To maintain this low Canadian price for the U.S. dollar, the Bank of Canada must add to the supply of U.S. dollars entering the country each period, so that the overall supply curve — that involving both the private traders and the Bank of Canada — shifts over to intersect the demand curve on the fixed exchange rate line. So the Bank must sell foreign exchange every period, and that per-period amount is labelled excess demand in Figure 15.9. Of course, there is a limit to how long the Bank can intervene in the market since the Bank will eventually run out of its foreign exchange reserve holdings. The Bank can print Canadian dollars, but it cannot print other currencies.

Market traders become wary in the situation depicted in Figure 15.9, in which foreign exchange is traded at an artificially low price (or, equivalently, the domestic currency is overvalued). They know that the central bank cannot maintain this policy indefinitely, since, by reading the central bank's published balance sheet each month, they can see how rapidly the Bank's holdings of foreign exchange are running out. They can easily calculate when that supply is likely to be exhausted, and they know that when it is, the Bank can no longer intervene in the market and will therefore have to let the domestic currency fall in value (depreciate). Speculators then scramble to ensure that their wealth is not denominated in Canadian dollars, for those dollars are about to drop in value. Thus, speculators attack an overvalued currency.

Speculators know that, when the Bank of Canada's foreign exchange reserves run out, the U.S. dollar is going to rise in value. This is just another way of saying that the Canadian dollar will depreciate. Once they expect this change, they sell off their Canadian-based assets and use the funds to buy U.S.-based assets. They want to avoid the capital loss that will be involved for those holding Canadian bonds, and they want to benefit from the capital gain that will be enjoyed by holders of American bonds. So all speculators move in this direction, demanding even more U.S. dollars so that they can purchase American bonds.

So the demand for U.S. dollars shifts to the right, as shown in Figure 15.10. For the same reasons, the supply of U.S. dollars shifts to the left. No one wants to sell the currency that is about to appreciate. So the magnitude of the excess demand for U.S. dollars gets much larger. If the Bank of Canada was already running short of foreign exchange reserves before this speculation effect set in, then it is sure to run out once this effect has taken place. This analysis exposes a fundamental problem with a fixed exchange rate policy. It involves a large capital gain opportunity for speculators. By simply observing central bank behaviour, speculators know which way the exchange rate will move if it moves, and they know that the moment they act to take advantage of this movement, they magnify the size of the market imbalance so much that they may force the very change in the exchange rate that they were expecting. Thus, the speculators' own actions can guarantee the outcome from which they can profit.

Two central bank reactions to a speculative attack of this sort are common. Sometimes central banks push domestic interest rates up (temporarily). By making domestically issued bonds more appealing to savers in this way, they try to reverse the shifts in the supply and demand curves for U.S. dollars shown in Figure 15.10. But this approach can cause a recession. A more thoroughgoing solution to speculation is to stop fixing the exchange rate al-

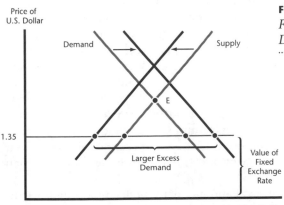

Price of
U.S. Dollar

Demand

Supply

E

1.35

Larger Excess
Demand

Value of
Fixed
Exchange
Rate

Quantity of U.S. Dollars

FIGURE 15.10
Fixed Exchange Rates:
Destabilizing Speculation

together. Thus, as a result of the speculative opportunities that a system of fixed exchange rates creates, many economists favour a flexible exchange rate policy. We will discuss other advantages and disadvantages of a flexible exchange rate in Chapters 17 and 18. Our task at this stage has been simply to understand how the Bank of Canada fixes the exchange rate, not why it sometimes does so.

SUMMARY

We can now summarize how monetary policy works in both large and small economies. In an economy such as that of the United States, which is big enough that its financial markets are a significant part of the world financial system, monetary policy works through changes in interest rates. A decrease in the money supply raises the interest rate and thus lowers the investment component of aggregate demand.

But a smaller economy such as Canada's can affect domestic interest rates only temporarily. In full equilibrium, we must accept interest rates as determined in world financial markets. Monetary policy works through changes in the exchange rate. A decrease in the domestic money supply pushes our interest rates up temporarily. Funds flow into the country as savers in the rest of the world acquire the currency that they need to buy our high-yield bonds. The result is that the international value of the Canadian dollar rises. This rise squeezes the profits of Canadian exporters, and it makes imports cheaper for Canadians. Thus, contractionary monetary policy works by reducing the net export component of aggregate demand.

So a reduction in the quantity of money has a contractionary effect in either case. But to understand the process fully, we needed to study both the domestic money market (to determine the interest rate effects even if they are only temporary) and the foreign exchange market (to determine the exchange rate effect).

Here is a review of the key concepts covered in this chapter. By combining **supply and demand for money**, we have realized how **interest rates** are determined. We have distinguished two effects of changes in money growth on market interest rates: the **liquidity effect** operates in the short run, while the **inflationary expectations effect** operates in the long run. By deriving both the supply and the demand curves for **foreign exchange**, we have learned that a **flexible exchange rate** exists if free market forces prevail. The alternative is that the Bank of Canada can **fix the exchange rate**, but this policy leads to **speculative attacks** if the domestic currency is overvalued. Finally, we have understood that monetary policy works primarily by affecting interest rates in a large economy such as that of the United States and primarily by affecting the exchange rate in a small economy such as Canada's.

We can now discuss both fiscal and monetary policy in a truly integrated fashion. In the next two chapters, we will pull together our analysis of money markets and our analysis of the market for goods and services so that we can fully examine the effectiveness of stabilization policy.

SUGGESTIONS FOR FURTHER READING

N. Cameron, *Money, Financial Markets, and Economic Activity*, 2nd ed. (Don Mills, ON: Addison Wesley, 1992), Chapters 2–6 — much detail on financial markets.

D. Laidler and W. Robson, *The Great Canadian Disinflation: The Economics and Politics of Monetary Policy in Canada: 1988–1993* (Toronto: C.D. Howe Institute, 1994) — an analysis of the Bank of Canada's determined drive to eliminate inflation.

D. Laidler and W. Robson, *Two Nations, One Money* (Toronto: C.D. Howe Institute, 1991) — how Canada's monetary system would function following a Quebec secession.

WEB ACTIVITIES

www.bank-banque-canada.ca
The semi-annual *Monetary Policy Report* gives the Bank of Canada's explanations of recent changes in interest rates and exchange rates.

www.cabe.ca
Click on "Links" to get many useful Web sites concerning economic issues, including those for the economic analysis divisions of Canada's private banks.

CHAPTER SIXTEEN
Stabilization Policy

LEARNING OBJECTIVES

After reading this chapter, you should understand

- how money market and goods market analyses can be combined for an integrated analysis of monetary and fiscal policy;

- why monetary policy was weak and fiscal policy was powerful back in the 1930s and why this ranking of the effi-

cacy of each policy changed in later decades; and

- why government policy faces a temporary — not permanent — trade-off between unemployment and inflation and why recognition of this fact has led our government to favour a passive approach to stabilization policy — one that emphasizes automatic stabilizers.

INTRODUCTION

Monetary and fiscal policy are the two tools that can be used to help stabilize the economy. In earlier chapters, we analyzed monetary policy by studying a supply and demand graph depicting the nation's money market, and we analyzed fiscal policy by studying a supply and demand graph depicting the nation's market for goods and services. In this chapter, we pull together these two partial analyses. The result will be a much clearer understanding of what we can reasonably expect from government policy.

MONETARY POLICY IN A LARGE ECONOMY

We start by reviewing the chain reaction that summarizes how monetary policy works in a country large enough to have a lasting effect on its own interest rates (the left side of the flowchart in Table 14.1 on page 168). An increase in the money supply reduces the interest rate; lower borrowing costs raise investment spending; higher total spending raises real GDP (at least temporarily) and the price level. This summary (and flowchart) seems to suggest that cause and effect run in one direction — from the money market to the goods market. But a careful review of our supply and demand graphs indicates that this analysis is incomplete, since some of the causal mechanisms run in the reverse direction.

Figure 16.1 summarizes equilibrium in both the money and goods markets. The money market graph has been used to show the first part of the monetary policy story, while the goods market graph has been used to show the second half. Recall the major things that can cause a shift in each curve. The level of bank reserves is the key shift influence for the money supply

FIGURE 16.1

An Integration of Goods and Financial Markets

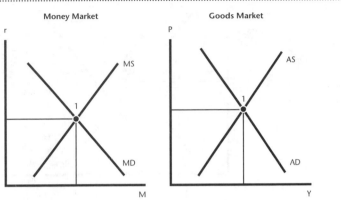

curve. The overall level of transactions (nominal GDP) is the shift influence for the money demand curve. Anything that can affect total expenditures (e.g., government spending, taxes, investment, and net exports) is a shift influence for the aggregate demand curve for goods. And remember that, since investment depends on interest rates, and since net exports depend on the exchange rate, these financial variables are indirect shift influences on the aggregate demand curve. Finally, the position of the short-run aggregate supply curve depends on input prices such as the level of wages.

We can now appreciate that the outcome in each market affects what happens in the other. The interest rate determined in the money market affects the position of the aggregate demand curve for goods, and the values for price and output determined in the goods market define nominal GDP and thus govern the position of the money demand curve. So the money and goods markets must be considered simultaneously. In this chapter, we accomplish this task for the case of a large economy that can have a lasting effect on its own rate of interest. A similar analysis for a small economy is provided in Chapter 17.

Let us assume that the economy starts out at the points numbered 1 in both markets in Figure 16.1. Now consider a monetary policy intended to expand economic activity. The increase in bank reserves shifts the money supply curve to the right, and the short-run equilibrium in the money market shifts to point 2, as shown in Figure 16.2. The important result is the lower interest rate. Since investment spending is increased by lower interest rates, the aggregate demand curve shifts to the right, and the outcome in the goods market shifts to point 2 in Figure 16.3. The important results are a higher level of real economic activity and higher prices.

This cannot be the end of the story. The economy now has higher prices and higher real output, so nominal GDP, which is the price level times real

FIGURE 16.2
Expansionary Monetary Policy: Financial Market Effects
··

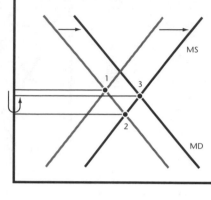

FIGURE 16.3
Expansionary Monetary Policy: Goods Market Effects
·····································

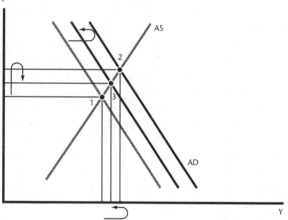

output, must be higher, and nominal GDP is the shift influence for the money demand curve. So there must be further developments back in the money market. The higher level of transactions means an increased need for the means of payment, and that is shown as a shift to the right of the money demand curve. So the final outcome in the money market is point 3, not point 2 (refer back to Figure 16.2). By comparing the heights of these two points in Figure 16.2, we see that we were overestimating the fall in interest rates in our earlier analysis, in which discussion ended at point 2. But this secondary move from point 2 to point 3 means that our description of what happens in the goods market has been exaggerated as well. If we overestimated the fall in interest rates, then we must have also overestimated the rise in investment spending. Thus, to be thorough and consistent, we must show the shift in the aggregate demand curve to be less dramatic. In Figure 16.3, we see the aggregate demand curve shifted back somewhat, with the final equilibrium being point 3. This feedback between the markets continues in ever decreasing amounts, but (since that further discussion is simply a repetition of what I have now clarified) we take the final equilibrium as point 3 in both markets.

What we have now seen is that, while the more simplified explanation of how monetary policy works (which we discussed in earlier chapters) predicts the direction of the effects correctly, it overestimates the degree to which monetary policy can be used to regulate the economy. And we know from before that even point 3 in Figure 16.3 exaggerates the effect on real output if it corresponds to a level of production that exceeds the economy's long-run potential. In that case, an inflationary gap has been created, so that rising wages cause the aggregate supply curve to shift up, and the level of output is pulled back down.

A MORE COMPLETE ANALYSIS OF FISCAL POLICY

We have just seen that the nation's money and goods markets interact in important ways and that, if we do not appreciate this fact, we will exaggerate expectations concerning the power of monetary policy to regulate business cycles. We now see that a similar warning applies to fiscal policy.

As before, we consider the economy starting at points numbered 1 in both the money and the goods markets (as shown in Figure 16.1). Suppose the government increases its spending. Government expenditure is a shift influence for the aggregate demand curve in the goods market, so the outcome in that market moves from point 1 to point 2 in Figure 16.4. The important short-run results are shown along the axes: an increase in real output (so some jobs are created) and an increase in the price level. So there is a short-run trade-off between job creation and inflation.

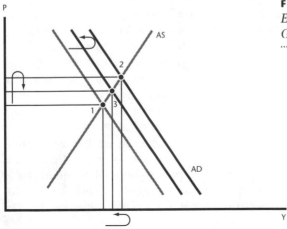

P

FIGURE 16.4
Expansionary Fiscal Policy:
Goods Market Effects

AS

2

1 3

AD

Y

FIGURE 16.5

Expansionary Fiscal Policy: Financial Market Effects

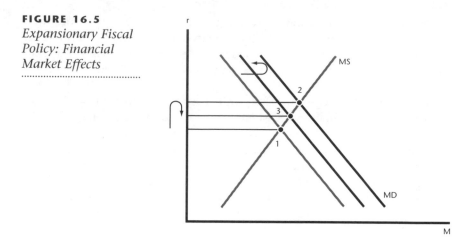

But this is not the end of the story. With higher prices and real output, nominal GDP must be higher, and this is a shift influence for the money demand curve. So fiscal policy causes indirect effects in the money market — effects that we did not consider adequately in earlier chapters since we concentrated on simpler analyses. More transactions mean an increased desire to hold money, so the money demand curve shifts to the right. The outcome in the money market moves from point 1 to point 2, as shown in Figure 16.5. The important result is a higher rate of interest. Remember, with higher interest rates, investment spending is lower, so the aggregate demand curve (in Figure 16.4) must shift back somewhat to the left.

Initially, the demand for goods shifts out to the right (to position 2) because of the higher government-spending component of total demand. But since that policy results in higher interest rates, some investment spending gets choked off, and the aggregate demand curve shifts back to the left (to position 3). For completeness, we should note that, since this subsequent shift back in aggregate demand causes a reduction in both price and real output, the money demand curve also shifts back somewhat. The final position is at an intermediate point such as 3 in both markets (Figures 16.4 and 16.5).

Once again, the lesson of this more complete story is that, even when we ignore the longer-run effects of wage changes, fiscal policy is less powerful than we previously thought. Our introductory analysis that abstracted from the financial market implications of fiscal policy got the direction of effect right but exaggerated the job-creation potential of fiscal policy.

Economists have called the effect that we have just emphasized — that higher government spending leads to some reduction in private investment spending — the **crowding-out effect**. It is often mentioned in the media as one of the major costs of what some regard as excesses in government spending. It is worth appreciating the intuition behind this crowding-out effect in more detail.

Aggregate demand is the sum of several components: consumption spending by households, investment spending by firms, government spending, and net spending by foreigners for our output. When government expenditure is increased, aggregate demand is raised directly. In Chapter 12, we placed great emphasis on the fact that the increase in government spending has an indirect effect as well. Higher demand leads to an increase in national income, and consumption spending by households depends positively on how much they earn. Thus, there is an induced increase in consumption that follows an increase in government spending. We called this a multiplier effect since the overall increase in output is the sum of the two component increases. (In the equation below, the overall increase in aggregate demand is estimated to be the sum of both the upward-pointing arrows.)

$$\text{Aggregate Demand} = C + I + G + X - IM$$

But now we know that one implication of higher spending is an increased need for money. With money more scarce (relative to demand), interest rates rise, and investment spending declines. So the downward-pointing arrow must be inserted above the equation as well to show the crowding out of the investment component of aggregate demand. It is even possible that this reduction in total spending can be as large as the total of the other two. If so, then the attempt to add to aggregate demand by increasing government expenditure and creating jobs in the government sector just replaces preexisting demand by destroying jobs in the investment goods sector. When the government borrows more to finance its higher spending, it "uses up" more of households' savings. With less funds remaining to finance firms' investment spending, they are "crowded out" of the bond market.

It is important to determine whether this crowding-out effect on investment spending by firms is large or small. It turns out that the magnitude of this effect depends on the slope of the money demand curve.

A MORE COMPLETE ANALYSIS OF MONEY DEMAND

To keep things simple so far, we have drawn the money demand curve as a straight line. But it is curved as shown in Figure 16.6, and it is easy to appreciate what may lie behind this empirical finding. Given any society's institutional arrangements, there is a minimum amount of money that must be held to carry on any level of spending. Once the rate of interest on bonds has risen to the point that people have to cut back on money holdings all the way to the minimum, further increases in the interest rate cannot cause further decreases in the quantity of money demanded. So the money demand curve becomes vertical at that point (at the upper end of the curve in Figure 16.6).

Similarly, at the low interest rate end, people become nearly indifferent about holding money or bonds. At some point, with very low yields, buying

FIGURE 16.6

The Money Demand Curve Revisited
....

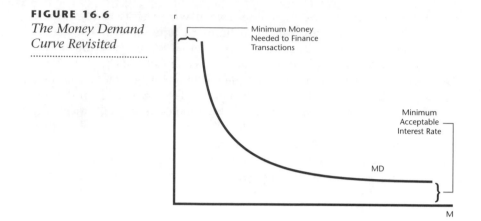

bonds is not worth the brokerage costs. So there is a minimum acceptable rate of interest on bonds. Once the rate of interest has fallen low enough to make people want to hold all their wealth in the form of money, further reductions in the rate of interest are not required to increase the demand for money. So the money demand curve flattens out at that minimum acceptable rate of interest.

Now we explore the implications of the resulting curve in the money demand function. This is best done by comparing the North American experience during the 1970s and 1980s with the years of the Great Depression (the 1930s). In the 1970s and 1980s, we had high interest rates, so the money supply and money demand curves must have intersected well above the flat region of the money demand curve. When the money supply curve was shifted to the right during these years, interest rates fell noticeably. So monetary policy worked in the 1970s and 1980s because it had a significant effect on interest rates.

But back in the 1930s, we had the lowest rates of interest that we have ever observed. The relevant graph for the 1930s shows the supply curve for money intersecting the demand curve for money down in the flat region, as in Figure 16.7. In this instance, when the money supply curve is shifted to the right, such a policy simply moves the intersection along the flat region, so the interest rate does not fall. As a result, monetary policy has no expansionary effect on the economy. If policy cannot cause interest rates to drop, then it cannot stimulate investment spending.

Intuitively, we can understand the Depression as follows. An increase in the money supply gives people more wealth, and all that new wealth is in the form of money. Normally, people want to diversify their holdings, so they try to turn some of that new wealth into bonds. But people do not want to invest in the bonds of firms about to go bankrupt, and people did think that many firms were in that position in the Great Depression. Thus, people were

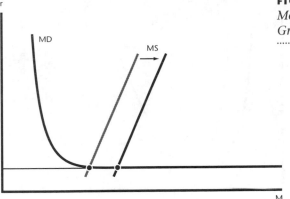

FIGURE 16.7
Monetary Policy in the Great Depression

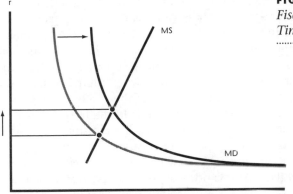

FIGURE 16.8
Fiscal Policy in Recent Times

unwilling to buy bonds and to diversify during the 1930s. They preferred to keep all their wealth in the form of money, and they hoarded any new money given to them. Clearly, when people just hoard new currency, monetary policy accomplishes little. So increases in the money supply have been much more important in recent times than they were back in the 1930s.

What about fiscal policy? We can now see why the crowding-out effect is much more important today (as it was in the 1970s and 1980s) than it was during the Great Depression. As noted already, in recent decades money supply and demand curves have intersected in the higher interest rate region, as shown in Figure 16.8. Recall that when there is a fiscal expansion the indirect effect is that people have increased needs for money, so the money demand curve shifts to the right. When interest rates rise by a significant amount (as we see in Figure 16.8), there is a noticeable crowding-out effect.

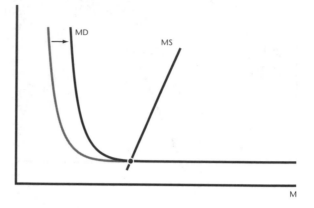

FIGURE 16.9
*Fiscal Policy in the
Great Depression*
·····································

Things were different back in the 1930s, as is shown in Figure 16.9. The same stimulation of demand by higher government spending caused the same shift to the right in the negatively sloped part of the money demand curve. But because the money demand and money supply curves intersected in the flat region, the shift to the right did not change the interest rate. With borrowing costs not rising, the crowding-out effect was minimal. Thus, fiscal policy was at its most powerful in the Depression of the 1930s.

Many economists think that Figure 16.9 applied to the Japanese economy in the late 1990s. The Japanese economy was in recession for several years, and interest rates were below 1 percent. In earlier years, the Japanese prided themselves on not running fiscal deficits, so there was no political support for expansionary fiscal policy; however, because expansionary monetary policy was of no use in that setting, the Japanese were in an awkward position. One policy instrument — monetary policy — could not work (for economic reasons), and the other — fiscal policy — could not be used (for political reasons). No wonder that the Japanese recession was prolonged.

PITFALLS IN POLICY-MAKING

As we have just seen, the relative power of fiscal and monetary policy to affect aggregate demand appears to have changed significantly over the decades, and we now understand why. Unfortunately, some of this understanding comes with the benefit of hindsight. Sometimes government officials have applied the lessons learned in one decade to the policy problems of the following decades without realizing that doing so can be inappropriate. For example, printing a lot of money during the Great Depression would not have stimulated demand to a great extent. Some policy-makers reacted to this lesson by simply assuming that printing money would not have much effect in later periods either. This assumption was wrong. But before this fact was widely understood, all Western central banks printed a lot of money during the late 1960s and 1970s, and they created a worldwide inflation.

A similar lag in appreciating the limitations of fiscal policy has also been evident. During much of the 1930s, 1940s, and 1950s, interest rates were low, and the crowding-out effect was small. As a result, fiscal policy could be counted on to provide a fairly significant stimulus for job creation in the short run. However, policy-makers continued to try to use fiscal policy for job creation in later decades without appreciating that the crowding-out effect was much more important then. With interest rates rising appreciably in these later decades, the national debt was driven up to a great extent, and the policy did not create the number of jobs that had been (unreasonably) expected.

In summary, both fiscal policy and monetary policy were too expansionary as the lessons of the 1930s were applied in later decades when the situation had changed. Rising inflation was the result of the inappropriate monetary policy, and rising debt was the result of the inappropriate fiscal policy. Much hardship was incurred during the 1980s as monetary policy was thrown in reverse to pull the inflation rate back down. Similarly, much hardship was incurred in the 1990s as fiscal policy was reversed to slow down the growth of the national debt.

So stabilization policy has not always worked out as well as government officials have hoped. Even when there is no mismatch between the underlying theory and the characteristics of that decade, there are other problems, such as **time lags**.

There are several lags in the process of implementing government policies. One is the *recognition lag*. It takes government officials quite a while to find out whether the economy needs to be stimulated or pulled back. It takes several months just to estimate what GDP was in the previous quarter. Then there is an *implementation lag* because officials cannot raise government spending immediately. They have to decide which category of spending is most needed, and they must allow private firms time to submit tenders (in attempts to win the government contracts). On average, it has taken between eighteen months and two years after the need for an expansionary fiscal policy was first recognized before the higher spending has been implemented. So, by the time that the stimulative effect on aggregate demand takes hold, the recession could already be over, and the policy might actually worsen inflation in the boom half of the cycle rather than ease the previous recession.

Implementation lags are shorter with monetary policy. Deposit switching and open market operations can be decided quickly. But firms sometimes wait quite a while after a decrease in the interest rate before increasing their investment spending. Firms want to be sure that the recession is almost over before expanding their operations. So there are discouraging long lags involved with both monetary and fiscal policies.

The general problem of time lags is summarized in Figures 16.10 and 16.11. In each case, the solid line shows the time path for real GDP. Its wavy nature illustrates the existence of business cycles. If government policy can dampen demand in boom periods and fill in troughs during recessions, then it can change

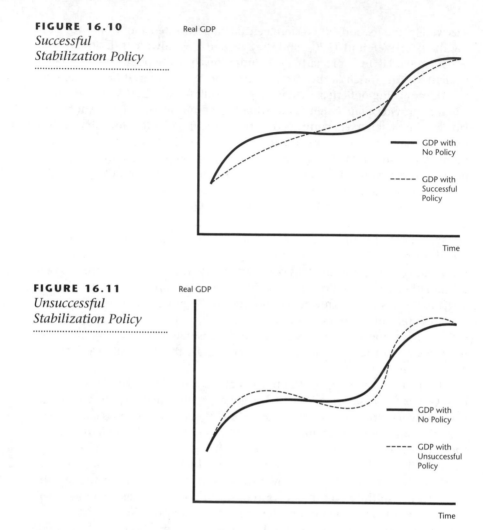

FIGURE 16.10
*Successful
Stabilization Policy*

Real GDP

GDP with
No Policy

----- GDP with
Successful
Policy

Time

FIGURE 16.11
*Unsuccessful
Stabilization Policy*

Real GDP

GDP with
No Policy

----- GDP with
Unsuccessful
Policy

Time

the time path of real GDP from the solid line to the dashed line in Figure 16.10. But, unfortunately, the impact of policy can be so delayed that the government has sometimes pushed the economy up in the booms and down in the recessions. In the latter case, the government has transformed the real GDP graph from the solid line to the dashed line in Figure 16.11. Well-intentioned policy can, and sometimes does, worsen the business cycle.

THE SHORT-RUN TRADE-OFF BETWEEN INFLATION AND UNEMPLOYMENT

Time lags do not represent the only impediment to a successful stabilization policy. Even if government officials could time their interventions perfectly, they must be careful not to overdo things in terms of the size of the government initiative. Too much stimulation in an attempt to create jobs simply drives up the rate of inflation.

To appreciate this trade-off, which is equally relevant for large economies and small open ones such as Canada's, we must appreciate two things: that there are different types of unemployment, and that the economy has a self-correcting mechanism.

When actual output is at the potential level of GDP, unemployment is equal to what we call the *frictional* (or sometimes *structural*) amount. Even when overall demand and potential output are in balance, some industries are contracting (perhaps in the Maritimes) while others are expanding (say, in Alberta), and there is excess demand for labour in the latter area. There is incomplete information, and it takes time for people to retrain and relocate. Thus, there is always some unemployment that has nothing to do with the overall state of demand in the economy. The amount of unemployment that occurs even when overall demand and supply are balanced is called **frictional unemployment**. Whenever output exceeds its long-run potential level, the unemployment rate is lower than the frictional amount, and whenever we have a recession, unemployment exceeds the frictional level. This additional unemployment is called **cyclical unemployment**.

It is useful at this stage to review the self-correction mechanism. In Figure 16.12, aggregate demand and supply intersect initially at point A, and unemployment is equal to the frictional amount. When the demand curve moves to the right (say, due to a boom in the United States that stimulates our export sales), the economy moves from point A to point B. With higher

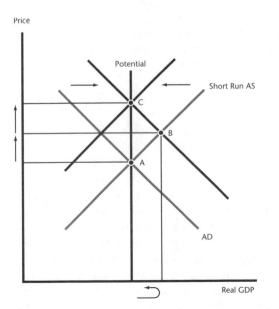

Price

Real GDP

FIGURE 16.12
*Demand Management
and the Self-Correction
Mechanism*

production, unemployment goes down, but prices rise to some extent as well. We have learned that point B is not a sustainable outcome because the economy is producing more than it can on an ongoing basis. Machines are not being maintained, and men and women are working overtime and thus are not getting enough rest time. Because of this high-level input use, once the contracts for the use of inputs have expired, their prices are bid up. We have focused on labour because wages represent roughly three-quarters of the average firm's costs. Scarce labour means higher wages, and with higher unit costs, the short-run aggregate supply curve shifts up over time. So the economy gradually drifts from point B to point C, and the inflationary gap is automatically cured by the self-correction mechanism. This mechanism is the automatic adjustment of input prices (e.g., wages).

Figure 16.12 indicates that we get some temporary inflation in exchange for a temporary reduction in unemployment. We now recast this trade-off in terms of a different picture. To do so, we focus on the very things that connect the short run and the long run — the self-correcting mechanism of wage adjustment and the short-run aggregate-supply relationship. We now summarize each mechanism in the form of a simple equation, and we use these equations to generate a trade-off relationship between unemployment and inflation.

Before considering the equations, we must be clear on notation. We use W to stand for the wage rate, so $\Delta W/W$ stands for the percentage change in wages. Similarly, we use P to stand for the price level, so $\Delta P/P$ stands for the inflation rate. Furthermore, we add a superscript e to denote the rate of price inflation that people are *expecting* at any point in time. The mark-up of selling prices over wage costs depends on how productive labour is; we use A to stand for the average productivity of labour (with $\Delta A/A$ then denoting the percentage change in productivity). Finally, we let u and u^f stand for the overall unemployment rate and the frictional level of unemployment.

The first equation is the wage change relationship:

$$\Delta W/W = (\Delta P/P)^e + (\Delta A/A) - b(u - u^f).$$

This equation says that wages change for three reasons, and they are summarized by the three terms on the right-hand side. The first is the expected change in the cost of living. Workers care about the real purchasing power of their wages, and this is why some contracts have cost-of-living clauses. We say that such wages are indexed to the rate of inflation, so that workers receive one-for-one compensation for increases in the cost of living. That is why there is a coefficient of one in front of this first term.

Now consider the other important determinants of wage changes. First, workers want to receive a raise whenever they become more productive. The tendency for workers' wages to increase one-for-one with increases in labour productivity is captured by the coefficient of one in front of the productivity growth term. Finally, wage changes depend on the state of the market. If the labour market is overheated and there is excess demand for labour, then wage increases exceed the amount needed to cover expected inflation and productivity increases. The third term in the equation captures this fact. When the labour market is in excess demand, the overall unemployment rate is smaller than the frictional unemployment rate, so this expression in parentheses is negative. With b standing for a positive number, this third term is positive, implying that wage changes exceed the sum of the first two terms. Similarly, if there is a recession, then labour's bargaining power is weak, u exceeds u^f, the third term (including the –b part) is negative, and this implies that wage changes fall short of the cost-of-living and productivity growth targets. By letting parameter b represent either a big or a small number, we can allow the market forces term to be either a big adjustment or a small adjustment in wage changes.

This three-part explanation of wage changes fits the facts well for Canada. Since this relationship indicates how wages are adjusted whenever actual GDP does not coincide with potential GDP, it is a formal representation of the self-correction mechanism.

We now consider the aggregate supply curve, written in equation form as well:

$$P = cW/A.$$

This equation is the simplest one that is both consistent with the supply and demand diagrams that we have been drawing and consistent with the workings of the Canadian economy. It simply says that firms mark up prices over unit costs, where unit costs are the ratio of the wages that firms have to pay for the labour (W) divided by the average productivity of that labour (A); c is the mark-up factor. Recall that we have assumed diminishing returns as an economic fact of life in the short run. Thus, as more labour is hired (having to share the fixed quantity of capital more widely across the increased workforce), the productivity of each worker decreases. This means that A falls as firms produce more items, and to maintain profit margins, firms raise prices. This is why the aggregate supply curve slopes up as we move to the right. Higher employment and output push down the denominator on the right-hand side of this equation. For given wages, then, this mark-up equation implies higher prices (P). So the upward slope of the short-run supply curve is built into this equation through the variation in the average productivity term. Wages enter the picture as a shift variable: the higher the wage rate, the bigger the right-hand side of the mark-up equation, so the higher prices become. Thus, the supply curve moves up and to the left as wages rise. This aggregate supply relationship can be rewritten in percentage change form:

$$\Delta P/P = (\Delta W/W) - (\Delta A/A),$$

which says that the inflation rate for prices equals the excess of the percentage change in wages over the rate of change of productivity.

To get one summary relationship between the rate of price inflation and the unemployment rate, we substitute the wage change equation into that for price changes. The result is

$$\Delta P/P = -b(u - u^f) + (\Delta P/P)^e,$$

which says that actual inflation is negatively related to the unemployment rate and positively related (responding one for one in fact) to people's underlying expectations of inflation.

We now graph this summary relationship between inflation and unemployment. There are four variables involved: actual inflation, expected inflation, overall unemployment, and frictional unemployment. Since the graph is in two dimensions, we focus on the two ultimate goals of stabilization policy in the short run: actual inflation and overall unemployment. We graph these two measures on the axes of our summary picture and then account for changes in either of the other two influences (frictional unemployment and inflationary expectations) by moving the entire position of the partial relationship between actual inflation and overall unemployment.

The slope of the partial relationship is $-b$, so it is a negatively sloped line, as shown in Figure 16.13. The intercept of this short-run trade-off line shifts one for one with changes in expected inflation. This fact is indicated in Figure 16.13 by two members of the entire family of short-run trade-off lines: one for 0 percent underlying inflationary expectations, and another for 10 percent underlying inflationary expectations. Given the unity coefficient in front of expected inflation in the equation version of this trade-off relationship, every point on the 10 percent expectations trade-off line is precisely 10

FIGURE 16.13
The Trade-off Relationship

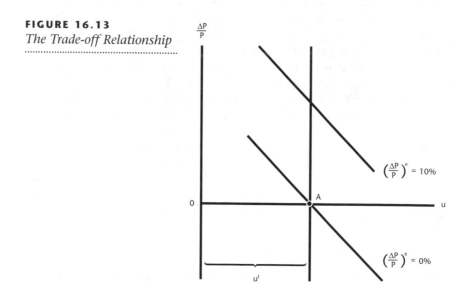

percentage points above the corresponding point on the 0 percent expectations trade-off line.

To appreciate how this analysis can provide an understanding of Canadian history, assume that overall unemployment is equal to the frictional amount and that inflation is zero. In other words, suppose the economy is at point A in Figure 16.13, as Canada's economy was in the early 1960s. At that time, our government decided to use expansionary aggregate demand policy to drive down the unemployment rate. This policy caused the economy to move from point A to point B, as shown in Figure 16.14. As the diagram predicts, unemployment fell, but inflation rose. The estimates of Canada's trade-off relationship (in the 1960s) indicated that Canadians did not have to pay much in terms of higher inflation to get lower unemployment. In other words, coefficient b was estimated to be fairly small so that point B in Figure 16.14 was estimated to be not too far above the horizontal axis in this graph. The trouble with focusing on point B, however, is that it is *not* sustainable in the long run. At point B, actual inflation is positive, but inflationary expectations are still zero. (If it were not so, then the economy would be on a different short-run trade-off line.) Surely it is not plausible to expect people to go on experiencing positive inflation while continuing to expect *no* inflation. Indeed, this did not happen. After inflation had remained at point B for a while, people started to build higher inflationary expectations into their wage settlements, and Canada's trade-off line drifted up and out to the right. To maintain the lower unemployment rate, the government had to expand spending even more. As long as actual inflation exceeded expected inflation (as at point B), unemployment could be kept lower than its frictional level. But with rising inflationary expectations, the point showing the economy's

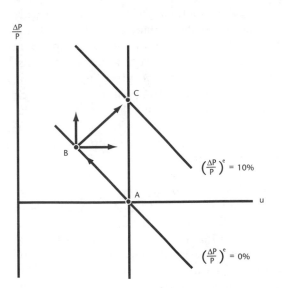

FIGURE 16.14
The Temporary Nature of the Trade-Off

outcome was being pushed above point B. And, as the government realized that we were experiencing more inflation than anticipated, officials began to contract aggregate demand again. This contraction caused a move to the right from point B in the graph.

The scaling up of inflationary expectations is represented by the upward arrow in Figure 16.14, and the backing off of policy is represented by the rightward arrow. The overall result was a move toward both rising inflation *and* rising unemployment. Canadians were not trading off one evil for the other; they were getting more of both evils. By about 1980, we had reached point C, so it took about fifteen years, from the mid-1960s to about 1980, to get back to roughly the same unemployment rate that we had in the early 1960s, but this time with an ongoing rate of inflation of about 10 percent. The policy error was that the government thought there was a long-term trade-off between unemployment and inflation. In fact, by ignoring the inevitable adjustment in inflationary expectations, the government confused the short-run trade-off (which does exist) with a long-run trade-off (which does not).

Point C is sustainable because both actual and expected inflation are the same there. People do not find their forecasts to be wrong, so they do not change their behaviour from one period to the next. As a result, we can stay at point C indefinitely. But it is less desirable than the original situation — point A. As of 1980, then, the challenge facing the government was how to get from point C back to point A with the least cost. Basically, the government had to embark on the same policy, only this time in reverse. The strategy was to contract the economy by decreasing aggregate demand, thereby pushing the economy down the high-inflationary expectations trade-off line from point C to point D in Figure 16.15. Canadians had to remain at point D with high unemployment until their inflationary expectations gradually diminished. Eventually, with lower anticipated inflation, the trade-off line shifted down, and the government could then reintroduce some spending and push the economy back to point A. But since it took us about fifteen years to travel through the A-to-B-to-C cycle, it is not surprising that it took us another fifteen years to go through the C-to-D-to-A part of the cycle. Even in the mid-1990s, we still had high unemployment. This was the painful legacy of the earlier policy error.

As already noted, this episode taught us that the trade-off between unemployment and inflation is not permanent. The best way to appreciate the true nature of the trade-off is to phrase it in terms of the policy dilemma that faced the government in the early 1980s. To bring down inflation, do we want a bit of extra unemployment for a long period, or do we want a lot of extra unemployment for a short period? Under the first option, we choose a point D a little over to the right. With inflation coming down just a little each period, it takes a long time for people's inflationary expectations to be reduced. Under the second option, we pick a point D far over to the right by recessing the economy dramatically. In this situation, people are so fright-

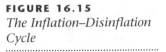

FIGURE 16.15
The Inflation–Disinflation Cycle
....

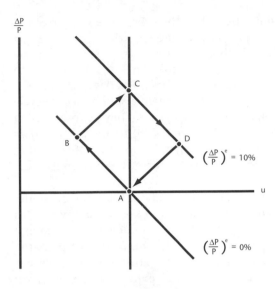

ened about losing their jobs that they do not care about cost-of-living bonuses. Inflationary expectations dissipate quickly.

Our government rejected this second — "cold turkey" — approach. What the government would have liked to see was a bit of extra unemployment for a short time only (during this C-to-D-to-A sequence). This is why our central banker adopted such a harsh tone in all speeches at the time, promising sustained contractionary policy. The hope was that people would adopt low expectations even before actual inflation diminished appreciably and that Canadians could thereby avoid prolonged high unemployment.

The finance minister has also tried to speed up the self-correction mechanism by indicating that never again will the government commit fiscal policy to target a low unemployment rate. If workers and firms think that the government might lose this new resolve, then they would wait for a stimulus to demand to raise employment and thus avoid the need for wage and price concessions. This would weaken the self-correction mechanism, and this is why the government has adopted such a dogmatic position. In a sense, there is a parallel to the dilemma that parents face when their child misbehaves and pleads to have the threatened punishment waived. In the short run, it is appealing to drop the punishment since a major family upset is thereby avoided. But this policy sends a signal that violations of the parents' rules will be tolerated in the future. In the long run, the appealing policy is never to negotiate the consequences after the fact. Obviously, firms and wage earners are not badly behaved children. The analogy simply clarifies that aggregate demand policy faces a similar trade-off — what is appealing in the short run is not appealing in the long run. Our government has now switched its emphasis to the long run. This stance makes the government appear to be insensitive, like parents who embrace the "tough love" approach, but at least the new stance should strengthen the economy's self-correction mechanism by making wages and prices adjust more quickly.

In retrospect, we have incurred a high cost (periods of high unemployment in the 1980s and 1990s and inflation in the 1960s and 1970s) just to have unemployment temporarily lower in the earlier decades. Many economists have concluded that the costs of going through a several-decade cycle like this are not worth the temporary benefits. Thus, they advocate using structural policies (e.g., those discussed in Chapter 18) to attack *equilibrium* unemployment and leaving *cyclical* unemployment to the self-correction mechanism. They advocate the following **rules for governing macroeconomic policy**.

Monetary policy should focus on limiting inflation. Fiscal policy should be used to help stabilize the business cycle but only in a responsible way. This means balancing the budget over the time involved for each full cycle so that the national debt does not rise over time. This also means relying primarily on **automatic stabilizers**. Our income tax and employment insurance systems operate in the same way as would a fiscal policy-maker who never makes mistakes. For example, during a business downturn, people earn less, so they automatically pay less tax and receive more unemployment insurance benefits. These institutional arrangements involve fiscal policy turning expansionary without any recognition or implementation lags, and that is why they are called automatic stabilizers.

In recent years, the Canadian government appears to have accepted this more passive approach to stabilization policy. The government has published its inflation target — that the annual inflation rate be between 1 and 3 percent — and it has instructed the Bank of Canada to conduct monetary policy so that this target is achieved. The government has also set firm targets for its budget balance. With fiscal policy committed to achieving a deficit or surplus target and monetary policy focused on the inflation target, there is no other policy instrument left for addressing high cyclical unemployment. For that problem, then, we must rely on the economy's self-correction mechanism.

SUMMARY

Here is a review of the key concepts covered in this chapter. We learned that **stabilization policies are sometimes weak** and **sometimes powerful**. For example, an expansionary monetary policy has no effect on aggregate demand when money is hoarded (as it was when interest rates were low and bonds were risky during the 1930s). Another example is provided by the **crowding-out effect**: higher government spending pushes up interest rates and thus decreases pre-existing investment spending. This effect is a bigger problem today than it was in the Great Depression.

Stabilization policies operate with **long lags**, so they can accentuate business cycles instead of mitigating them. Another impediment to implementing stabilization policy is that there can be trade-offs between objectives. Because of the economy's **self-correction mechanism**, there is a **short-run, but not a long-run, trade-off between inflation and unemployment**. Ultimately, employment is determined by the economy's potential, not by temporary variations in the positions of the short-run aggregate supply and demand curves. Given the long-run capacity constraint, the **benefit of higher inflation** is just a **temporary reduction in unemployment**.

These facts lead many analysts to favour a "hands off" policy in which the central bank has the limited objective of avoiding inflation and in which fiscal policy is limited to the provision of **automatic stabilizers** such as employment insurance and progressive taxes.

SUGGESTIONS FOR FURTHER READING

T.G. Buchholz, *New Ideas from Dead Economists* (New York: Penguin, 1990), Chapters 9, 10, 12, 13.

S.E. Landsburg, *The Armchair Economist: Economics and Everyday Life* (New York: Free Press, 1993), Chapters 22, 23.

WEB ACTIVITIES

www.oecd.org
The Web site of the Organisation for Economic Co-operation and Development; click on "Free Documents," then "Policy Briefs," for studies on macroeconomic issues as well as broad public sector questions such as the aging society; see also the individual country reports.

CHAPTER SEVENTEEN

Options for a Small Open Economy

LEARNING OBJECTIVES

After reading this chapter, you should understand

- why fiscal policy works better under fixed exchange rates;
- why independent monetary policy is possible only under flexible exchange rates; and

- why there is controversy concerning whether a flexible exchange rate acts as an important shock absorber for the economy.

INTRODUCTION

In the previous chapter, we discussed monetary and fiscal policy from the vantage point of a large economy — one whose financial markets are a large enough proportion of the world financial system that the country's policies can affect interest rates. We learned an important lesson for all economies: we must have modest expectations for stabilization policy because of time lags and the short-run nature of the unemployment–inflation trade-off. In addition, what we learned about stabilization policy in a large economy is needed as a stepping stone for understanding the options for a small open economy, such as Canada's, whose financial markets are highly integrated with world financial markets, especially those in the United States.

Since Canada is such a small part of the North American financial market, it is impossible for us to maintain interest rate levels different from those in the United States for long periods. Competitive pressure simply forces our effective yields to be in line with those in the United States.

When we look at data for Canadian and U.S. interest rates, there is a slight difference that analysts call the **risk premium**, and this premium does vary over time. For instance, it widened in 1992 when there was uncertainty about the constitutional referendum and whether Quebec would separate from Canada. The risk premium remained substantial during much of the 1990s, partly because of the continuing uncertainty concerning the future of Quebec, and partly because foreign lenders were concerned that Canadian government debt levels were out of control. But by the end of the decade, the government's deficit had been eliminated, and the Canadian inflation rate had been slightly less than the American inflation rate for quite a few years. These developments, and a perception that Quebec separation was less likely, made the risk "premium" a small negative amount. In this chapter, we do not analyze variations in this risk premium. Indeed, for convenience, we assume the risk premium to be zero so that we can focus on short-run stabilization issues rather than on considerations of longer-run political stability.

For the analysis in this chapter, then, the small open economy constraint is that the Canadian interest rate must equal the U.S. interest rate in full equilibrium. In the graphs, this constraint involves abbreviations: $r_{CAN} = r_{US}$. We do consider temporary gaps between Canadian and American interest rates, and Canadian government policy is one of the things that can cause these gaps to occur for a while. But we always follow through how these interest rate differentials are eventually eliminated by the flow of savings out of the low-interest rate country and into the high-interest rate country.

This flow of funds either changes the exchange rate (if our central bank policy permits that to happen) or forces our central bank to adopt whatever monetary policy is necessary to keep fixing the exchange rate. In this chapter, we explore how either development eliminates the temporary interest rate differential.

Broadly speaking, there are two tools available for affecting aggregate demand: fiscal policy and monetary policy. And there are two possible exchange rate policies that we can follow. So we consider a set of four analyses: fiscal policy undertaken in either a flexible or a fixed exchange rate environment, and monetary policy undertaken in each of those two exchange rate regimes. Our goal is to determine whether or not there is a lasting effect on aggregate demand in each case.

FISCAL POLICY WITH A FLEXIBLE EXCHANGE RATE

We start by assuming that both the economy's money market and its goods market are in equilibrium at the points numbered 1 in Figure 17.1. Recall the major influences that can cause a shift in each supply and demand curve. The level of bank reserves is the key shift influence for money supply, and the

FIGURE 17.1

Macroeconomic Equilibrium with Domestic Interest Rates Matching Foreign Yields

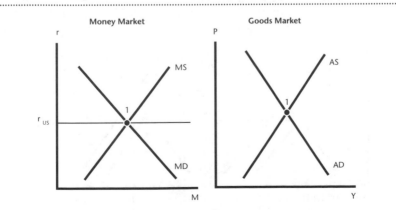

level of transactions (nominal GDP = PY) is what shifts money demand. Changes in any of the major expenditure components can shift the aggregate demand curve for goods. The exchange rate is particularly important for a country such as Canada since it affects our large export and import components of total spending. Finally, the position of the short-run aggregate supply curve depends on input prices, such as wages.

Compared with the analysis in Chapter 16, what is new in Figure 17.1 is the world interest rate line. Initial point 1 is a full equilibrium since the Canadian rate of interest (given by the height of the intersection of the money supply and money demand curves) is equal to the foreign rate of interest (given by the height of the U.S. interest rate line). With equal yields, there is no incentive for bond holders to switch their holdings from one country to the other. But keep in mind that our analysis of any government policy will not be complete unless the final equilibrium point in the money market also occurs somewhere on this U.S. interest rate line.

We now consider an increase in government spending, with the economy starting from point 1 in each of the money and goods markets. The first effect is that the demand for goods shifts to the right, and for a short interval the outcome is point 2 in the goods market in Figure 17.2. The usual results occur: higher real output and higher prices. These developments mean that nominal GDP (the product of the price level times real output) must have increased, so that people want to hold more money for transactions. We show this effect as a rightward shift of the money demand curve, so the outcome in the money market moves to point 2 as well.

Now comes the part of the story specific to a small open economy. Point 2 in the money market is above the U.S. interest rate line, so the fiscal policy has caused an interest rate differential between Canada and the United States. We must now follow through the implications of this temporary differential.

FIGURE 17.2
Fiscal Policy under Flexible Exchange Rates

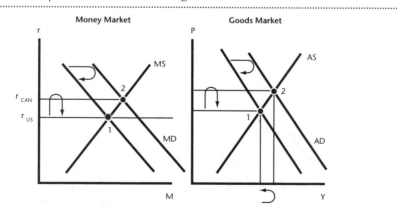

With our rate of interest higher, savings from the rest of the world flow into Canada, and, since we are considering a flexible exchange rate, this means that our currency will be bid up in value. When the Canadian dollar becomes more expensive for foreigners to buy, it makes our exports more expensive. So our exports begin to fall. For the same reason, we find imports cheaper, so we do more importing. The combination of lower exports and higher imports pulls the aggregate demand curve in the goods market back to the left. Point 2 slides back down toward point 1.

As the aggregate demand curve drifts back toward its starting position, both price level and real output decline, so nominal GDP slips back down. In the money market, as nominal GDP declines, people's desire to hold money declines as well, so the money demand curve moves back toward its starting position. But as long as that move back is only partial, the Canadian interest rate remains above the yield available in the United States, so funds continue to flow into the country. Thus, the Canadian dollar continues to appreciate, our exports continue to be crowded out in world markets, and the adjustment process has not been completed. It can end only when the demand curves shift the full distance back, so that point 2 in both markets is all the way back to, and then coincides with, the initial point 1.

So in the end, fiscal policy has no lasting effect on aggregate demand under flexible exchange rates. All that an increase in government expenditure does is push up the value of the Canadian dollar, so that instead of adding to aggregate demand it simply replaces some pre-existing private demand in the form of net export expenditures. Jobs are created in the government sector, but they are destroyed in the export and import competing sectors. This process is the open economy version of the **crowding-out effect** — it works through the exchange rate, not the interest rate.

Because of the exchange rate–induced crowding-out effect, then, fiscal policy has no lasting effect on aggregate demand when it is undertaken in a flexible exchange rate environment. This has been proved in many episodes in Canadian history, the most famous being one in 1960 when the Diefenbaker government introduced a large budgetary change in an attempt to lower unemployment. But this fiscal policy did no good because our central bank governor at the time, James Coyne, was determined to pursue a flexible exchange rate policy. There ensued a crisis: the governor of the Bank was forced to resign, and Canada moved to a fixed exchange rate policy. This crisis was perfectly predictable on the basis of our analysis, and this fact (among others) gives economists confidence concerning the applicability of this analysis. We now consider whether an attempt to expand aggregate demand with fiscal policy works any better under a fixed exchange rate environment.

FISCAL POLICY WITH A FIXED EXCHANGE RATE

Once again we start at point 1 in both markets (as in Figure 17.1), and once again the increase in government expenditures shifts the aggregate demand

FIGURE 17.3
Fiscal Policy under Fixed
Exchange Rates
....

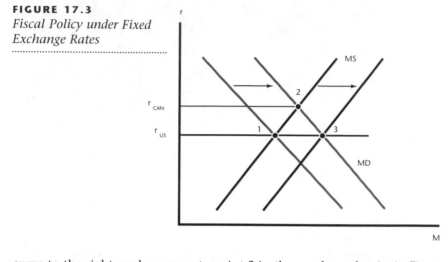

curve to the right, and we move to point 2 in the goods market (as in Figure 17.2). As before, the higher level of nominal GDP means an increased desire to hold money, so the money demand curve moves to the right (as in both Figures 17.2 and 17.3). As we have seen, point 2 is the initial, but not the final, outcome since the Canadian interest rate cannot remain above the American interest rate indefinitely.

Again, funds flow into Canada, but this time the Canadian dollar is not bid up in value because the Bank of Canada simply does not allow that to happen. To keep the exchange rate from changing, the bank buys the otherwise unwanted U.S. dollars coming into the country. (The owners of these funds want to turn them into Canadian dollars to buy the relatively high-yield Canadian bonds.) But when the Bank of Canada buys incoming foreign exchange, it has to pay with newly issued Canadian money, and doing so increases the reserves of our chartered banks. Thus, the money supply curve shifts to the right, as shown in Figure 17.3. As this curve shifts, the Canadian interest rate comes down, and this process must continue as long as any interest rate differential persists.

A full equilibrium is possible only when point 3 is reached and the Canadian interest rate has fallen back to the level of U.S. yields. There is no reason for any shifting back of the demand curve for goods in this case because there has not been any exchange rate change to alter the competitiveness of our exporters or importers. Thus, fiscal policy can have a lasting effect on aggregate demand. But we have learned that this conclusion applies only in a fixed exchange rate environment, when that commitment forces the Bank of Canada to alter the money supply in a way that supports the fiscal initiative.

So the first thing you should check when forming an opinion on the government's annual budget policy is whether Canada is currently following a flexible exchange rate policy or not. If so, then the budget changes will be largely irrelevant for aggregate demand, and any claims about major job creation are simply not credible. However, if Canada is adjusting monetary policy to limit changes in the exchange rate, then the budget changes will have an effect on aggregate demand.

MONETARY POLICY IN A FIXED EXCHANGE RATE ENVIRONMENT

Now we consider the options for monetary policy. As before, the initial equilibrium is point 1 in both markets (in Figure 17.1); however, since we are now considering monetary policy, the first shift occurs in the money market. Let's examine a contractionary monetary policy. It involves a decrease in chartered bank reserves, so the initial effect is a leftward shift in the money supply curve. We move from point 1 to point 2 in the money market, as shown in Figure 17.4. We see that the Canadian interest rate rises above the U.S. interest rate.

We know that this interest rate differential cannot last. As before, with the Canadian rate of interest being higher, foreign funds flow into the country. With a fixed exchange rate, the Bank of Canada is obliged to buy the otherwise unwanted foreign exchange entering the country. Issuing new Canadian money to pay for these purchases simply pushes the money supply curve back to the right, as shown in Figure 17.5. The Bank of Canada is forced to allow this to happen as long as the interest rate is higher here than in the United States. In other words, the money supply curve drifts all the way back, so that point 2 recedes back to and becomes point 1.

So this temporary shift in the money market, from point 1 to point 2 and then back again, is all that happens. With competition precluding any lasting interest rate effect, and with the Bank of Canada fixing the exchange rate, there is no mechanism through which the aggregate demand for goods can be affected. The Bank of Canada has merely performed two open market operations that cancel each other. The Bank started off with

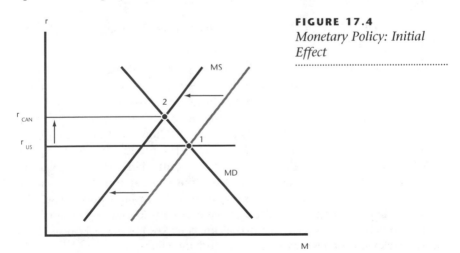

FIGURE 17.4
Monetary Policy: Initial Effect

FIGURE 17.5

*Monetary Policy under
Fixed Exchange Rates*

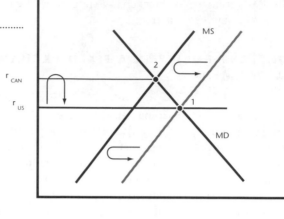

an open market sale of government bonds. But this sale just set up a temporary interest rate differential that, given the commitment of the Bank to fix the exchange rate, forced the Bank to make an open market purchase of foreign exchange. So the open market sale of government bonds and the open market purchase of foreign exchange simply offset each other, and there is no net effect on the position of the money supply curve.

In 1970, the Bank of Canada embarked on what was intended to be the most contractionary policy that it had tried up to that time during the postwar period. But we had a fixed exchange rate. The attempt to use monetary policy at a time when, as we have just seen, it simply could not work caused an exchange rate crisis. Within a few months, Canada was forced to give up its fixed exchange rate policy. We now consider the same monetary policy undertaken in a flexible exchange rate environment.

MONETARY POLICY IN A FLEXIBLE EXCHANGE RATE ENVIRONMENT

As before, the initial equilibrium is point 1 in both markets (see Figure 17.1, page 215), and then the reduction in bank reserves moves the money supply curve to the left. The equilibrium moves from point 1 to point 2 (as in Figure 17.4), and the now familiar temporary interest rate differential emerges. With the Canadian interest rate temporarily higher, funds flow into Canada. With the Bank of Canada not bothering to intervene in the foreign exchange market in a flexible exchange rate environment, the Canadian dollar is bid up in value. As this happens, foreigners find it more expensive to buy Canadian goods, so our exports fall. For the same reason, Canadian imports rise. The fall in net exports then causes the aggregate demand curve of goods to shift to the left, and the results are shown along the axes in Figure 17.6 — lower prices and lower real output.

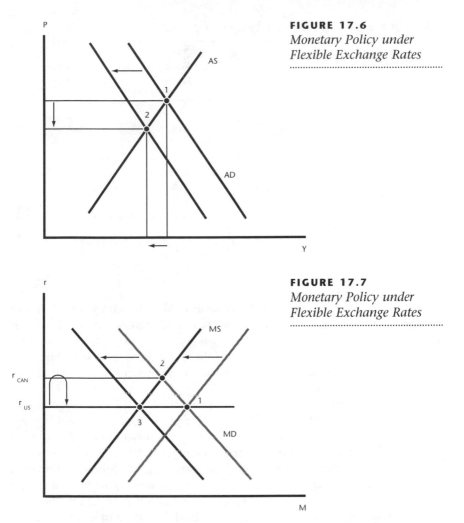

FIGURE 17.6
Monetary Policy under
Flexible Exchange Rates

FIGURE 17.7
Monetary Policy under
Flexible Exchange Rates

Both developments mean that nominal GDP is lower, so the demand for money is less. As usual, we show this effect by shifting the money demand curve to the left, and this sequence of events must continue until the shifting money demand curve moves the observation point from 2 to 3 in Figure 17.7, and the Canadian interest rate is pulled back down to the point that the interest rate differential is eliminated. So a contractionary monetary policy works under flexible exchange rates, but it works because the exchange rate change affects net exports, not because interest rate changes affect investments.

Table 17.1 summarizes this analysis of domestic policy options for a small open economy. There is an exchange rate environment in which fiscal policy and monetary policy can each have a lasting effect on aggregate demand. But each instrument must be used at the appropriate time if it is to

TABLE 17.1 *Lasting Effects on Aggregate Demand*

	Fiscal Policy	Monetary Policy
Fixed Exchange Rate	Yes	No
Flexible Exchange Rate	No	Yes

meet its objective of stabilizing the economy. Also, it is important to recall that having a lasting effect on the position of the aggregate demand curve is not enough for policy to have a significant effect on job creation. It is necessary but not sufficient. The impact on jobs will still be limited if the short-run aggregate supply curve is fairly steep and if wage increases cause that supply curve to start shifting up.

Space limitations preclude our using this model of a small economy to analyze the effects on Canada of various foreign developments. But you are now fully equipped to do so, and you can use the formal model on your own to consider things such as increases in foreign interest rates or increases in foreign tariffs. To allow you to check your reasoning, the following intuition is provided. Foreign tariffs are like a decrease in domestic government spending: both decrease the aggregate demand for Canadian products. We have learned that this effect will last only in a fixed exchange rate environment. Thus, a flexible exchange rate policy is recommended for better insulating the Canadian economy from foreign trade restrictions.

Foreign interest rate increases can be analyzed by shifting up the U.S. interest rate line in the money market graph. This shift results in an initial flow of funds out of Canada. In a fixed exchange rate environment, there is no exchange rate change that can possibly counter the depressing effect of higher interest rates on firms' investment spending, so aggregate demand falls. But in a flexible exchange rate environment, the flow of funds out of the country causes a depreciation of the Canadian dollar, which stimulates net export demand. Thus, there is a mechanism to offset the depressing effect of higher interest rates on aggregate demand, so once again a flexible exchange rate policy appears to provide better insulation from disruptive foreign events.

IS A FLEXIBLE EXCHANGE RATE A SHOCK ABSORBER?

Thus far, the analysis in this chapter suggests that a flexible exchange rate *is* a shock absorber; when aggregate demand falls, a depreciating dollar provides one way for demand to increase again, and this degree of freedom is lost if the exchange rate is fixed. But there are three reasons why the applicability of the analysis thus far may be limited.

First, while allowing a flexible exchange rate, the Bank of Canada rarely holds the money supply constant. Instead, it adjusts the money supply, period by period, in an attempt to maintain price stability. We will examine this version of a flexible exchange rate below. Second, to simplify, we have ignored one important fact: some of Canada's imports are intermediate products. They are not bought for consumption directly; instead, these items go into production operations within Canada. If the value of the Canadian dollar falls, then these inputs to business operations in Canada become more expensive. These higher costs cause our aggregate supply curve to shift up whenever the value of the Canadian dollar falls. Thus, the exchange rate is a shift influence for both the aggregate supply and the aggregate demand curves. Third, we must reconsider our assumption concerning complete integration of the Canadian and American financial markets.

Let us first clarify the financial market integration issue. We have imposed this assumption by specifying

$$r_{CAN} = r_{US} + \text{risk premium.}$$

Thus far, we have assumed that the risk premium depends on longer-term issues such as political stability, so we have set this term to zero. By doing so, we have assumed that the risk premium is not affected by short-run changes in fiscal and monetary policy. It is now time to reconsider this simplification. When bond holders expect the Canadian dollar to depreciate vis-à-vis the U.S. dollar, say, at a rate of 2 percent per year, they are reluctant to have their wealth denominated in Canadian dollars. To compensate lenders for such anticipated capital losses, Canadian borrowers must offer an interest rate that is 2 percent higher than what lenders can earn by buying bonds denominated in U.S. dollars. Thus, still ignoring issues of political stability, we must specify the risk premium as equal to the expected depreciation of the domestic currency. As a result, the extended model involves

$$r_{CAN} = r_{US} + \text{expected depreciation of the Canadian dollar.}$$

Now we are ready for a more complete analysis. Assume that the economy is initially at point 1 in Figure 17.8: actual GDP (given by the intersection of the aggregate demand and short-run aggregate supply curves) coincides with potential GDP. Then assume that the economy is hit with an adverse demand shock — a leftward shift in the demand curve that results from a loss

FIGURE 17.8
A Decrease in Demand:
Fixed Exchange Rates
....

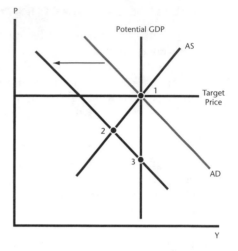

in export sales. The economy moves to point 2: the lower real output means job losses, while the lower price level means deflation. Under fixed exchange rates, this is all that happens in the short run. Over time, however, unemployment weakens labour's bargaining position, and wages gradually fall. This decrease in firms' costs is shown graphically by a downward shift in the short-run supply curve. The economy shifts gradually to point 3, where the cyclical unemployment has been eliminated. But with sluggishly adjusting wages, there is a significant hardship for a noticeable period.

Proponents of flexible exchange rates argue that there is no reason for us to endure this prolonged recession. Under flexible exchange rates, the domestic central bank can pursue its own price stability program. We implement this program in Figure 17.8 by assuming that the bank adjusts the money supply (and therefore the position of the aggregate demand curve) to ensure that the price level is constant — that is, to ensure that the intersection of the aggregate supply and demand curves always occurs somewhere on the horizontal line that passes through point 1. In this case, the bank will react to the lower price level that emerges in the impact period by increasing the domestic money supply, thereby depreciating the domestic currency. The cheaper domestic currency stimulates net exports and shifts the demand curve right back to its starting point. In principle, with such a policy, there is no need to have *any* wage decreases; the recession is *avoided*.

As far as it goes, this analysis makes a compelling case for a flexible exchange rate. But let us consider the other complications. With intermediate imports, a cheaper domestic currency pushes the short-run supply curve up at the same time as it pulls aggregate demand back to the right. If the central bank is successful in maintaining price stability, then the short-run outcome is point 3 in Figure 17.9. To peg the price level, then, the central bank cannot let the domestic currency depreciate enough to avoid a recession. So the

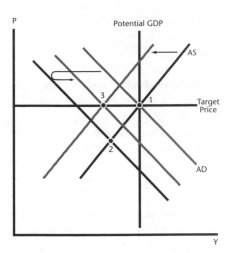

FIGURE 17.9
A Decrease in Demand:
Flexible Exchange Rates

issue is not a recession under fixed exchange rates versus no recession with a flexible exchange rate; it is an issue of a demand-induced recession under fixed exchange rates and a supply-induced recession with a flexible exchange rate.

The final complication involves adding the expected depreciation term in the interest arbitrage relationship. Since part of the adjustment process under flexible exchange rates is a depreciating domestic currency, and market participants know this, arbitrage forces the domestic interest rate to be higher than it otherwise would be in that case. This development puts additional downward pressure on aggregate demand since the investment component is depressed. With aggregate demand shifting more to the left under flexible exchange rates, point 2 must be more to the left in Figure 17.9 than it is in Figure 17.8. This means that point 3 in Figure 17.9 can be more to the left than point 2 is in Figure 17.8, so that — in the extended model — a flexible exchange rate policy may not be a shock absorber after all.

When eleven European countries adopted a common currency, the Euro, in 1999, they argued (on the basis of our extended analysis) that they were not risking much in terms of macroeconomic stability by rejecting a flexible exchange rate. During that year, Canada suffered a major loss of export sales as world commodity prices fell dramatically. Many analysts in this country took the opposite view from their counterparts in Europe; they regarded Canada's flexible exchange rate as essential for limiting the damage that accompanied the commodity price shock. Resolving these different views is part of ongoing research in macroeconomics.

SUMMARY

Here is a review of the key concepts covered in this chapter. A small open economy must accept that in full equilibrium its **rate of interest is determined in**

the rest of the world. In Canada's case, ignoring variations in risk, the Canadian interest rate always gravitates to the American interest rate. There are two implications. First, **monetary policy works by changing the exchange rate**, not the interest rate, so monetary policy cannot be performed once the decision to fix the exchange rate has been made. Second, since the **crowding-out effect** involved with fiscal policy works through the exchange rate, not the interest rate, it can be **avoided only if the exchange rate is fixed.**

Fiscal policy has a lasting effect on aggregate demand only under fixed exchange rates, and an independent monetary policy is possible only under flexible exchange rates.

A flexible exchange rate can act as a **shock absorber** in the face of foreign disturbances since a depreciating domestic currency can stimulate foreign demand for our products when sales are lost for other reasons. But a depreciating currency has two adverse effects: it raises the price of **intermediate imports**, so it increases unit costs for domestic producers; and, since asset holders adjust their expectations of **exchange rate depreciation**, it pushes domestic interest rates higher.

As we have seen, stabilization policy involves many problems, such as lags, crowding-out effects, and trade-offs. As a result, many economists have turned their attention to the longer-term issue of how a country can achieve a high rate of growth in the potential output. It is to this long-term consideration that we turn in the final chapters of this book.

SUGGESTIONS FOR FURTHER READING

D. Laidler (ed.), *Where Do We Go from Here?* (Toronto: C.D. Howe Institute, 1997), Policy Study 29, and L. Osberg and P. Fortin (eds.), *Hard Money, Hard Times: Why Zero Inflation Hurts Canadians* (Toronto: James Lorimer, 1998) — two collections of essays by economists who debate the wisdom of recent Canadian monetary policy.

WEB ACTIVITIES

www.bank-banque-canada.ca
The short speeches by the governor of the Bank of Canada explain how the bank is implementing its inflation target policy and why it has reacted as it has to recent developments in financial markets.

www.fin.gc.ca
Finance Canada's monthly *Fiscal Monitor* explains how well the year's fiscal targets are being met; the annual budget documents evaluate fiscal policy.

CHAPTER EIGHTEEN
The Global Economy

LEARNING OBJECTIVES

After reading this chapter, you should understand

- how the international financial system has evolved over time;
- how proposed currency arrangements may help to limit speculative crises without blocking the international

loans necessary to finance the world's most productive investments; and

- how both globalization and skills-biased technical change can generate greater income inequality and how governments can react to this challenge.

INTRODUCTION

As the twenty-first century begins, there is widespread concern that rising economic prosperity may be more difficult to secure in the future. We enjoyed rapid increases in living standards from the end of World War II to the early 1970s. Then, from the mid-1970s to the mid-1990s, we encountered two setbacks: much slower growth in average living standards and increased income inequality. Finally, in the late 1990s, seven economies — those that produced one-quarter of the world's output — experienced a decrease in economic activity that resembled what Western countries endured in the Great Depression of the 1930s. Many individuals became concerned that the major economies of the world had become so integrated that there was a new level of fragility in the system. They feared that problems in one area of the world would spread quickly to other areas without individual governments being able to do anything about the problems.

This chapter explores these concerns. We begin by tracing the history of the international monetary system. Then we discuss speculation and currency crises, some reform proposals, and whether it is international integration or skills-biased technical change that is the primary cause of increased income inequality.

THE HISTORY OF THE INTERNATIONAL MONETARY SYSTEM

We have had three different international monetary systems. The first was called the gold standard, and it was the method of financing world trade from the earliest days until the Depression of the 1930s. Then we shifted to a system that has been called the U.S. dollar standard, and it was in place from World War II until about 1970. Between 1970 and the late 1990s, much

TABLE 18.1 *The Gold Standard*

Surplus Country		Deficit Country
X > IM		X < IM
	Gold ←	
↑M		M↓
↑P, ↑Y		P↓, Y↓
↓X, ↑IM		X↑, IM↓

of the world adopted a third system of flexible exchange rates. Finally, in recent years, there has been a return to fixed exchange rates in several parts of the world, particularly in Europe, where eleven countries adopted a new single currency, the Euro, in 1999.

For centuries, precious metal coins served as money within individual countries, so it should be no surprise that gold became the international medium of exchange. Table 18.1 shows how the gold standard worked. Consider a country with a surplus in its trade with the rest of the world. Such a country was exporting more than it was importing. Also consider a country with a deficit in its trade with the rest of the world. Such a country was importing more than it was exporting. The gold standard eliminated such imbalances in trade automatically.

Since the deficit country was spending more than it was earning, it had to ship some of its gold over to the surplus country as payment. Shipments of gold entering the surplus country meant an increased money supply in that country. This increase raised aggregate demand and thus pushed up prices. Higher prices made the country less competitive, so its exports fell. Similarly, in the deficit country, with some of its money supply being shipped over to the other country, it was as if the deficit country had adopted a contractionary monetary policy that caused a recession and decreased prices. Lower prices made this country more competitive, and that stimulated its exports.

This **automatic adjustment process** meant that there were inflations in surplus countries and recessions in deficit countries. Sometimes in world history, of course, there were worldwide inflations. They occurred when there were major gold discoveries. At such times, even though deficit countries shipped gold over to surplus countries, they still had more gold than before, so money supplies in all countries rose, as did prices.

After World War II, most traders found it convenient to use the currency of the dominant country as the international medium of exchange, so U.S. dollars replaced gold. The system worked exactly as before, except that deficit countries shipped U.S. dollars over to surplus countries instead of gold. (Just envision "gold" being replaced by "U.S. dollars" in Table 18.1. This change in labelling has no effect on the underlying causal mechanisms.) The whole sequence of the adjustment in trade balances was the same — enforced monetary expansion in surplus countries, and enforced monetary contraction in deficit countries.

Worldwide inflation could still occur in the U.S. dollar system. It occurred whenever there was the equivalent of major discoveries of U.S. dollars, and this happened most dramatically in the late 1960s. President Lyndon Johnson was waging both a war against poverty on the home front and the Vietnam War on the international front. He was paying for them by printing large quantities of U.S. dollars. By shipping many U.S. dollars to other countries of the world (countries that maintained fixed exchange rates with the U.S. dollar), the United States effectively forced those countries to adopt very expansionary monetary policies, as in the United States. The result was worldwide inflation.

After some years, the rest of the countries in the Western world did not want to endure this inflation any longer. Since they could not affect U.S. monetary policy, their only remedy was to break out of the U.S. dollar system, so they simply refused to continue trading their currencies for U.S. dollars at a fixed rate of exchange. Thus, the world moved to a flexible exchange rate system.

Flexible exchange rates involve a self-correction mechanism as well. When a surplus country is selling to the rest of the world more than it is buying from it, the price of its currency is bid up. This change makes the country less competitive and reduces its trade surplus. Similarly, there is a low demand for the deficit country's currency, so it is bid down, and its firms become more competitive. Thus, eventually, trade imbalances are automatically corrected.

For a long time, economists argued that the automatic correction that operates under flexible exchange rates is more appealing than the one that operates under fixed exchange rates. This is because volatility in currency values seemed to be less disruptive than sustained periods of inflation and unemployment, and, as we have just seen, these hardships are part of the adjustment mechanism under fixed rates. But experience with flexible exchange rates has indicated that speculators can accentuate the variations in exchange rates. Many analysts have become concerned that — instead of being an alternative to variations in real output and employment — a flexible exchange rate can become a mechanism that magnifies these undesirable swings in real economic activity.

SPECULATION AND EXCHANGE RATE VOLATILITY

Economists have long argued that speculators need not be a cause for alarm. After all, a speculator makes money by purchasing an item when the price is low and selling it when the price is high. And, since the speculator's purchases raise prices when they otherwise would be lower and her sales reduce prices when they otherwise would be higher, speculators are benign — they help to stabilize markets. This argument implies that speculators who lose money destabilize markets, but this is no problem since that very loss of money drives them to other pursuits.

But there is an important exception to this traditional analysis of speculators. Some markets have multiple equilibria, and speculators can push these markets from one (preferred) equilibrium to another. Consider the market for a paper asset — such as an equity. A stock is a ticket that entitles its owner to a stream of profits that the company earns over the years. In principle, if only the fundamental earning capacity of the company's operations is considered, no one should pay more than the present value of this stream of expected profits when purchasing the stock. But this value is just one equilibrium that can be observed in the market. Suppose investors suddenly believe that the price will go much higher than this amount. If they try to buy the stock for this reason, they bid up the price, and these expectations are fulfilled. This outcome is a second equilibrium for this stock market. In general, any item whose *present* value depends on its *expected future* price can settle on a *self-fulfilling* equilibrium that bears no relationship to the underlying fundamental determinants of value. Of course, such non-fundamental equilibria tend not to last, but they are observed, and just when the expectational "bubble" will burst in each case, cannot be predicted by economic theory. As matters of market psychology — guesses about the **average opinion** of other traders — they are independent of economic fundamentals.

Exchange rates are asset prices, so it should be no surprise that we have observed bubbles in foreign exchange markets. In fact, before institutional reforms, we used to observe similar bubbles in domestic banking as well. Recall our discussion of gold warehouses (the precursors of modern banks) in Chapter 14. We noted the classic crisis-of-confidence problem that is always present when an institution promises to convert one item (in that case, the IOU slip) into another (gold) but has only a fraction of the reserves necessary to back up this promise. If people believe that no one will test the situation, then the system is in its "normal" equilibrium. But if people come to fear that the average opinion is that the system might collapse, then they try to withdraw their gold, the warehouses go bankrupt, and most depositors lose their wealth.

Several institutions have been devised to cope with this problem within any one country. First, to avoid having an insufficient supply of gold to convert into Canadian dollars, our government no longer makes any promise of convertibility. Our currency is simply defined as legal tender. This is an example of government intervention: within our borders, no one is allowed to refuse Canadian dollars as the settlement of any debt. Second, to lessen the chance of a "run" against private banks to test their commitment to convert passbook entries into Canadian currency, the Bank of Canada is committed to act as the "lender of last resort." Canadian banks (which are deemed solvent) are allowed to borrow whatever reserves they need from the central bank (on the understanding that they will pay the going Bank Rate as interest). As a result, knowing that private banks cannot run out of reserves, depositors have little incentive to test their particular institution. Third, we have deposit insurance (whereby the federal government pays depositors if their particular institution fails) and a well-developed set of regulations and supervision procedures for banks. It is no wonder, then, that, domestically at least, runs against banks have become a thing of the past.

But things are different in a world setting, principally because there is no world government to define legal tender, to set up a central bank, and to tax citizens to cover deposit insurance obligations. For a time, the development of the world financial system parallelled domestic monetary history. After World War II, we began using IOU slips (U.S. dollars) instead of gold. The system was underpinned by a commitment of convertibility by the United States: its government promised to give one ounce of gold to anyone who presented $35. A fractional reserve situation developed, since by the 1960s there were many more U.S. dollars outstanding in the rest of the world than there were ounces of gold in Fort Knox to back up the promise of convertibility. By the end of that decade, the United States had "solved" this problem by simply removing any future promise of convertibility between the dollar and gold. Americans could not define their currency as legal tender for the world, but they could drop its connection with gold. People no longer hold and use the American dollar because it is deemed to be "as good as gold" or because it is international legal tender. Now this use is based on the judgement that the U.S. dollar is at least as safe a medium of exchange as anything else available.

As already noted, the U.S. dollar system involved fixed exchange rates. The United States fixed one exchange rate (the price of gold in terms of the U.S. dollar), and each other country pegged the value of its currency in terms of the U.S. dollar. But just as Americans could not maintain a high value for their currency when they ran out of gold to offer at that price, no other country could maintain a high price for its currency if it ran out of U.S. dollar reserves. The system became increasingly unstable as speculators staged a run against any country that appeared to be in danger of running out of reserves (see page 190 for a review). Just as in the domestic banking setting, such runs generated self-fulfilling outcomes. Whenever there was a widespread fear of a currency depreciation, speculators could bet that the exchange rate could move only in one direction. With no possibility of losing the bet, speculation was rampant, and the depreciation occurred. The only way that these other countries could stimulate Americans' refusal to peg any particular price of gold in the future was to refuse to defend any particular value of their own currencies in the future. With this decision came the move to flexible exchange rates. Many analysts expected that, with the one-way speculation guarantee removed, as it is under flexible exchange rates, speculators could revert to their "normal" function of adding to, not detracting from, market stability. But this expectation ignored the **average opinion problem**.

A second consideration is that economic systems can behave in complicated ways when key variables adjust at different speeds. For example, wages tend to be set according to long-term contracts. As a result, when a shock hits the economy, wages cannot adjust to take much of the brunt of that shock until much later. With some variables "under reacting" in this way in the short run, other variables have to adjust more in the short run than they will in the longer term. The variables that pick up the slack in the short run are paper asset prices since they are traded every second. Thus, the exchange rate can "overshoot" (adjust more immediately than it does later on) in response to many disturbances. So high volatility in exchange rates is not surprising after all.

DEALING WITH EXCHANGE RATE VOLATILITY

What are we to do if we think that exchange rate volatility is costly? We cannot just go back to fixed exchange rates as before — both domestic history and international history have demonstrated that a promise of convertibility with fractional reserves is simply not credible. And, with the openness of financial markets today, runs are much more immediate and severe than in the past. Other than simply accepting the volatility of exchange rates under a flexible rate system, there are only two options:

1) tax the "hot" money in some way that does not reduce the important contribution that open capital markets make to long-term growth in living standards (they transfer scarce savings to the most productive investment opportunities); or
2) fix the exchange rate in some way other than making a promise to buy or sell unlimited quantities of foreign exchange that the central bank does not have.

The first option is called the **Tobin tax** — a financial transactions turnover tax — originally suggested by Keynes in a domestic context, but made popular as a reform proposal at the international level by Nobel Laureate James Tobin in 1974. Many analysts see serious administrative problems with the Tobin tax, but simple forms such as that used by Chile are feasible. Until the late 1990s, 30 percent of all foreign loans entering Chile had to be deposited with the central bank for the first year. Since this provision limited the return on investment only for the first year, the long-term allocation of funding was little affected. However, since it represented a major loss if funds were pulled out of the country in less than a year, the short-term "hot" money flows were discouraged. Some economists advocate further study of capital market controls of this sort.

The second option involves fixed exchange rates *without* a confidence problem. There are two ways in which this can be done. One way stipulates that the domestic central bank (the Bank of Canada in our case) conduct monetary policy so that it perfectly mirrors the policy of the key-currency country (the United States in our case). This behaviour ensures that the private supply and demand curves for foreign exchange always intersect at a height equal to the target exchange rate. With no gap between private demand and supply ever emerging, no exchange market intervention in the traditional sense is necessary. Of course, speculators could bet against the central bank's maintaining this policy, but there is no reason to suspect that speculators would want to do so when the exchange rate is the target — any more than they want to do so now, when the Bank targets the consumer price index.

The second way that speculative attacks may be reduced is by eliminating the fractional reserve dimension of the standard arrangements. To accomplish this, we must convert the central bank into a vending machine that simply turns foreign exchange into domestic currency at a fixed price with *100 percent reserves*. This is called a **currency board**. However, there are three disadvantages: the central bank cannot undertake any domestic initiatives, such as acting as a lender of last resort in times of domestic crisis; the bank must have a large supply of foreign exchange in the first place; and runs against the country's currency can still occur (as Hong Kong's currency board discovered in 1998). It may seem to be irrational for speculators to attack a currency board. After all, by definition, it cannot run out of foreign exchange reserves. But what the country can still run out of is the political will to maintain the currency board. When the Hong Kong currency board was attacked, speculators turned in Hong Kong dollars for foreign currencies. With a large part of the previously circulating domestic currency then in storage at the central bank, the speculators had forced a large contractionary monetary policy on Hong Kong. Interest rates rose dramatically, and the speculators bet that the country would have to end the currency board regime to undo this recessionary pressure.

So currency boards are not that much different from traditional fixed exchange rates. The only truly credible commitment to a fixed rate is the complete giving up of a country's own currency. In Canada's case, this option is currency union with the United States — which became a cover story in newspapers and in *Maclean's* magazine in 1999. We discussed the short-run pros and cons of a fixed exchange in the previous chapter. The main long-term issue involved in this debate is that an independent monetary policy requires a flexible exchange rate. One reason to want an independent policy is to have lower inflation; however, since the United States appears to share Canada's commitment to low inflation, there is not much at stake on this point. The second reason to want an independent monetary policy is to have the ability to run one's own lender-of-last-resort facilities. If Canada adopted the U.S. dollar unilaterally, then we would have no say regarding U.S. monetary policy, and we would not have access to American automatic lending arrangements. While it is possible to arrange lending that is not connected with the central bank (as our life insurance companies do), loss of the traditional lender of last resort is a serious concern. This concern could be met only if currency union is adopted through explicit agreement with the United States.

Opponents of flexible rates argue that — even if inflation were the same — nominal interest rates could be lower under currency union. The reasoning can be appreciated by recalling the interest arbitrage equation from the previous chapter:

$r_{CAN} = r_{US}$ + expected depreciation of the domestic currency.

This relationship implies that Canadian interest rates can be expected to exceed U.S. interest rates if, for whatever reason, lenders demand a depreciation risk premium. Such risk premiums emerge whenever there is general uncertainty about exchange rates. For example, during the uncertainty in late 1998, yields in Norway bulged to 1.5 percentage points above German yields. Although both Norway and Finland were exposed to the same commodity price drop and chaos in Russia, Finland's risk premium was only a quarter of a percentage point. Analysts attributed this difference in risk premium to the commitment by Finland to join the common currency arrangements a few months later. In short, commitment to a credible form of fixed exchange rates can lower interest rates.

It was the currency crises in Asia during 1997 and 1998 that most stimulated interest in reforming the international system. Asian banks got into precarious situations. They expanded rapidly, and all their assets (loans to firms and to individuals investing in real estate) were long-term (they were difficult to liquidate quickly) and were denominated in domestic currency. The banks made these loans on the basis of a flood of deposits coming in from savers in the rest of the world. These liabilities of the banks were denominated in foreign currency, and they were short-term (the foreign lenders could withdraw their funds on short notice). The Asian banks were in very risky positions; any loss in asset values or depreciation in their domestic currencies could quickly make their assets worth less than their liabilities.

Why did these banks (and the foreign investors) not appreciate this risk? Partly because there was limited regulation and supervision of banking, so there was incomplete information, and partly because of what we referred to as **moral hazard** in Chapter 7 — the fact that the provision of insurance makes people less careful about avoiding the very outcomes against which they are insured. No company provides fire insurance to establishments that do not abide by the fire code. Similarly, no government should provide insurance for financial institutions unless various rules of prudent behaviour are followed. If this proviso is not attached, then investments become gambles with a dimension of "Heads I win, tails the government loses." Many analysts believe that Asia suffered the explosive combination of insufficient supervision and regulation, on the one hand, and too many government guarantees, on the other.

This diagnosis leads to a central uncertainty regarding the appropriate action in helping out in such situations. If we argue that the fundamentals were basically satisfactory and that — despite short-run liquidity problems — most firms and banks were solvent, then the rest of the world should act as a lender of last resort. As such, it should arrange an influx of cash with "no strings attached" other than the condition that the funds be repaid with interest. A *rapid* response of this sort can stop a contagious series of runs before they get out of control. On the other hand, we could argue that some of the fundamentals were not right. Moral hazard was underappreciated, and we would make this problem even worse in the future by demonstrating that any such mess would be bailed out after the event.

This dilemma complicates suggestions for reforming the international financial system. But let us apply some of the lessons that we learned in earlier chapters. In Chapter 7, we saw that any institutional arrangement that induces individuals to self-select into different groups automatically eliminates some incomplete information. We saw this principle applied in pollution policy with the use of emission taxes and tradeable emission permits (Chapter 8). In that application, individual polluters self-select between the group that reduces emissions and the group that purchases the right to keep polluting.

What is the analogue of tradeable emission permits in the area of international financial reform? The answer has been provided by two British economists who call their proposal **UDROP**: Universal Debt Rollover Option with a Penalty. The idea is based on the proposition that (just as with pollution) there is a third-party effect in the act of international lending. If investors become worried about risk, then they pull their money out of a country as soon as their short-term loans expire — without any regard for what the resulting exchange rate crisis will do to the residents of that country.

The proposal is that all foreign loans must involve an option that the borrower can extend the loan beyond its retirement date — by something like six months — at a penalty rate of interest. Knowing that the borrower could choose to exercise this option, the lender would find it in her interest to assess this risk and reallocate loans accordingly. Loans would be less forthcoming for riskier borrowers — whatever the state of incomplete supervision and regulation within that country. Since there would be no risk that truly worthwhile projects would lead to the exercise of this provision, this scheme discourages only less desirable capital flows — as judged by market participants themselves. Co-ordination among the major Western countries is needed for implementation of this proposal, however, to prevent risky foreign borrowers from simply going to countries whose individuals and institutions can make loans without the UDROP feature. But it is worth pursuing this co-ordination since no other reform proposal makes private market participants such a central part of the solution. Limited government funds always lead to official loans being slow and conditional (as they have been with the International Monetary Fund), and these are not desirable features if a crisis is one of liquidity, not solvency.

INCOME INEQUALITY

Beyond volatility, the primary concern about the new global economy is **income inequality**. Compared with many low-wage countries, Canada has an abundance of skilled workers and a small proportion of unskilled workers. The opposite is the case in the developing countries. With increased integration of the world economies, Canada specializes in the production of goods that emphasize our relatively abundant factor, skilled labour, so it is the wages of skilled workers that are bid up by increased foreign trade. The other side of this development is that Canada relies more on imports to supply goods that require only unskilled labour, so the demand for unskilled labour falls in Canada. The result is either lower wages for the unskilled in Canada (if there is no legislation that puts a floor on wages here) or rising unemployment among the unskilled in Canada (if there is a floor on wage rates, such as that imposed by minimum wage laws and welfare). In either case, unskilled Canadians can lose income in the new global economy.

There is a second hypothesis concerning rising income inequality. It is that, during the final quarter of the twentieth century, **skills-biased technical change** has meant that the demand for skilled workers has risen while that for unskilled workers has fallen. Just as with the free-trade hypothesis, the effects of these shifts in demand depend on whether it is possible for wages in the unskilled sector to fall. The United States and Europe are often cited as illustrations of the different possible outcomes. The United States has only a limited welfare state, so there is little to stop increased wage inequality from emerging, as indeed it has in recent decades. Europe has much more developed welfare states that maintain floors below which the wages of unskilled workers cannot fall. When technological change decreases the demand for unskilled labour, firms have to reduce their employment of these individuals. Thus, Europe has avoided large increases in wage inequality, but the unemployment rate has been high there for many years.

Most economists favour the second hypothesis — skills-biased technical change — for explaining rising income inequality. This is because inequality has increased so much within each industry and occupation, in ways that are unrelated to imports. The consensus has been that only 11 percent of the rising inequality in the United States can be attributed to the expansion of international trade. But whatever the causes, the plight of the less skilled is dire.

In searching for a policy response, many analysts focus on payroll taxes, often called "job killers." Canada's main payroll taxes are the contributions that employers and employees make to the Canada and Quebec Pension Plans and to the Employment Insurance fund. If these taxes are job killers, then some tax cuts in this area seem to be warranted, given the plight of unskilled workers. Consider Figure 18.1. The left-hand panel depicts the skilled labour market, while the right-hand panel illustrates the unskilled labour market. There is unemployment in both sectors. In the skilled labour market, unemployment is due to incomplete information, as explained in Chapter 7 (page 80). In the unskilled labour market, unem-

FIGURE 18.1
Unemployment

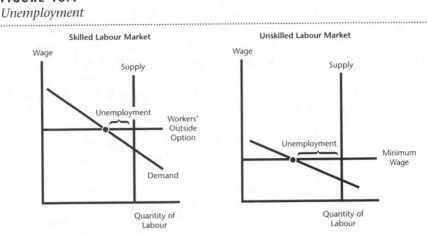

FIGURE 18.2
A Cut in the Employer Payroll Tax on Skilled Workers

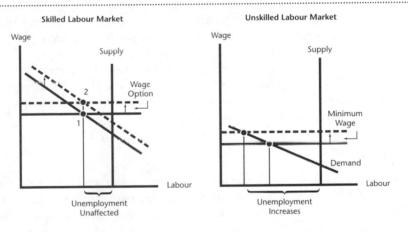

ployment is due to welfare and minimum wages. Let us consider a decrease in the employer payroll tax using these diagrams. Cutting the tax that employers must pay when hiring skilled workers results in a shift up in the demand for skilled labour. But since all firms react in the same way, the workers' outside option rises to the same extent, so the market outcome moves from point 1 to point 2 in the left-hand panel of Figure 18.2. No jobs are created. Indeed, some jobs may be eliminated. If the value of the minimum wage is set as a fixed proportion of wages in the skilled sector, then there is a further effect. The minimum wage line shifts up in the right-hand panel of Figure 18.2, and unemployment among the unskilled is higher. So cutting the employer payroll tax associated with skilled workers is not recommended.

Cutting the tax that employers must pay when hiring unskilled workers results in a shift up in the demand for unskilled labour. Since the position of no other curve in either market is affected directly by this policy, it is obvious — without providing a separate diagram — that it reduces unemployment in the unskilled labour sector. So the elimination of payroll taxes levied on employers for hiring unskilled workers is recommended. Indeed, offering employment subsidies (a negative payroll tax) for low-wage workers has been recommended by all leading economists who have addressed the issue of rising income inequality.

It is worth noting that wage subsidies for hiring low-wage workers have a beneficial effect on productivity. When firms hire more unskilled workers, the productivity of their complementary factors — capital and skilled labour — rises. With high capital mobility in today's globalized economy, firms react by hiring more capital, and this further raises productivity — and therefore wages — for skilled workers. As a result, low-wage subsidies are an example of what has been called "percolate-up" (as opposed to "trickle-down") economics. (For a detailed analysis of trickle-down economics, see the next chapter, pages 248–51.)

Of course, some individuals view any active labour market initiative, such as employment and low-wage subsidies, as a backward step — one in opposition to the trend of freeing the market economy from excess regulation. But even the most conservative must admit that in principle the government has a role to play when markets fail. Conservatives prefer corrective action in the form of adjusting *private incentives* through taxes and subsidies, rather than having direct government involvement. The employment subsidy for low-wage workers respects this preference.

SUMMARY

Here is a review of the key concepts covered in this chapter. There is an **automatic correction mechanism** for **eliminating trade imbalances** with all international monetary systems. Under fixed exchange rate systems, such as the gold standard and the U.S. dollar system, countries with trade deficits experience recession, whereas countries with trade surpluses experience inflation. With flexible exchange rates, these effects can be tempered: deficit countries have depreciating currencies, while surplus countries have appreciating ones.

If there is no **average opinion problem**, then speculators decrease market volatility. But with waves of optimism and pessimism, asset prices — including exchange rates — can wander a long way from what determines their fundamental value. In this setting, speculators can accentuate volatility. With integrated world financial markets, they can quickly withdraw massive amounts of money from individual countries. Those countries then face recessions — either because financial institutions fail in the face of withdrawn deposits or because the domestic central bank must raise interest rates in an attempt to defend the exchange rate. This need to play a "confidence game" with speculators can take precedence over normal macroeconomic policy.

These problems may be counteracted by applying a **Tobin tax** — preferably one like **UDROP**, which respects the key issues of administrative feasibility, **moral hazard**, and **self-selection**. Instead of taxing capital flows, some countries may opt for a **currency board** or **currency union** with a more stable currency.

Beyond volatility, the primary complaint concerning the new global economy has been that it has caused the large rise in **income inequality**. But evidence shows that this problem stems mostly from **skills-biased technical change**, and it can be counteracted by a policy of payroll tax cuts and employment subsidies, for the employers of low-wage workers.

History has shown that society's interest in the redistribution of income is dependent on significant growth in the living standards of those financing that redistribution. For this reason, we turn to issues of long-term growth in the remaining chapters of the book.

SUGGESTIONS FOR FURTHER READING

D. Cohen, *The Wealth of the World and the Poverty of Nations* (Cambridge, MA: MIT Press, 1998) — a brief and fascinating account of the trend toward rising inequality and the role of globalization in this process.

P. Krugman, *The Return of Depression Economics* (New York: Norton, 1999) — an entertaining short book on the causes of the "Asian crisis" in 1998 and on other instabilities in the international monetary system.

L. McQuaig, *The Cult of Impotence: Selling the Myth of Powerlessness in the Global Economy* (Toronto: Penguin, 1999), and W. Watson, *Globalization and the Meaning of Canadian Life* (Toronto: University of Toronto Press, 1998) — different perspectives on how Canada's economic policy should react to increased global integration.

WEB ACTIVITIES

www.imf.org
The Web site of the International Monetary Fund; click on "Publications," then "Economic Issues," for articles on fixed versus flexible exchange rates, globalization, and income inequality.

www.imfsite.org
A Web site maintained by the Hoover Institution at Stanford University containing the text of a book (published in 1999) that evaluates the IMF; many of the short chapters are reprints from magazines and newspapers; some contributors support the IMF, while others want it disbanded immediately.

CHAPTER NINETEEN

Growth and Development

LEARNING OBJECTIVES

After reading this chapter, you should understand
- which factors are conducive to raising labour productivity and economic growth and how analysis of growth has developed over time;
- why "trickle down" policy initiatives have limited effectiveness in a small open economy such as Canada's; and
- why there is a built-in feature of the growth process that helps to solve some of the problems of natural resource scarcity.

INTRODUCTION

Most people are aware of the desperate poverty endured by a large part of the world's population. These countries have not shared in the process of economic growth that the developed economies have enjoyed in the past 300 years. This chapter considers how growth in the standard of living occurs and what government policy can do to affect this process.

Thus far, our focus in macroeconomics has been on stabilization policy. The difference between growth policy and stabilization policy can best be appreciated by looking back at the first graph that we considered in macroeconomics — Figure 11.1 in Chapter 11 (on page 132). We saw there that potential GDP has a smooth time path but that the level of actual GDP is buffeted about, so that we endure a series of business cycles. We have learned that this cyclical time path for actual GDP is due to major shifts in the aggregate demand and supply curves that occur in the short run.

The whole point of stabilization policy is to try to fill in the troughs and shave off the peaks — to make the actual GDP time path more closely approximate that for potential GDP. From a growth point of view, we are interested in the longer-run outcomes of the economy, and in that respect we tend to ignore the short-run dips and swings of the business cycle. Thus, in the remaining chapters, we focus only on the time path for potential GDP. The purpose of growth policy is to shift up the time path for potential GDP — either in a parallel fashion or by pivoting it counterclockwise — so that people can enjoy a larger quantity of goods and services in the future.

Is it legitimate to assume that the long-term growth path is independent of short-term cycles? Some analysts say no — that a series of recessions is good for growth. Recessions force less productive firms out of business, and other firms choose to restructure more during recessions when the disruption costs (lost sales) are smaller. Other analysts argue that recessions are bad for growth. For one thing, productivity growth requires learning by doing, and during recessions there is less doing. In addition, recessions involve uncertainty, which reduces investment. Empirical studies have not resolved this debate.

Growth in real GDP is only necessary for higher living standards; it is not sufficient. After all, if the number of people grows faster than the total quantity of goods, then the amount available for each individual actually shrinks. So economists focus on a concept called labour productivity.

LABOUR PRODUCTIVITY

Labour productivity is defined as the total quantity of goods and services that the economy produces divided by the number of workers who produce that total. This ratio is an important determinant of our standard of living since it defines the level of real wages that workers can earn. Workers cannot generally have a rising standard of material welfare unless output grows at a faster rate than does the labour force, so that **output per worker** is rising.

Over the first 125 years following Confederation, Canada had an average rate of growth in labour productivity of just less than 2 percent per year. This growth rate has raised our standard of living by a factor of eight. Small changes in either the growth rate or the number of years during which growth takes place can make an even more dramatic difference. For instance, a 3 percent growth rate in labour productivity operating for 200 years allows the standard of living to go up a staggering 300 times. So a bit of stimulus to raise the growth in labour productivity even a fraction of a percentage point is important for the growth of real wages.

In recent years, there has been a marked slowdown in the growth in labour productivity and therefore in real wage growth. Figure 19.1 shows the evidence. For example, income growth fell from 36 percent in the 1960s to 8 percent in the 1970s, and to just 2 percent during the final two decades of

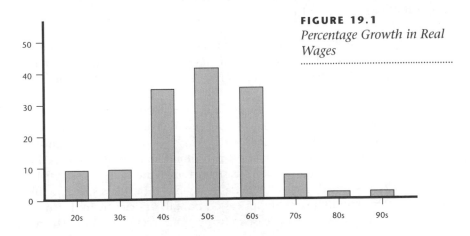

FIGURE 19.1
Percentage Growth in Real Wages

the century. There is simply no way that we can afford better health care, more thoroughgoing environmental cleanups, or other valuable things if we do not have higher income growth. Many economists regard the productivity growth slowdown during the past three decades to be one of the most important economic events of the twentieth century.

While most people react to the slowdown of productivity growth by asking what we can do to reverse it, others do not. This difference of opinion may be explained by the fact that Canadians have chosen to consume more services and fewer manufactured items. Since many services require one-on-one consultation, it is more difficult to achieve productivity improvements in services. Despite this fact, competition forces firms to pay similar wages in both sectors. As a result, rising productivity in manufacturing *must* cause rising costs in services. Hence, in the long run, we must either accept ever fewer services or devote an ever larger fraction of GDP to services (and accept falling *overall* productivity growth as a result).

POLICIES THAT CAN LEAD TO HIGHER ECONOMIC GROWTH

Now we know how growth is measured and that growth can bring large benefits. But many questions remain. Why do some countries grow more rapidly than others? What are the costs associated with higher growth? Can growth proceed when the world has limited amounts of key resources? We now turn to the first of these issues. Which policies lead to higher economic growth?

The factors conducive to higher economic growth are

1) a high savings rate,
2) education,
3) research,
4) social acceptance of the profit motive, and
5) flexibility in the workplace.

Let us focus on a **high savings rate**. It has been stressed in earlier chapters that the only way in which workers can have more capital equipment to work with is if society chooses not to consume all of the output that it produces in any one year.

The role of savings differs when we shift our focus from short-run to long-run issues. In the short run, our primary focus is on stabilization policy, since many people believe that the economy's self-correction mechanism needs time to fully operate. In that short-run time frame, we focused on the circular flow of income and spending, as shown in Figure 12.1 of Chapter 12 (on page 142). We noted that an increase in savings meant less spending by households. Since interest rates and prices do not fall sufficiently in the short run, there is not an offsetting increase in firms' investment spending. The result is that aggregate demand falls and a recession occurs. That analysis is relevant for the short run.

But in the longer run, there is no problem of insufficiency of demand. After all, if saving becomes larger than investment, then banks can raise their profits by lowering interest rates — both on deposits to discourage saving and on loans to encourage investments. Thus, given enough time, the self-correction mechanism of interest rate adjustments in a large economy (or an analogous process involving exchange rate adjustments in a small open economy) solves any aggregate demand problem. In the longer run, then, when the focus is on economic growth and not on cycles, any temporary dislocation caused by a higher savings rate can be de-emphasized. Instead, we concentrate on the lasting implication of higher saving — a higher ratio of investment to GDP, which means more productive equipment for each labourer to work with and thus higher incomes.

The circular flowchart also points to the opportunity cost of higher growth. To obtain the increased quantity of investment goods, we must save — that is, forgo some current consumption. There is a trade-off: to have higher standards of living in the future, we must accept lower standards of living now. This trade-off is also involved when we try to promote growth through **investment in education and research** (factors 2 and 3 listed above) instead of through investment in equipment. Investment in higher skills can raise productivity, but these investments also mean less current consumption.

Another important factor for growth is that the **profit motive**, and **entrepreneurial activity** in general, not be regarded as antisocial behaviour. In some societies, people who search for profit opportunities are not well accepted, and these countries have low growth rates.

Finally, an important consideration is **flexibility in the workplace**. When new production methods are invented, management and labour need to embrace them in a constructive fashion rather than resist them. Countries that have co-operative labour relations, as opposed to confrontational ones, seem to have higher growth performance.

Let us assess how well some of these prerequisites for growth are satisfied in other countries. We consider both the developing countries and the former centrally planned economies. It is easy to see why the developing countries are having a great deal of trouble. They possess little capital equipment, and they have low levels of education and research activity. Furthermore, some of these societies do not support making profits, so they fall short on essentially all the main criteria for rapid growth. Low growth rates in these countries represent a staggering problem because many of them have high population growth rates. They need a high growth rate in GDP, more than other countries do, just to keep living standards from falling even lower.

One constructive solution is to drop the significant **barriers to trade** that industrialized countries have erected against products from the developing countries. Many of these latter countries get all their foreign exchange from selling a few primary commodities. While there have been large reductions in tariffs among Western countries, this process has not happened with agricultural commodities. Indeed, restrictions that favour the developed countries at the expense of the less developed ones have become more prevalent, with the result that income growth in the developing countries has been severely limited.

What about the former centrally planned economies? These countries have little experience with the market mechanism and the profit motive. Decentralized trades between individuals and firms require a system of well-established **property rights** and a legal system to enforce those property rights. After all, you will not pay me for something if you are not confident that it is actually mine to sell. But when countries move abruptly from a centrally planned system in which everything is state-owned, there simply are not any private property rights. Institutions cannot be created quickly.

Indeed, Western countries took centuries to develop the institutions that support free enterprise. The reliance on markets occurred very gradually, starting in feudal times with a tiny proportion of the economy involving itinerant traders. So the formerly planned countries are trying to develop market systems much more quickly than we ever did, and these countries are trying to assign property rights in fair ways. We never did that; property rights were distributed through political decisions and historical accidents centuries ago as our market system gradually evolved. On both fronts, then, the time frame and the emphasis on equity, Eastern countries are trying to do something that has never been done before.

Considering the plight of other countries provides valuable perspective, but to examine growth policy within Canada in a more thorough manner, we must understand basic growth theory.

GROWTH THEORY

Figure 19.2 summarizes the labour market of a traditional, pre-industrial society. In such a society, all adults had to work full-time at menial tasks just to live, so the supply curve is completely wage-inelastic; it simply reflects the size of the population. The demand for labour is downward sloping for the usual reason — diminishing marginal productivity. The larger the population, the smaller the share of the fixed capital stock (the supply of agricultural implements) with which each individual has to work. Since we are interested in the growth process — starting from a subsistence level — we assume that the initial equilibrium in Figure 19.2 is point A.

Thomas Malthus, an economist writing about 200 years ago, made a prediction that caused others to label economics as the "dismal science." Malthus predicted that, except for relatively brief periods of higher living standards, people were doomed to a subsistence level of existence. To appreciate his reasoning, we consider the implications of an increase in the quantity of capital in Figure 19.2. With more capital, labour's marginal product increases, and the equilibrium outcome moves from point A to point B.

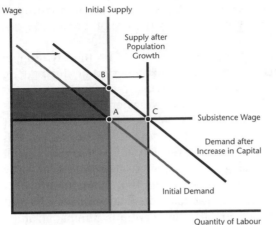

FIGURE 19.2
The Labour Market In Pre-industrial Society

Labour's total income grows from the medium grey rectangle initially to the sum of both the medium and the dark grey rectangles. Income per person, and therefore material living standards, have increased.

But Malthus predicted that this happy circumstance would not last. He argued that, with wages now above the subsistence level, fewer individuals — especially infants — would die, and families would become larger. The growing population is shown in Figure 19.2 as a rightward shift in the labour supply curve. Gradually, as the larger quantity of capital is shared over a larger number of workers, labour's marginal product is bid down again. This process continues until the wage returns to the subsistence level, so that population growth is no longer possible, at point C. Total labour income is higher than it was initially (it is now the sum of the light grey rectangle and the original medium grey area). But with the number of people rising by the same proportion, living standards are no higher.

While Malthus's analysis has relevance for some countries that remain traditional societies today, overall his prediction has been rejected by economic history. There has been a spectacular rise in material living standards in many countries over the two centuries since Malthus wrote. The main reason for the inapplicability of his theory appears to be that people have acquired a taste for things other than large families, so they have not "spent" their higher incomes — which Malthus expected to be temporary — on increased numbers of children. To show this in Figure 19.2, we simply assume that the population does not expand, so that point B becomes the final outcome. So modern growth theory predicts a permanent rise in standards of living following capital accumulation.

Since today's economists do not embrace Malthus's view regarding fertility, they believe that the "dismal science" epitaph is no longer so appropriate. In one sense, however, it still is. This fact can be appreciated by realizing that the increase in living standards shown in Figure 19.2 is once and for all.

How can we achieve *ongoing* increases in living standards? You might think that the answer is obvious — just keep increasing the size of the capital stock with which people can work.

The problem with this strategy, however, is that — with the fixed supply of labour — capital's marginal product keeps falling over time. In the long run, saving equals investment, so the yield on savings is dictated by the marginal productivity of capital. People refuse to save when that return is less than what economists call their rate of time preference. People prefer current to postponed consumption. Once the payoff for waiting fails to exceed this impatience factor, people stop saving. Once a society stops saving, its capital stock stops growing. In short, when growing living standards are achieved by acquiring more physical capital, the process cannot last. The faster that capital is accumulated, the more rapidly capital's marginal product is pulled down, so the incentive for further capital accumulation is eliminated, and a dismal prediction remains. It is not that we will have to give up what we have gained — as Malthus predicted — but that *further* increases in living standards cannot be expected if all that lies behind our past success is the accumulation of physical capital.

Fortunately, physical capital is not the only form of investment. Knowledge capital has been expanded through investment in education. Both forms of investment affect Figure 19.2 in the same way — by shifting labour's marginal product curve to the right. But they affect the market for physical capital, shown in Figure 19.3, in quite different ways.

The demand curve in Figure 19.3 is the marginal product of capital schedule, and the long-run supply relationship graphs the condition discussed above. Let r, t, and i represent the yield on capital (its marginal product), the tax rate that people pay on that yield, and the household rate of impatience. Households save — that is, they allow current output to take the form of new physical capital instead of current consumption goods — as long

FIGURE 19.3
The Market for Capital
....

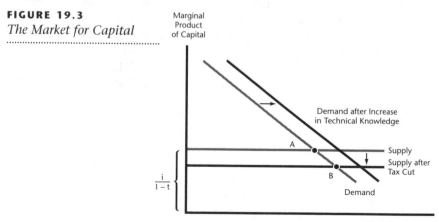

as capital's yield (after tax) is at least as great as the rate of time preference — that is, as long as r(1 – t) is greater than or equal to i. Thus, the supply curve for capital in Figure 19.3 is perfectly elastic at the lowest acceptable level of the pre-tax marginal product: r = i/(1 – t).

Government policy can stimulate capital accumulation. For example, a cut in the tax rate lowers i/(1 – t), so lower taxes shift down the position of the supply curve in Figure 19.3. The outcome moves from point A to B. The "good news" part of this outcome is the bigger stock of capital, which is what shifts the labour demand curve to the right in Figure 19.2 — raising total labour income. The "bad news" part of this outcome is that capital's marginal product falls. Hence, further application of this initiative in the future is more difficult since capital's marginal product is being pushed down ever closer to the household rate of impatience.

There is an important difference with investment in knowledge capital. Increased technological knowledge shifts the marginal product curves for *both* labour and physical capital to the right. In Figure 19.3, this means "good news" without any "bad news" — labour gets more physical capital to work with, and there is no fall in the marginal product of physical capital. As a result, there is not the same dismal prospect that investments of this sort cannot be repeated in the future. The underlying reason is that it is not plausible to assume diminishing returns for knowledge.

Figure 19.4 summarizes the difference between investment in physical capital and that in knowledge capital. It shows the time path for per-capita output not growing at all until point A along the time axis. Then the economy invests either in physical capital — achieving time path 1 — or in education — achieving time path 2. One difference is that only investment in education can permanently raise the slope of the per-capita output time line. Given this fact, using government funds to invest in education seems to be the superior approach, since eventually time path 2 must be higher, and by

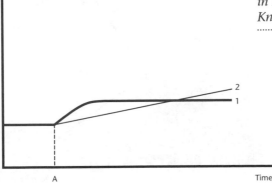

FIGURE 19.4
The Effects of Investment in Physical Capital and Knowledge Capital

a big margin. The higher living standards can come more quickly, however, when government funds are used to stimulate saving (as assumed in Figure 19.4). In a discounted present value sense, then, investment in physical capital should not be neglected. With this in mind, we now consider what has come to be called **trickle-down economics**.

TRICKLE-DOWN ECONOMICS

The basic approach to growth policy within Western countries has been to focus on what was listed as the first item important for growth — savings. The general advice is that we should use our tax system to discourage consumption and to stimulate saving. There are various ways of doing so. One option is tax-free registered retirement savings plans. A second is an increased reliance on sales taxes, such as the GST, instead of general income taxes. Sales taxes must be paid only when individuals spend; they can be avoided by saving.

A number of people oppose these kinds of tax measures on equity grounds; they believe that only the rich have enough income to do much saving and to benefit from these tax breaks. Those who favour these programs argue that this assumption is incorrect — that most of the benefits go to those with lower incomes. But since the process by which these benefits "trickle down" the income scale is indirect, they argue, many people do not understand it and thus reject these tax initiatives inappropriately. We now examine whether this trickle-down view is correct, first in a large economy, and then in a small open economy.

Figure 19.5 is a graph of the market for capital with a more general specification of the supply curve than that shown in Figure 19.3. People do more saving when the rate of interest is higher, and that is why the supply curve has a positive slope. Both the amount of capital and the return on capital

FIGURE 19.5
The Size and Distribution of Income: A Closed Economy

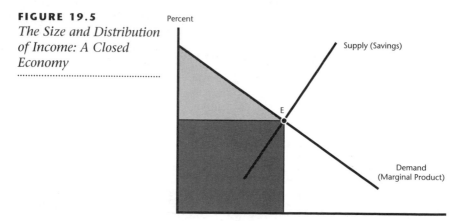

get determined by the intersection of supply and demand (at point E in Figure 19.5).

The graph also determines the overall level of output and income. Think of the economy having just two factors of production: capital equipment and labour. If we add up all the area under the marginal product of capital curve, we get the total product, the country's GDP. Thus, GDP is the entire shaded area in Figure 19.5. Since each unit of capital is receiving a rate of return equal to the height of point E, capital's share of national income is the dark grey rectangle. Labour gets the residual amount — the light grey triangle. So the graph shows both the size and the distribution of national income.

Now consider a tax measure designed to stimulate savings. This initiative shifts the capital supply curve to the right, as shown in Figure 19.6. Equilibrium moves from point E to point A. Total production increases by the additional area under the marginal product curve — that is, by an amount equal to the shaded trapezoid in Figure 19.6. So the growth policy works. By stimulating savings, we get more output. How is this additional material benefit distributed? The owners of capital get the dark grey rectangle, and labour gets the light grey triangle. So even if capitalists do all the saving and become the apparent beneficiaries of the tax break, and even if labour can afford to do no saving, labour does get something.

Furthermore, labour's benefit is not just the small light grey triangle in Figure 19.6. With capital being more plentiful, its rate of return has been bid down to a lower level. Since that lower rate is being paid on all units of capital, there has been a transfer to labour of the rectangle formed by the horizontal lines running through points E and A. By comparing Figure 19.5 and 19.6, we can see that this area used to be earnings of capital, but with the policy that stimulated savings it is now part of labour's income. So, in the end, capitalists as a group may not win from the stimulation of savings. Capitalists gain the dark grey rectangle in Figure 19.6, but they lose the unshaded

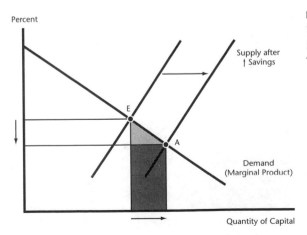

Percent

E

A

Supply after
↑ Savings

Demand
(Marginal Product)

Quantity of Capital

FIGURE 19.6
*Trickle-Down Economics
in a Closed Economy*

rectangle that we have just discussed. The only group that is a clear winner is labour — it gains both the light grey triangle and the unshaded rectangle. That is, labour gains the entire trapezoid formed by the horizontal lines going through points E and A. Recall that labour was assumed to be too poor to benefit directly from any tax break that stimulated savings. But labour benefits indirectly because workers become more productive when they have more capital with which to work.

We conclude that, in a large economy that can set its own interest rate, tax breaks that stimulate savings do not benefit just high-income capitalists; the benefits also trickle down to low-income wage earners. While the term "trickle down" has acquired a kind of pejorative interpretation, we have just seen that this standard analysis supports the trickle-down process. But one question remains. Can this standard analysis be legitimately applied to a small open economy such as Canada's?

In earlier chapters, we noted that domestic policy cannot have a lasting effect on the domestic rate of interest in a small open economy. Thus, while the standard analysis just presented (which assumes the contrary) can be used to support the trickle-down approach in a large economy such as the United States, it does not apply in Canada. We now modify the trickle-down analysis so that it is applicable to the Canadian case.

In Figure 19.7, the marginal product of capital curve appears as before; it is the demand for capital equipment in Canada. Again, as before, the supply of domestic savings is part of the analysis. But Figure 19.7 contains one additional relationship — a line that shows the supply of savings on behalf of lenders in the rest of the world. These individuals are ready to buy capital equipment employed in Canada should the return be adequate. To satisfy foreign lenders, the return must equal the risk-adjusted rate of return that capital can earn when it is employed in the rest of the world. We assume that this alternative yield is given by the height of the foreign supply curve in Figure 19.7.

FIGURE 19.7
The Size and Distribution of Income: An Open Economy
....

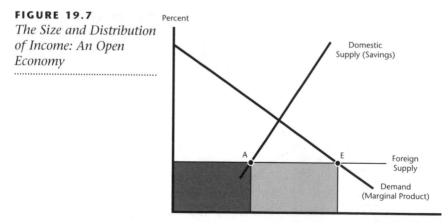

Equilibrium occurs at point E, and GDP is the entire trapezoid under the marginal product curve up to point E. The rate of return for each unit of capital is given by the height of the foreign supply curve, so capitalists earn the shaded rectangles under that line, while labour receives the white triangle. The domestic supply of savings curve indicates the proportion of capital's income that goes to Canadian-owned capital (the dark grey rectangle) as well as the proportion that is the income of foreign capitalists (the light grey rectangle).

We now consider, as before, a tax break for domestic capitalists if they save more income. This policy shifts the domestic supply curve to the right, as shown in Figure 19.8. In this case, equilibrium remains at E. There is no growth in the amount of goods produced. But there is growth in the amount of income that Canadian residents can achieve from that output, because the income of Canadian capitalists increases by the amount of the shaded rectangle between points A and B in Figure 19.8 (and the income of foreign capitalists decreases by the same amount).

Since labour is still working with the same overall quantity of capital, labour's income — the white triangle — is unaffected. So the entire increase in national income goes to capitalists. This is a very different conclusion from the one we reached when we applied this tax policy to an economy not constrained by international competition. So critics of trickle-down economics are justified in a small open economy such as Canada. The benefits of tax breaks that stimulate savings do not trickle down to labour in any direct fashion. Of course, many workers are indirectly partial capitalists. Their pension funds and insurance companies own capital. Nevertheless, this analysis suggests that investing in better education and training, which directly raises labour's skills and therefore labour's marginal product, may be a more direct way of helping labour while stimulating growth.

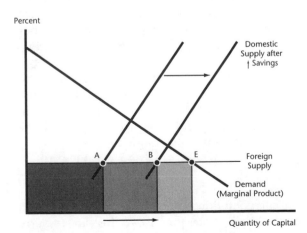

Percent

Domestic
Supply after
↑ Savings

A   B   E

Foreign
Supply

Demand
(Marginal Product)

Quantity of Capital

FIGURE 19.8
*Trickle-Down Economics
in an Open Economy*

IS CONTINUED ECONOMIC GROWTH SUSTAINABLE?

The analysis of tax breaks to stimulate higher output through increased saving assumes that continued growth is possible. Many individuals focus on the world's rapidly growing population and limited supply of non-renewable resources, and they doubt this assumption.

To many concerned individuals, it seems to be a hopeless rat race — all countries trying to keep output growing just to keep pace with their growing populations. If the current rate of world population growth continued for just 650 years, then there would be ten persons on every one square metre of the Earth's surface (including all the oceans). Since such population density is impossible, however, population growth will slow down — either painfully through dwindling incomes and death for millions of people or less painfully through rising income levels and improved education, both of which lead to dramatic declines in birth rates. Perhaps paradoxically, then, one of the most important things that we can do to make economic growth sustainable in the longer term is to help the developing countries grow more now. Only with higher incomes can the citizens in these countries achieve higher levels of education and lower birth rates.

Population growth is not the only reason to be concerned that the growth process may not be sustainable. What about non-renewable resources? Many people worry that, if we run out of some of the key inputs to the production process, the whole economic engine will grind to a halt, so that income standards will plummet. Economists are less worried than others about the non-renewable resource issue because they have identified a self-correction mechanism that operates in a free market for resources.

Suppose you are the owner of a non-renewable resource and are trying to make a difficult decision. Should you sell some of your scarce resource now and invest the proceeds? Or should you leave it in the ground and sell it at a future date, say, next period? If today's price of the resource is P_1 then you would get a sum of money equal to P_1 should you sell it today. You could then invest this sum for a period and earn rate of interest r. So if you mined the resource, sold it now, and invested the proceeds, the amount of money that you would have by next period would be the selling price P_1 scaled up by the factor $(1 + r)$.

Your second option is to leave the resource in the ground for now and then sell it in the second period for price P_2. You would choose this option if the return, P_2, is bigger than the return of the first option, $P_1(1 + r)$. An equilibrium does not exist unless you are indifferent about whether you sell the resource now or keep it for the future. Thus, in equilibrium

$$P_1(1 + r) = P_2.$$

Consider what happens if this condition is not met. For instance, if P_1 is high, then the expression on the left is greater than P_2. In this case, resource owners would mine the resource quickly, bringing a great quantity to the market. By flooding the market now, they would reduce the current price, P_1, reducing the left-hand side and bringing it into line with the right-hand side. Similarly, if the current price, P_1, is very low, then resource owners would tend to withhold supply today, shifting the supply curve for today dramatically to the left. That shift forces P_1 up, and once again the two sides of the equation are brought into balance.

If we transpose terms, divide by P_1, and re-express the equilibrium condition, then it becomes

$$(P_2 - P_1)/P_1 = r.$$

This version of the equilibrium condition states that in equilibrium, the private incentive for profit among resource owners will ensure that, on average, the prices of natural resources will rise at a rate equal to the rate of interest.

Consider the implication of this fact for a graph showing any natural resource price over time. In such a graph, we must obtain an exponential growth curve. Eventually, the price of a non-renewable natural resource must go to infinity — and at an ever faster pace. Hence, there must eventually be tremendous profit incentives for people to invent substitutes for these natural resources. If people are not doing so now, then it simply means that we are still on the fairly flat region of the exponential growth path for prices. But once prices really start taking off, many people will engage in activities to find ways to do without these resources.

So the truly daunting issue that follows from natural resource use is not a problem of availability; rather, it is the effect on the environment. We can expect the market mechanism to automatically solve the availability issue, but we cannot expect it to cope with pollution problems automatically, because of all the spill-over issues, the property rights issues, and the equity issues (which we discussed in Chapter 7). No one owns the environment, so there is no self-correction mechanism to regulate its use.

SUMMARY

Here is a brief summary of some of the key concepts covered in this chapter. Growth in living standards stems from rising **labour productivity**. Some of the factors that lead to more rapid increases in productivity are **investment** in physical capital (which requires **saving**), investment in **education** and **research**, a culture that accepts the **profit motive** (entrepreneurial activity), and institutions and tax structures that facilitate **flexible labour markets**.

Since diminishing returns apply to the investment in physical capital but not to the investment in knowledge capital, the former initiative raises the growth rate only temporarily, while the latter policy can raise the growth rate permanently. However, since a long wait may be involved before this relative advantage of investment in education becomes important, both policies are worthwhile.

In a small open economy, increases in national saving do not increase the stock of physical capital with which labour can work. Since the benefits come in the form of decreased foreign debt, they do not **trickle down** to those receiving only labour income.

There is an automatic control mechanism regarding the running out of natural resources, since the incentive to invent substitutes grows exponentially over time. Nonetheless, growth is **sustainable** only if pollution and population growth can be controlled. Since these challenges require sacrifices, it will be easier to meet them if we can secure rising living standards in the relatively near future. We pursue this possibility in more specific terms in the final chapter.

SUGGESTIONS FOR FURTHER READING

T.G. Buchholz, *New Ideas from Dead Economists* (New York: Penguin, 1990), Chapter 3.

P. Krugman, *Peddling Prosperity: Economic Sense and Nonsense in the Age of Diminished Expectations* (New York: Norton, 1994) — this brief book traces the evolution of economic ideas on economic policy.

D. Landes, *The Wealth and Poverty of Nations: Why Some Are Rich and Some So Poor* (New York: Norton, 1998) — this lengthy book argues that certain cultural traits are central for economic growth.

J. Rifkin, *The End of Work* (New York: G.P. Putnam, 1995), and R. Lipsey, *Economic Growth, Technological Change, and Canadian Economic Policy* (Toronto: C.D. Howe Institute, 1996) — opposing views on the effects of rising labour productivity in the information age.

WEB ACTIVITIES

www.csls.ca
Web site for the Centre for the Study of Living Standards in Ottawa. Click on "Conference on Canada in the 21st Century: A Time for Vision." Several papers there make excellent reading, such as R. Harris, "Determinants of Productivity Growth and the Prospective Development in Productivity Trends."

www.fraserinstitute.ca
The Fraser Institute's *Public Policy Sources* series includes "Productivity and Economic Performance: An Overview of the Issues."

www.strategis.ic.gc.ca/sc_ecnmy/engdoc/homepage.html
Industry Canada's *Micro-Economic Monitor* contains articles on the slowdown of productivity growth and the Canada–U.S. productivity gap.

CHAPTER TWENTY

Alternatives for Raising Living Standards

LEARNING OBJECTIVES

After reading this chapter, you should understand
- how benefit–cost analysis is used to evaluate policies that involve short-term pain for long-term gain;
- how initiatives such as free trade and debt reduction receive support from this analysis; and
- why certain aspects of benefit–cost analysis — in particular, the treatment of income distribution effects and uncertainty — remain controversial.

INTRODUCTION

Over the past two decades, the Canadian government has made raising prosperity a priority. Part of the rationale for free trade (the primary initiative of the 1980s) was that it would facilitate longer production runs and, through increased competition, spur domestic firms to become more productive. Part of the rationale for government debt reduction (the main focus of the 1990s) was to lower interest payment obligations in order to make room in the budget for public investments and tax cuts that might raise productivity. It is hard to exaggerate the importance of this goal. An increase in the productivity growth rate of just one-quarter of 1 percent can — over a period of 30 years — raise living standards by 7.5 percent. At 1999 values, that's an extra $9 000 *every* year for an average family of four.

While the goal of raising prosperity seems to be uncontroversial, important questions remain. Can our government's policies deliver anything approaching an extra one-quarter of 1 percent per year of growth? How much short-term pain must be incurred to achieve this long-term gain? How can we assess whether this trade-off is worth it? These are the questions that concern us in this final chapter.

BENEFIT–COST ANALYSIS

Since the benefits of growth policies extend over many years, it is difficult to compare them to the current costs. If you need to review the calculation of present values, then read the rest of this section. It concerns the decision of an individual firm to invest in a new computer. If you do not need this review, then move straight to the next section, where we use the benefit–cost approach to evaluate a country's decision to invest in a free-trade agreement.

Consider a computer that costs $5500 today. Assume that, if a firm buys the computer, it will save clerical and other expenses equal to $2000 per year in each of the subsequent three years. For simplicity, assume that the computer is useless after three years. Is it worth investing in the computer? The sum of the three benefits, $6000, exceeds the cost, $5500, but this comparison ignores the fact that the firm is not indifferent about whether money is received today or received in the future. Funds received earlier can be used to earn interest or pay back loans.

We can obtain a consistent answer to this investment question by calculating the present value of the benefits, thereby making both sides of the ledger comparable. The first component of the stream of benefits is the $2000 received at the end of the first year of using the new computer. Suppose the interest rate that the firm can receive on any loan is 5 percent. The firm loses the opportunity of lending out the $2000 and earning 5 percent (or $100) on that loan, since it does not receive the $2000 saving until the end of the year. Thus, the present value of that $2000 is $2000/(1.05) or $1905. The second component of benefits is the $2000 received at the end of the second year. Since, by waiting that long, the firm loses two years of (compound) interest earnings, the present value of this second benefit is $2000/(1.05)^2$, or $1814. Given the rate of interest available to the firm, it is indifferent about whether (on the one hand) it receives $1814 immediately (which it could lend out for two years and — through compound interest — turn into a sum equal to $2000) or (on the other hand) it simply receives the $2000 two years later. Finally, the third component of benefits is the $2000 received at the end of the third year. By similar reasoning, the firm loses interest compounded for the three years. Thus, the present value of this component is $2000/(1.05)^3$, or $1728. The present value of the entire stream of benefits is the sum of the three component present values: $5447. In this example, the firm is essentially indifferent about whether it buys the computer or not. The firm would care more if the interest rate was not 5 percent; for example, a higher interest rate makes the future benefits have a smaller present value. Now you are ready to consider the more complicated investments made by entire nations.

INVESTING IN FREE TRADE

In Chapter 10, we learned that free trade allows countries to exploit the principle of comparative advantage by concentrating on those industries in which each is more productive and by achieving the cost savings that follow from producing for a larger world market. We learned that, in the case of Canada's 1989 free-trade arrangement with the United States, it was estimated that the deal would increase total Canadian income by about 3 percent of GDP each year. Let us pretend that we are back in 1989 trying to decide whether this long-term annual gain is worth the short-term pain involved in acquiring it. Costs exist because some firms previously protected from competition by tariffs are forced out of business, and some jobs are lost. Eventually, more jobs are created in the industries that expand after free trade, but some individuals are hurt for a significant time while these adjustments take place.

To permit an illustrative calculation, let us assume that the free-trade deal was expected to be *very* disruptive. It was expected to cause 10 percent of our labour force to be unemployed for a full five years — beyond those who were already unemployed. This assumption implies that total output would be lower by about 10 percent for this five-year period. This is much more disruption than what actually took place, but it is useful to exaggerate the costs in the illustrative calculation. With this assumption, then, the costs involve five components: the loss of 10 percent of the first year's GDP, the present value of 10 percent of the second year's GDP, and so on for four years — as specified in the equation that follows this paragraph. It is a historical fact that, on average, GDP grows each year. Let us use n to stand for this average annual growth rate; similarly, let r stand for the rate of interest. On average, then, GDP in year 2 can be expected to be $(1 + n)$ times GDP in year 1, and, to discount this amount back to year 1 values, it must be divided by the discount factor $(1 + r)$. This explains the second term in the square brackets in the equation below.

Present Value of Costs
$$= (0.1)(\text{today's GDP})[1 + (1 + n)/(1 + r) + (1 + n)^2/(1 + r)^2 + (1 + n)^3/(1 + r)^3 + (1 + n)^4/(1 + r)^4].$$

The final three terms involve both the growth factor compounding for one more period each time in the numerator (because GDP continues to grow) and the discount factor compounding for one more period each time in the denominator. Since the average annual growth rate for real GDP (3 percent in recent decades) is slightly less than the average real interest rate (5 percent), the present value of this sum is slightly less than five times the annual loss of 10 percent of GDP. According to these illustrative calculations, then, the disruption caused by adjusting to free trade is equivalent to a one-time loss of 48 percent of the first year's GDP.

The following equation is an explanation of how we add up the benefits of the free-trade deal. We have assumed that, during the first five years, only disruption occurs. Then, starting only in year 5, we receive the bonus of 3 percent of GDP each year. Since the GDP will have grown at rate n for five years by then, the first benefit component is 3 percent of today's GDP scaled up by the compound growth factor $(1 + n)^5$. But since we do not receive that benefit for five years, its present value equivalent is calculated by dividing by $(1 + r)^5$. This explains the first term in the equation:

Present Value of Benefits
$$= (0.03)(\text{today's GDP})\{[(1 + n)/(1 + r)]^5 + [(1 + n)/(1 + r)]^6 + \ldots + [(1 + n)/(1 + r)]^{\text{infinity}}\}.$$

The other terms represent the present value of the benefits received in the sixth, seventh, and all future years. In each future period, growth compounds for one more year (making the numerator larger), but the discount factor is ever larger as well, since we have to wait ever longer to receive these benefits (so the denominator is larger too). Using our illustrative values (growth averaging 3 percent and interest rates averaging 5 percent), the *net* benefit of the free-trade deal is calculated as the excess of benefits over costs:

Net Benefit = [(0.03)(43.72) − (0.1)(4.8)](today's GDP) = 83% of today's GDP.

Despite having assumed that the disruptions would be dramatically larger than what occurred in reality, we see that the free-trade agreement still leads to a net benefit equivalent to a one-time gift that is more than five-sixths of an entire year's GDP. At 1999 values, that is $750 billion — a truly staggering amount of material items. Rejecting free trade means refusing to accept these items. The amount is enough to give *each* member of the losing group (assumed to be 10 percent of the labour force) half a million dollars as compensation. While there were some adjustment assistance policies, those who were hurt by the 1989 initiative were not offered an explicit compensation package of this sort. But it is still worth going through the calculation, since it demonstrates that more than adequate compensation could have been offered, and the rest of the population would still have had significant net benefits left over.

INVESTING IN EDUCATION

Embracing free trade is just one of the ways in which society can choose to accept short-term pain for long-term gain. Other such policy initiatives are investment in education and deficit reduction. In this and the following section of the chapter, the focus shifts from a comparison of the pain and gain associated with one particular policy to a comparison of the long-term gains that can be expected from two alternative policies. First we consider investment in education; then, in the next section, we explore an increase in national savings. Since governments have limited budgets, and since individuals have limited tolerance for short-term pain, we need to understand which method of raising living standards can be expected to bring "more bang for the buck."

Many cross-sectional studies have estimated the higher earnings that accompany education; it turns out that, on average, formal education is an investment with a 10 percent private return. This finding does not necessarily mean that education actually creates ability at this rate. After all, in a world where reliable information is costly, employers find it difficult to know which individuals are more capable. By pursuing formal education, more able individuals may simply be acquiring a signal that employers can use at no cost to decrease the risk that they incur when hiring these individuals. People who invest in the signal get higher-paying jobs — even if education does not increase their ability much. Perhaps, then, we should not apply the 10 percent return to *nationwide* decisions concerning investment in education. Despite this concern, we proceed to do just this; later we return to address the resulting bias.

We consider a permanent transfer of one percent of GDP out of the provision of consumption goods and into the education sector. The assumption of 10 percent return implies that, by the end of the first year alone, this reallocation is equivalent to society's buying an equity that pays a dividend equal to 10 percent of 1 percent of each year's GDP every year into the indefinite future. In a formula, the benefit of just this year's "equity purchase" is

$$(0.1)(0.01)(\text{today's GDP})[a + a^2 + a^3 + \ldots + a^{\text{infinity}}],$$

where $a = (1 + n)/(1 + r)$. The term in square brackets is needed to allow for two facts: that GDP grows over time (at rate n), and that future benefits must be discounted (at rate r) to be expressed in present value terms. This term can be re-expressed as $[(1 + a + a^2 + \ldots) - 1]$, and, using the simplification explained on page 148, this expression simplifies further to $V = [(1 - n)/(r - n)]$. By choosing units of measure so that today's GDP is unity, we can write the benefit of the first year's equity purchase as $(0.1)(0.01)(1 - n)/(r - n)$. The cost of this resource reallocation is a reduction in consumption equal to (0.01). The net benefit, therefore, is $NB = (0.01)[((0.1)(1 - n)/(r - n)) - 1]$. Finally, since a permanent shift of resources into the education sector involves an "equity purchase" every year from now on, the present value of this entire package is $NB(1 - n)/(r - n) = NB \times V$.

We are interested in the percentage improvement in living standards — that is, the increase in the present value of the nation's consumption possibilities. Without the investment in education, that present value is simply the discounted value of GDP into the indefinite future, which is today's GDP times the present value factor, or V. Thus, the percentage change in living standards is calculated as: $([NB \times V] - V)/V = NB$. Representative values for r and n (0.05 and 0.03, respectively) yield $NB = 0.039$, so the improvement in living standards is equivalent to a one-time increase of about 3.9 percent.

When examining growth theory in the previous chapter, we found that more education is like a permanent increase in the economy's growth rate. But now we see that it is equivalent to only a small increase in that growth rate — less than one-tenth of 1 percent. This amount can be verified by considering n rising from 0.03 to 0.0308. This increase (along with r = 0.05) raises the present value factor, $(1 - n)/(r - n)$, by 4 percent. Today we invest only a few percentage points of GDP in education. Thus, an increase of 1 percent would be a major initiative. Even when the analysis has overstated the aggregate benefit of education (given the signalling controversy), we see that a very large investment is equivalent to a very small increase in the growth rate. This result suggests that prudent policy-makers should not emphasize the *permanent* growth *rate* effects of investment in knowledge capital. Nevertheless, since a once-for-all increase in living standards of 3.9 percent is significant, and since the equity dimensions of investment in education are appealing, the initiative is not rejected by this analysis.

DEFICIT AND DEBT REDUCTION

In Chapter 19, we considered higher national savings; we learned that, for a small open economy, the benefits come in the form of smaller foreign debt service obligations. Let us explore the likely magnitudes involved with this initiative. Using F, X – IM, and r to denote the level of foreign debt, net exports, and the interest rate, we can write the relationship that defines how our foreign indebtedness changes over time:

$$\Delta F = rF - (X - IM).$$

This equation states that debt increases during any year in which our interest payment obligations to foreigners exceed the net revenue that we earn by selling goods to the rest of the world. Long-run equilibrium requires that the debt-to-GDP ratio stay constant. Since the GDP growth rate is n, this equilibrium condition stipulates that the percentage change in debt, $\Delta F/F$, equals n — that is, $\Delta F = nF$. By substituting this expression for ΔF into the previous equation, we have

$$(r - n)F = X - IM.$$

We combine this relationship with two others: the GDP identity, GDP = C + I + X – IM (ignoring government for simplicity), and the consumption function C = (1 – s)(GDP – rF). The variable s is the marginal propensity to save; consumption is proportional to disposable income, which in turn is GDP minus foreign debt service payments.

We eliminate X – IM and F by substitution and divide so that aggregates are measured as ratios to GDP. With c and i standing for the ratios of C and I to GDP, these steps lead to

$$c = (1 - s)(n - ri)/(n - rs).$$

We focus on the percentage increase in c. Illustrative values for the parameters are r = 0.05, n = 0.03, i = 0.20, and s rising from 0.20 to 0.23 (a change in the savings rate roughly equal to what federal fiscal policy accomplished through deficit reduction in the 1990s). When these values are substituted into the equation, we see that living standards rise by 4 percent.

As just noted, increasing the national savings rate by 3 percent should not be seen as a particularly large initiative. It appears, then, that a politically feasible increase in national savings raises living standards by about the same amount as a large investment in education. We conclude our illustrative comparison of the long-term benefits that accompany these two initiatives by noting that — from a practical point of view — it would not be prudent for the government to stress the distinction between permanent and temporary growth *rate* effects.

CONTROVERSIAL ASPECTS OF BENEFIT–COST ANALYSIS

There are at least two reasons why benefit–cost analysis is controversial; the issues concern income distribution and uncertainty. First, even though the present value of long-term benefits exceeds the current costs, a policy should not necessarily be supported. After all, if you are among those who suffer the short-term pain, then it is little consolation that future generations will enjoy benefits that are bigger than your losses. Some people have asked, "What have future generations ever done for me?" Even restricting attention to future generations, it is rare for the benefits to be distributed equally. For example, we have learned that an increase in national savings brings no direct benefit to wage earners in a small open economy. For this reason, investments in education are important. In addition, governments should ensure that significant portions of the new programs and tax cuts that follow debt reduction go to labour.

Once again, we confront the trade-off between efficiency and equity. But a benefit–cost study is not intended to be the complete examination of any policy issue; it is just an applied efficiency analysis. When net benefits are positive, economists are not saying that everybody wins if that policy is adopted. Instead, they are saying that the winners could fully compensate the losers and still have some winnings left over. Thus, benefit–cost analysis is based on the principle of hypothetical compensation. Economists approach policy in two stages: first, we ask whether the policy does or does not increase the size of the pie; and second, we ask how a policy of supplementary redistribution can ensure that everyone's slice of that larger pie can be made bigger. Benefit–cost analysis is the profession's stage 1 tool. As a result, we should not expect it to address income distribution questions. Nonetheless, income redistribution is controversial, and as a result policy-makers often do not move on to stage 2. Also, even when not ignored, redistribution can be difficult. For example, if it calls for redistributing from capitalists to workers and capital is mobile internationally, it cannot be accomplished (as we learned on page 107). When these difficulties are encountered, policies are adopted without compensation for those who lose. My hope is that books like this one can decrease the likelihood that benefit–cost analysis will be misapplied in this way.

As just noted, beyond the income distribution question, the most controversial aspect of benefit–cost analysis is the treatment of uncertainty. The most uncertain costs and benefits are those expected to occur in the distant future. If we are certain that they will materialize, then we will discount them at a risk-free rate of interest, such as 5 percent, as we did in the examples discussed earlier. But if there is a strong chance that they will not materialize, then we will discount them more heavily — say, with a 15 percent discount rate. This is what firms do when investing in new plant and equipment. The larger the risk, the larger is the risk premium added to the interest rate.

To see why this is controversial, consider the prospect of global warming and a benefit–cost analysis of a major expenditure intended to lessen this problem 200 years from now. Since we know so little about global warming and about events that may happen years from now that could negate the beneficial effects of the current investment, standard practice calls for a high discount rate. As a result, even very large future benefits (e.g., the avoidance of global warming) have very small present values, and many investments of this sort cannot pass a benefit–cost test. Needless to say, environmentalists are not impressed. Nor are economists. Along with psychologists, some economists use experiments and surveys to learn more about how people react to fundamental uncertainty. In time, we hope to refine this aspect of benefit–cost analysis.

In the meantime, it is important to be aware of this arbitrary dimension of the analysis. All policies should be examined with several discount rates considered. Only then can we be confident that support for a particular policy is fairly general.

THE FUNDAMENTAL CHALLENGE

The problems of global warming and world pollution highlight the connection between developing countries and developed ones such as Canada. Just to stay alive, citizens in developing countries have strong incentives to cut down rainforests at an alarming rate, and there are spill-over effects for the entire planet. The citizens of developing countries cannot afford to cease this activity for the general benefit of everyone. In the short run, transfer payments to these developing countries are necessary. In the longer run, we need to foster economic growth (not discourage it), especially in the developing countries, so that transfers do not need to be permanent.

But where are developed countries to find the resources to offer this help? Economics is the study of choices. Is there any advice that the discipline can offer to society about how we might set priorities among the many claims on our governments?

One of the biggest challenges we face is how to increase efficiency within the public sector. With all the competing demands on government funds and a commitment to compassionate social policy that seems to be part of the Canadian identity, we just cannot afford inefficiency. Hence, economists advocate the adoption of voucher systems for pollution control, education, and health care, among other policy areas. The key feature of voucher programs is that they maintain universal access while harnessing the **efficiency** of **private incentives** in the **provision** of **public services**. Our desire to do so many things through the government can then be pursued in a realistic fashion that accepts human nature as we know it.

SUMMARY

Perhaps the central theme of this book has been how, by relying on our knowledge of private incentives when designing social and economic policies, we can minimize the trade-off between equity and efficiency objectives. My hope is that you are now more equipped to form your own opinion on these important questions.

I have tried to show that it is possible to have both a soft heart and a hard head at the same time. The softness of one's heart concerns equity; the hardness of one's head concerns efficiency. We confront various combinations of hearts and heads every day in public policy discussions. Some people give overriding emphasis to a hard-head approach. They understand that we cannot spend beyond our means indefinitely, and they advocate deficit reduction even if it involves gutting social policies. Others give overriding emphasis to a soft-heart approach. They push for the expansion of social policies even when we cannot afford current spending levels. Economics shows that respect for both the principle of scarcity and a policy of compassionate social programs is possible, but only with increased awareness of, and reliance on, private incentives.

SUGGESTIONS FOR FURTHER READING

D. Cohen, *The Misfortunes of Prosperity: An Introduction to Modern Political Economy* (Cambridge, MA: MIT Press, 1995) — a fast-paced and insightful tour of the dominant ideas in political economy.

R. Heilbroner, *An Inquiry into the Human Prospect* (New York: Norton, 1974, revised 1980) — an optimistic, but at the same time troubling, essay challenging us to contemplate the gap in living standards between developed countries and developing countries.

J. Richards, *Retooling the Welfare State* (Toronto: C.D. Howe Institute, 1997), Policy Study 31 — a former MP for the New Democrats, now a professor of business administration, indicates how the market mechanism and incentives can be respected as a durable welfare state is rebuilt.

W. Robson and W. Scarth (eds.), *Equality and Prosperity: Finding Common Ground* (Toronto: C.D. Howe Institute, 1997), Policy Study 30 — three essays concerning debt reduction, income inequality, and economic growth.

WEB ACTIVITIES

www.brook.edu

The Web site of the Brookings Institution in Washington, DC; click on "Policy Briefs" for short essays on central topics such as reforming the international financial system and pursuing prosperity through tax reform.

www.cdhowe.org

Click on "Benefactors Lectures (1999)" for the article by P. Fortin, "The Canadian Standard of Living: Is There a Way Up?"

APPENDIX
Questions and Answers

If you have been reading this book to increase your literacy in economics, then you may not want to work through these practice questions. But if you are enrolled in a course in economics, then you will be writing examinations with questions like those that follow. Experience has shown that students can know a lot of the material but still do rather poorly on examinations. This is because most examinations test your ability to solve specific problems rather than ask you to review in your own words what you have learned. Without practice at problem solving, many students have difficulty showing how much they know. This appendix contains 100 questions (with answers provided on pages 281–88). You are strongly advised to struggle with the questions *before* checking the answers. It is only by struggling that you can identify which parts of the material you need to review.

Chapter 1

1. Which of the following assumptions is not typically made by economists?
   a. Rationality is sufficiently prevalent to engender order in observed behaviour.
   b. Wants will always exceed the means to satisfy them.
   c. People are generally altruistic.
   d. Resources are generally more productive in some uses than in others.
2. Assume that the demand and supply functions for beans are as follows:

   quantity demanded = 12 – P, and
   quantity supplied = 2P,

where P is the price in dollars, and quantities are measured in millions. Suppose that the government is interested in raising the incomes of bean farmers and tries to do so by setting a legal minimum price for beans at $6. Compare the quantity of beans bought and sold, as well as the total expenditure by households on beans, before and after the government policy.

3. "If economists restrict their attention to positive questions, then economics is a discipline that remains value-free." Is this statement true or false? Explain your answer.

4. "The concept of opportunity cost is illustrated by the area under the production possibility curve." Is this statement true or false? Explain your answer.

5. "When the Winter Olympics were held in Calgary, both the quantity and the price of rental accommodation shot up. This outcome proved that the assumption of negatively sloped demand curves is sometimes a bad theory." Is this statement true or false? Explain your answer.

Chapter 2

6. The wine industry is in the doldrums. Taxes on alcohol are rising and pushing up costs. Also, because people have become more health-conscious and more aware of laws against drinking and driving, they are drinking less. These factors combined imply that (I) the price of wine must have risen and/or (II) the quantity of wine sold must have declined.
   a. I and II.
   b. II, but not I.
   c. I, but not II.
   d. neither I nor II.

7. Consider the following demand and supply functions for commodity X:

   quantity demanded = 100 − 4P, and
   quantity supplied = 6P,

   where P is the price of X in dollars.
   a. If this market is in equilibrium, what is the price of X, and how many units are produced?
   b. Suppose the government buys some of good X to stockpile it in case there is an interruption in future supply. Assume that, in addition to the private purchases that follow from the demand function, the government buys 10 units of X each period. What is the increase in the total sales revenue received in each period by the producers of X as a result of this policy?
   c. Now consider that the price of X has been set at non-market-clearing levels.
      (i) If there is a shortage of 20 units, what must the set price be?

      (ii) If there is a surplus of 50 units, what must the set price be?

   d. Now suppose this country opens its borders to foreign trade.

      (i) If the world price of X is $6, how many units will this country export or import?

      (ii) If the world price of X is $12, how many units will this country export or import?

8. The government is considering alternative policies to restrict the consumption of beer. The supply and demand curves are

quantity demanded = 300 – P, and
quantity supplied = (1/2)P,

where P is price expressed in cents and quantity is measured in millions of bottles. What are the equilibrium price and quantity before the imposition of any government policy?

   a. The first policy considered is to impose a quota of 80 million bottles on the production and sale of beer (i.e., no more than this number could be sold). What would the new equilibrium price be if this policy were introduced? If the government auctioned off the quota rights, how much revenue would it receive?

   b. The second proposed policy is to impose a per-unit tax on beer. What level of tax would be necessary to restrict beer consumption to 80 million bottles? How much revenue would the government collect?

   c. Compare the effects of the two policies.

9. "Price controls — whether floors or ceilings — are likely to lead to a smaller volume of transactions and the development of black markets." Is this statement true or false? Explain your answer.

10. "Economic analysis supports the proposition that the highest sales taxes should be on luxuries, not necessities." Is this statement true or false? Explain your answer.

Chapter 3

11. Assume that Graeme has a demand curve for steaks given by

Q = 10 – 0.4P,

where Q and P stand for the quantity of steaks and the dollar price of steaks. If the price of a steak is $5, what is Graeme's consumer surplus?

12. Assume that the demand for wheat is given by the following equation:

Q = 10 – 0.5P,

where Q is the output of wheat and P is the price of wheat in dollars. Assume also that wheat can be produced for a price of $5, no matter how much wheat is produced (i.e., there are no diminishing returns in the wheat industry).

a. What are the equilibrium price and quantity for wheat?

b. Suppose the government wants to maximize the sales revenue for wheat farmers by setting a quota (a maximum amount of wheat allowed to be sold in the overall market). What quota would the government set?

c. Compared with a free market, how much does this quota policy cost society?

13. The demand curve for video tapes is given by $Q = 10 - P$, where Q stands for quantity in millions and P for price in dollars. Video tapes are produced in a competitive industry with constant costs, and the price is $4 each. When an excise tax of $2 per unit is levied on the sale of video tapes, it both raises revenue and imposes a cost on society. What is the ratio of the cost to society to the amount of taxes paid?

14. Water is essential to life, while diamonds are not. If market prices are supposed to represent underlying value, why is the price of diamonds so much higher than that of water?

15. "The higher the price elasticity of demand for good X, the less able are the producers of good X to pass the burden of a sales tax on to the buyers of good X." Is this statement true or false? Explain your answer.

Chapter 4

16. Consider a firm whose short-run production function is given as follows:

Workers Hired	Total Output
0	0
1	20
2	35
3	45

The firm's product sells at a fixed price of $10. The firm has no fixed costs and must pay wages at the rate of $120 per worker each period. Use these data to determine the optimal quantity of labour to hire (relying on the marginal product [in dollars] equals wage rule) and to determine the optimal quantity of output to produce (relying on the marginal cost equals price rule). Since the firm has only one variable factor in the short run (labour), you must check that your answers are internally consistent (i.e., once a certain quantity of labour is hired, the production function dictates what output is produced).

17. A firm can always increase its output by one unit at a marginal cost of $20. Its fixed cost is $200. The firm's average cost curve

a. crosses its marginal cost curve at the lowest point on the marginal cost curve.

b. crosses its marginal cost curve at the lowest point on the average cost curve.

c. never crosses its marginal cost curve.

d. is a straight line with a positive slope.

18. An airline is considering adding an extra flight from Toronto to Ottawa. The total cost of the flight, including overhead, is $5500. The variable cost of the flight is $2000. The revenue from the flight is expected to be $3000. Should the flight be added? Why?

a. No; the revenue ($3000) is below the cost ($5500).

b. No; the addition to profit is very small and not worth the effort.

c. Yes; profit is increased by $3000 – $2000.

d. Yes; profit is increased by $3000.

19. "Anything that raises marginal cost will raise average cost, but an item that raises average cost will not necessarily raise marginal cost." Is this statement true or false? Explain your answer.

20. Explain why you think that the law of diminishing returns is or is not consistent with the possibility of increasing returns to scale.

Chapter 5

21. Under perfect competition, price will equal minimum average cost

a. in the short run.

b. in the long run.

c. always.

d. never.

22. Consider a competitive industry that initially contains 100 identical firms. The short-run costs of each firm are

Output	Total Cost
0	$30
1	120
2	150
3	200
4	270
5	360

and the industry demand function is $Q = 820 - 6P$, where Q and P stand for industry output and price in dollars.

a. What is the short-run equilibrium price? How much does each firm produce? How much profit does each firm make?

b. Assume that this industry has constant returns to scale — that is, if new firms enter, they will have the same cost function as existing firms. When this industry reaches long-run equilibrium, what will industry output be, and how many firms will comprise the industry? (To answer these questions, assume that firms cannot produce a fraction of a unit. With this restriction, full equilibrium will not occur exactly at the minimum point of the average cost curve, but there will still be zero economic profit in the long run.)

23. Suppose good Y can be produced at a constant marginal cost of $4 per unit. Assume the demand function for Y is $Q = 100 - 5P$. Suppose the government takes over the production of good Y and makes it available free to all users. Compared with the competitive market outcome,

    a. there is a net gain to society of $40.
    b. there is a net loss to society of $40.
    c. there is a net gain to society of $20.
    d. there is a net loss to society of $20.
    e. none of the above statements is true.

24. "If market price falls below the minimum point of a competitive firm's average cost curve, then it should shut down to avoid a loss." Is this statement true or false? Explain your answer.

25. "If the demand for the output of a competitive industry (which involves constant returns to scale) falls, then each firm will end up producing at a reduced level of output." Is this statement true or false? Explain your answer.

Chapter 6

26. Suppose that a profit-maximizing monopolist facing a downward-sloping demand curve and constant marginal cost suddenly becomes subject to an excise tax of $T per unit of output. In reacting to the tax, the monopolist will

    a. not change her price per unit.
    b. raise her price per unit by less than $T.
    c. raise her price per unit by exactly $T.
    d. raise her price per unit by more than $T.

27. Consider a natural monopolist with the following total cost and demand functions:

    total cost $= 8 + 2Q$,
    $Q = 6 - (1/2)P$,

    where Q and P stand for quantity and price. If the monopolist chooses the largest output consistent with profit maximization, which output level is chosen? What is the maximum value of a licence fee that the government can levy on this firm without causing it to shut down?

28. This question is designed to show the effect of a maximum price law imposed in a monopoly setting. Suppose that the monopolist's demand schedule and total cost function are those given here:

Quantity	Price	Total Cost
0	$18	$10
1	16	13
2	14	15
3	12	18
4	10	22
5	8	27
6	6	33

a. If the monopolist is an unregulated profit maximizer, then at what level does she set her price and output? How much profit does she earn?

b. Suppose a law is passed making the maximum price for this good $6. What output level will the firm choose? What will be its level of profits?

c. Compare what you have learned from this question with what you learned about maximum price laws in Chapter 2.

29. "Agricultural marketing boards help producers at the expense of consumers." Is this statement true or false? Explain your answer.

30. "According to theory, a monopolist should never operate at a price–quantity combination that is on the inelastic portion of the demand curve for its product." Is this statement true or false? Explain your answer.

Chapter 7

31. "Cartels often break up because most markets are contestable." Is this statement true or false? Explain your answer.

32. "The prisoner's dilemma outcome is less likely to occur in a repeated game (than it is in a one-shot game)." Is this statement true or false? Make up a pay-off table to explain your answer.

33. Two concepts introduced in this chapter are asymmetric information and credible threats. Use the former to explain why a new car suffers such a loss in value the moment it is driven off the lot, and use the latter to explain why William the Conqueror burned all his own ships the moment he and his troops landed in England in 1066.

34. John Kenneth Galbraith, a famous Canadian economist, has levelled sarcastic jibes at the profession throughout his career. One of his allegations concerns the profession's attitude regarding taxes and transfers and the amount of work that people do. Apparently, poor people don't work much because they receive too much money, while rich people don't work much because they receive too little money. Is this characterization of the profession's views accurate? Use some of this chapter's analysis to discuss this proposition.

35. Consider three voters (A, B, and C) and three mutually exclusive options (1, 2, and 3) for dealing with a public policy question. The individual's preferences are as follows A: 1 > 2 > 3; B: 2 > 3 > 1; C: 3 > 1 > 2 (where > means "is preferred to"). The individuals are asked to vote on the alternatives in a sequence of either–or choices (e.g., 1 vs. 2 and then a vote between the winner and option 3) — in the same way that an amendment and then the original motion are considered in Parliament. Which policy will be adopted? Will the order of the votes matter? How do these questions contribute to our assessment of the role of government as an instrument for alleviating market failure?

Chapter 8

36. Detrimental externalities imply all but which one of the following?
    a. The marginal social cost of an increase in output exceeds the marginal private cost.
    b. A misallocation of resources will result from the fact that the private market supplies less output than is socially desirable.
    c. Private firms will concentrate on private costs, ignoring the cost burden that they are imposing on others.
    d. Taxes that impose additional private costs on those causing the externalities are, in principle, capable of correcting the misallocation.

37. Education, especially at the primary and high school levels, provides positive external benefits. A person who is illiterate or poorly educated is more likely to become a public burden or a criminal, so all taxpayers benefit from education. Economists therefore believe that
    a. the provision of education should be left to the free market without interference.
    b. education should be subsidized with public funds.
    c. education should be provided only by the private sector.
    d. teachers' salaries should be raised.

38. Under an emissions tax program, the government sets _____; under an emissions permit program, the government sets _____.
    a. the price of the right to pollute; the price of the right to pollute.
    b. the price of the right to pollute; the permitted total amount of pollution.
    c. the permitted total amount of pollution; the price of the right to pollute.
    d. the permitted total amount of pollution; the permitted total amount of pollution.

39. "It is impossible to charge a price for a pure public good, but this is no problem. Since the marginal cost to society of making the item available to one more person is zero, the optimal planner's rule supports a zero price." Is this statement true or false? Explain your answer.

40. In modern corporations, the owners (shareholders) are often not the same individuals who manage the firm. While profit maximization is the desirable goal for shareholders, it may not be for managers, whose salaries and prestige seem to be linked to the firm's size (as measured by total sales revenue). Examine the effectiveness of an emissions tax imposed on a monopolist who maximizes sales revenue subject to the constraint that economic profits are not negative.

Chapter 9

41. Consider an economy with just two factors of production, labour and capital, both of which are fully employed. Suppose that the supply of labour is ten units and that the marginal product of labour is given by

    marginal product $= 16 - 0.8L$,

    where L is the quantity of labour employed. What is labour's share of national income in this economy?

42. Assume the following demand and supply functions for a commodity:

    demand: $Q = 21 - 2P$, and
    supply: $Q = P$.

    Assume that an excise tax of 3 percent per unit is imposed on the sellers of this commodity.
    a. What percentage of the tax collected is paid by the buyers?
    b. What is the ratio of the net cost to society of this tax to the magnitude of the tax collected?

43. Consider a negative income tax scheme with a guaranteed minimum income level of $6000 for a family of four and a tax rate of 50 percent. Which of the following statements is false?
    a. The break-even level of income is $12 000.
    b. Reducing the tax rate below 50 percent would increase both work incentives and the break-even level of income.
    c. Increasing the minimum guarantee without changing the tax rate will increase the break-even level of income.
    d. If the Uptons earn $4000 in wages, then their total income (earnings plus negative tax receipts) will be $10 000.

44. An individual's personal income taxes rise from $3000 to $7500 when her income rises from $15 000 to $30 000. Calculate this person's average and marginal tax rates. Is the tax system progressive? How could the tax system be changed so that it becomes both more progressive and less of a disincentive to earn additional income?

45. "Sales taxes are particularly unpopular — compared with personal income taxes — since they shrink the size of the overall economic pie

more and cause that smaller total income to be more unequally distributed." Is this statement true or false? Explain your answer.

Chapter 10

46. The domestic demand and supply functions for good X are

    quantity demanded = 10 – P, and
    quantity supplied = P,

    where P is the price of X in dollars. The world price of X is fixed at $6. If free trade is allowed, then this small country
    a. will import one unit of X.
    b. will export one unit of X.
    c. will import two units of X.
    d. will export two units of X.
    e. none of the above is true.

47. The domestic demand and supply functions for good Y are

    quantity demanded = 20 – 2P, and
    quantity supplied = 2P,

    where P is the price of Y in dollars. Y is available from the rest of the world at a fixed price of $3, if this country imposes no tariff. Compared with free trade, what is the net loss to society when a tariff of $2 per unit is imposed?

48. "If a country must restrict imports, then it should impose a tariff, not a quota." Is this statement true or false? Explain your answer.

49. "The principle of comparative advantage implies that even if foreign labour is paid less than Canadian labour, Canadian workers cannot lose in the long run by embracing free trade." Is this statement true or false? Explain your answer.

50. "The one exception to the case for free trade concerns a country with a comparative advantage in producing *all* goods. Such a country is better off operating on a self-sufficient basis." Is this statement true or false? Explain your answer.

Chapter 11

51. In 1981, nominal GDP was $356 billion. In 1982, nominal GDP increased to $375 billion. On the basis of just this information, which of the following statements is true?
    a. The total real output of the economy was greater in 1982 than in 1981.
    b. The whole increase in nominal GDP was the result of inflation.
    c. Real GDP increased from $356 billion to $375 billion.

d. It is impossible to determine what happened to prices and real output from the data on nominal GDP alone.

52. Consider a country that taxes interest earnings at a rate of 33.3 percent. Suppose the nominal interest rate in this country is 6 percent when there is no inflation. If inflation rises to 6 percent and remains there indefinitely, what increase in the nominal rate of interest is required to keep the after-tax real rate of return unchanged? What does this example illustrate about the costs of inflation?

53. "A period of excessive aggregate demand is likely to be followed by a period of stagflation (falling output combined with rising prices) as the inflationary gap self-destructs." Is this statement true or false? Explain your answer.

54. Unexpected inflation redistributes wealth (I) from borrowers to lenders and (II) from the private sector to the government.
a. I and II.
b. I, but not II.
c. II, but not I.
d. neither I nor II.

55. When job seekers become discouraged and stop looking for work, (I) the unemployment rate usually rises, and (II) the participation rate usually falls.
a. I and II.
b. I, but not II.
c. II, but not I.
d. neither I nor II.

Chapter 12

56. Assume that consumption and investment expenditures are determined by the following decision rules:

$$C = 100 + 0.7Y \text{ and}$$
$$I = 200 + 0.1Y,$$

where Y stands for real GDP. What is the equilibrium value of GDP?

57. The greater the slope of the consumption function, (I) the smaller is the marginal propensity to save and (II) the greater is the expenditure multiplier.
a. I and II.
b. I, but not II.
c. II, but not I.
d. neither I nor II.

58. If all of every dollar of increased income goes to savings, taxes, or imports, then the government expenditure multiplier on GDP is
a. zero.

   b. one.
   c. infinity.
   d. $1/(1 - MPC)$.
   e. none of the above.
59. The self-correction process for a recessionary gap includes (I) a downward shift in the short-run aggregate supply curve and (II) an upward shift in the total expenditure line.
   a. I and II.
   b. I, but not II.
   c. II, but not I.
   d. neither I nor II.
60. If the horizontal shift in the aggregate demand curve is $10 billion and the multiplier is four, then what must have been the vertical shift in the total expenditure line?

Chapter 13

61. An increase in income tax rates will lead to all but which one of the following?
   a. a decrease in the size of the government spending multiplier on GDP.
   b. a movement along the aggregate demand curve to a lower price level.
   c. a reduction in the level of GDP.
   d. a shift of the total expenditure line.
62. "Government deficits may impose a burden on future generations if, as a result of crowding out, there is less private investment and a smaller capital stock in the future." Is this statement true or false? Explain your answer.
63. "A temporary cut in sales taxes is likely to have a smaller impact than a permanent change in sales taxes on the timing of household consumption spending." Is this statement true or false? Explain your answer.
64. If the GDP growth rate, the interest rate, and the debt-to-GDP ratio are 5 percent, 8 percent, and 75 percent, respectively, what proportion of GDP must the government collect in taxes just to pay for the interest on the debt?
65. "If government spending and tax rates are adjusted each year to keep the overall budget equal to a deficit of 1 percent of GDP and the GDP growth rate is 5 percent, then the debt-to-GDP ratio must eventually settle at 20 percent." Is this statement true or false? Explain your answer.

Chapter 14

66. Chartered bank deposits at the central bank are (I) one of the Bank of Canada's assets and (II) one of the chartered banks' liabilities.
   a. I and II.
   b. I, but not II.

    c. II, but not I.

    d. neither I nor II.

67. If banks hold currency as reserves in an amount equal to 30 percent of their deposit obligations, if households and firms hold $1 of currency for every $10 of their deposits, and if there is $1000 of currency in existence, what are the total amounts of bank deposits and loans?

68. "A large switch in government deposits from the Bank of Montreal to the Bank of Canada will cause an increase in the Bank Rate." Is this statement true or false? Explain your answer.

69. Deposit insurance

    a. reduces the likelihood of a run on a bank.

    b. protects the shareholders of a bank from losses.

    c. both a and b are true.

    d. neither a nor b is true.

70. The Bank of Canada defines both an operating band for the overnight money market and a monetary conditions index. (I) The operating band is narrowed whenever the Bank Rate increases; (II) the monetary conditions index must rise when both domestic interest rates go up and the domestic currency rises.

    a. I and II.

    b. I, but not II.

    c. II, but not I.

    d. neither I nor II.

Chapter 15

71. After reviewing the day's activity in the government bond market, analysts attributed the rise in bond prices to the activity of the central bank. This means that the central bank was probably (I) trying to lower interest rates (II) by purchasing government bonds.

    a. I and II.

    b. I, but not II.

    c. II, but not I.

    d. neither I nor II.

72. A movement along the money demand curve can be caused by (I) changes in either real GDP or the interest rate and (II) changes in either nominal GDP or the interest rate.

    a. I and II.

    b. I, but not II.

    c. II, but not I.

    d. neither I nor II.

73. With no intervention in the foreign exchange market by the central bank, (I) the balance of payments deficit must be zero and (II) both the government budget and the current account must be in deficit.

    a. I and II.

b. I, but not II.

c. II, but not I.

d. neither I nor II.

74. Which of the following statements is not true, if Mexico and Canada have a flexible exchange rate and a Mexican peso that used to cost 2 cents now costs 1 cent?

a. The Canadian dollar has depreciated relative to the peso.

b. Mexico's aggregate demand curve has shifted to the right.

c. Canada's aggregate demand curve has shifted to the left.

d. Mexico has a balance of payments deficit equal to zero.

75. Consider a country that is attempting to peg its currency at an unrealistically high value. Which of the following is not true?

a. Inflation will not be a serious worry for this country.

b. The country will have a balance of payments deficit.

c. The country will have a balance of payments surplus.

d. The country will be forced to use foreign exchange reserves — gold and holdings of other currencies — in order to buy its own currency.

Chapter 16

76. Which of the following is not a valid reason to oppose activist stabilization policy?

a. doubts about the accuracy of forecasting

b. uncertainties about the response of the private economy to any change in policy

c. a concern that activist policy necessarily means a growing public sector

d. a strong belief that the economy, if left alone, is apt to correct most problems by itself quickly

77. In what ways do policy-makers have to face a trade-off between inflation and unemployment?

a. The cost of reducing inflation via restrictive fiscal and monetary policies is a permanent rise in unemployment.

b. The cost of reducing inflation via restrictive fiscal and monetary policies is a temporary rise in unemployment.

c. The cost of reducing unemployment via expansionary fiscal and monetary policies is virtually nonexistent.

d. The inflationary cost of reducing unemployment via expansionary fiscal and monetary policies is higher in slack times than in boom times.

78. The economy's self-correction mechanism to eliminate a recessionary gap relies on

a. increasing prices, which shift the aggregate supply curve inward.

b. rising wage rates, which shift the aggregate supply curve inward.

c. falling interest rates, which shift the aggregate demand curve outward.

d. falling wage rates, which shift the aggregate supply curve outward.
79. Explain what North America in the 1930s and Japan in the 1990s had in common with respect to monetary policy.
80. Give three examples of automatic stabilizers and explain how they work.

Chapter 17

81. Following an increase in government spending in a small open economy with a flexible exchange rate, there will be
   a. a lasting increase in the price level and a lasting depreciation of the domestic currency.
   b. a lasting increase in the price level and a lasting appreciation of the domestic currency.
   c. a lasting decrease in the price level and a lasting depreciation of the domestic currency.
   d. a lasting decrease in the price level and a lasting appreciation of the domestic currency.
82. For a small open economy on a flexible exchange rate, a depreciation of the domestic currency can be caused by all but which one of the following events?
   a. an increase in the money supply
   b. a switch in government deposits to the central bank
   c. an increase in income tax rates
   d. a decrease in exports
83. If Canada has a fixed exchange rate, then a lasting increase in real GDP can be caused by either
   a. an increase in exports or a decrease in income tax rates.
   b. an increase in the money supply or a decrease in exports.
   c. a decrease in the money supply or an increase in income tax rates.
   d. an increase in the money supply or an increase in income tax rates.
   e. a decrease in the money supply or a decrease in income tax rates.
84. With intermediate imports, a depreciating domestic currency (I) must raise the country's price level and (II) must raise the country's real GDP.
   a. I and II.
   b. I, but not II.
   c. II, but not I.
   d. neither I nor II.
85. "The more that people expect inflation in Canada to exceed inflation in the United States, the more likely it is that Canadian interest rates will exceed U.S. interest rates." Is this statement true or false? Explain your answer.

Chapter 18

86. Under the gold standard, (I) countries with a balance of payments deficit had recessions and (II) countries with a balance of payments surplus had appreciating currencies.

a. I and II.

b. I, but not II.

c. II, but not I.

d. neither I nor II.

87. "Speculation represents behaviour that is unproductive from a social point of view; people make money, but no good or service is produced, and markets are necessarily destabilized." Is this statement true or false? Explain your answer.

88. A currency board (I) involves 100 percent foreign exchange reserves and (II) avoids the destabilizing speculation problem that otherwise characterizes fixed exchange rates.

a. I and II.

b. I, but not II.

c. II, but not I.

d. neither I nor II.

89. "With an effective Tobin tax, an independent central bank operating as a lender of last resort would not be needed." Is this statement true or false? Explain your answer.

90. Suppose the productivity of skilled workers rises, while that of unskilled workers remains the same. Explain what happens to unemployment in both the skilled and the unskilled sectors of the labour market.

Chapter 19

91. Over the longer run, lagging productivity growth in a single country is likely to lead to

a. a large increase in that country's unemployment.

b. greater exports from that country.

c. lower exports from that country.

d. a lower standard of living relative to other countries.

92. Thomas Malthus argued (I) that people were doomed to a subsistence level of existence in the long run and (II) that this prediction followed necessarily from the principle of diminishing returns.

a. I and II.

b. I, but not II.

c. II, but not I.

d. neither I nor II.

93. Consider a closed economy with a given population and state of technical knowledge. If the proportion of GDP saved increases, then (I) the standard of living rises in the long run and (II) the productivity growth rate increases in the long run.

a. I and II.

b. I, but not II.

c. II, but not I.

d. neither I nor II.

94. "Deficit reduction (an increase in national saving) helps capitalists more than labourers in a small open economy." Is this statement true or false? Explain your answer.
95. One ounce of the exhaustible resource zenon now sells for $200 in a competitive market. If the interest rate is 10 percent and if there are no changes in the zenon market over the next two years, how much will one ounce cost then?

Chapter 20

96. If the benefits of dropping a country's tariffs have been estimated to equal 3 percent of that country's GDP (starting at the end of one year and continuing into the indefinite future), if the annual growth in that country's GDP is 3 percent, and if that country's interest rate is 7 percent, what is the present value of the benefits of moving to free trade?
97. Suppose we could increase the annual labour productivity growth rate from 0.5 of one percentage point to 0.6 of one percentage point for the next 50 years. At the end of this period, how much higher would living standards be?
98. Explain how income distribution considerations are treated in benefit–cost analysis and why this practice is controversial.
99. Explain how uncertainty about the future is treated in benefit–cost analysis and why this practice is controversial.
100. Consider a small open economy with a government that always balances its budget. If this government gets smaller by cutting its annual tax collections and transfer payments by the same amount, what will happen to average living standards?

Answers

1. c
2. Before the minimum price law is enacted, P = $4 and quantity (Q) = 8 million, so total expenditure by households, P x Q, is 32 million. After the minimum price law is imposed, P = $6, quantity produced is 12 million, and the quantity sold (demanded) is 6 million. Thus, total household spending is 6 x 6 = 36 million.
3. False — by choosing to study some positive questions and not others, we impose value judgements.
4. False — opportunity cost is shown by the slope of the curve.
5. False — the demand curve simply shifted to the right.
6. b
7. a. P = $10, Q = 60
   b. Before the government purchase plan, P x Q = 600. After it, P x Q = 11 x 66 = $726, so the producers' sales revenue increases by $126.
   c. (i) shortage = demand – supply = (100 – 4P) – 6P = 20, so P = $8.

(ii) surplus = supply – demand = 6P – (100 – 4P) = 50, so P = $15.

d. (i) At P = $6, demand = 76, domestic supply = 36, so 40 are imported.

(ii) At P = $12, supply = 72, demand = 52, so 20 are exported.

8. P = 200, Q = 100

a. P = 220. To produce 80, firms need a price of 160. Total willingness to pay for the quota rights is (220 – 160) x 80 = $48 million.

b. 60 cents per bottle, $48 million.

c. Consumers of beer would be indifferent. The two policies differ only if the quota rights are given away, in which case the firms (not the government) get the extra revenue.

9. False — both lead to less output, but black markets occur only with price ceilings.

10. False — from an efficiency point of view, necessities should be taxed; from an equity perspective, luxuries should be taxed.

11. $80

12. a. Substitute P = 5 into the demand equation: Q = 7.5.

b. To determine maximum sales revenue (the maximum value for P x Q), try substituting several values of P into the demand function. You will find that the combination P = 10 and Q = 5 is the one that yields the biggest value for P x Q (equal to 50). Thus, the quota is that Q not exceed 5.

c. By cutting output from 7.5 to 5, some resources are saved. The value of these resources is 5 per unit, so the saving is 2.5 x 5 = 12.5. But when these 2.5 units of wheat are lost, there is a loss of satisfaction equal to the people's willingness to pay for these units. The area under the demand curve over the 5 to 7.5 quantity range is the amount of this willingness to pay. This area exceeds the value of resources saved by 6.25. Thus, the net loss to society of the quota is 6.25 each period.

13. The ratio is one-quarter. The tax collected is $2 on each of 4 units ($8), while the burden to society is the excess of the area under the demand curve (in the Q = 4 to Q = 6 range) over the cost of those two lost units.

14. According to the optimal purchase rule, prices are proportional to marginal, not total, utilities. Given that water is plentiful, its marginal utility is low (even though the total utility that it generates is high).

15. True

16. In dollar terms, the marginal product schedule is $200, $150, and $100 for employment levels 1, 2, and 3. Since the price of each worker is $120, two workers should be hired. The marginal cost schedule is $6, $8, and $12 for output levels of 20, 35, and 45 units. Since the selling price is $10, it pays to expand to 35 units of output, but not to 45. Thus, only two workers should be hired.

17. c

18. c

19. True

20. They are consistent because they apply to different situations. The law of diminishing returns involves just one input being increased while the other is fixed — for example, a pipeline company can raise its employment of labour while not expanding its pipeline network. Such a decision would likely lower each worker's productivity. Increasing returns to scale involve (say) doubling all inputs. In this case, each new worker is responsible for the same amount of pipeline. And, since the area of a circle rises at a faster rate than does the circumference — as the radius is expanded — a pipeline that involves double the construction material can conduct more than double the product.

21. b

22. a. P = $70, and industry output is 400. Each firm produces 4 and earns profits of (4 x 70) – 270 = $10.

    b. The lowest point on the AC curve that can be reached is $66.67, which occurs at an output level of 3 for each firm. Full equilibrium exists when enough firms have entered the industry to make economic profit equal to zero at this level of output. From the industry demand function, P = $66.67 implies Q = 420. The number of firms is then 420/3 = 140.

23. b

24. True in the long run, but not necessarily true in the short run, since the firm may still be able to make back some of its fixed costs.

25. False

26. b

27. Profits are highest (at 4) when Q = 3. The maximum licence fee is 4.

28. a. MR = MC at Q = 4. The firm charges P = $10, and profits are $18.

    b. The maximum price law makes the average and marginal revenue lines coincide over the Q = 0 to Q = 6 output range. They become a horizontal line up to Q = 6. Beyond that level of output, consumers are unwilling to pay a price as high as $6, so the law has no effect there. With the law, MR = MC = $6 at Q = 6. Thus, the firm charges $6 for each of six units and receives a profit of $3.

    c. With competition, a maximum price law must reduce the quantity available while pushing price down. With monopoly, a maximum price law can simultaneously push price down and increase the quantity available.

29. False — consumers are hurt, but current producers are not helped. Owners of farms at the time that the marketing board was created are the only ones who benefit.

30. True — marginal revenue is negative over the range of output for which demand is inelastic. As long as marginal cost is positive, the MR = MC intersection must occur in the range of output for which demand is elastic.

31. False

32. True

33. Some cars are lemons. Neither buyer nor seller knows which of the new cars will be lemons. But there is asymmetric information in the used-car market; in this case, the seller knows whether her car is a lemon, but the buyer does not. That she is selling the car suggests to buyers that there is a higher probability that the used car is a lemon (compared with the probability for a new car). The price must reflect this higher probability.

William the Conqueror had to accomplish two tasks: demoralize the opposing army, and get a full effort from his own troops. He did this by convincing everyone — in a *credible* fashion — that retreat would not be considered.

34. Economic theory focuses on income at the *margin*, while Galbraith tries to ridicule the analysis by appealing to our intuition about the *total* income received by rich and poor. Whatever a person's income level is, both high marginal tax rates and generous benefits (offered at the margin) for not working discourage that person from earning additional income.

35. There are three possibilities: pit 1 vs. 2, then the winner against 3; pit 1 vs. 3, then the winner against 2; pit 2 vs. 3, then the winner against 1. A different policy wins each time. Since the political process cannot reach a unique ranking of the policies, it is not reasonable to expect the government to act as a benevolent institution that can repair market failures without cost.

36. b

37. b

38. b

39. False — it is true that a zero user charge is appropriate, but we must still decide the appropriate amount of the public good to supply. This is difficult to determine if people have no incentive to reveal their preferences.

40. A sales-revenue-maximizing monopolist will expand output either to the point where the elasticity of demand has fallen to unity or to the point where the average cost curve cuts the demand curve — whichever comes first. If it is the former, then the fact that the emissions tax shifts up the cost curves can be irrelevant. In this case, the tax fails to limit pollution.

41. 2/3

42. a. Supply equals demand implies $P = 21 - 2P$, so $P = Q = 7$ before the tax is levied. If P denotes the price received by sellers, then $P + 3$ is the price paid by buyers. Thus, with the tax involved, supply equals demand implies $P = 21 - 2(P + 3)$, so $P = Q = 5$. The tax collected equals tax per unit times the Q, or $3 \times 5 = 15$. Since the producer price falls by 2, and the consumer price rises by only 1, one-third of the tax burden is borne by consumers.

   b. The payment of tax is not a net loss to society; it is simply a redistribution of funds. But there is a net loss to society involved with this tax, since there are two fewer units of the good being produced and enjoyed. The loss in satisfaction is the area under the demand curve in the Q = 5 to Q = 7 range, and the value of the resources freed up by this cutback is equal to the area under the supply curve over this range of output. The net loss to society is the amount by which the former exceeds the latter, which is 3. Since the net loss is 3 and the tax collected is 15, the net loss is 20 percent of the taxes collected.

43. d

44. At an income of $15 000, the average tax rate is 20 percent, while at $30 000 it is 25 percent. Since the average tax rate rises with income, the tax system is progressive. The marginal tax rate over this income range is 30 percent. Consider a linear tax schedule: tax = t(income – E), where t and E stand for the marginal tax rate and the value of income that is exempted from tax. To cut work disincentives, we need a smaller t; to increase progressiveness, we need either a larger t or a larger E. To achieve both goals, therefore, we need a lower t and a higher E. But this combination means less revenue collected and therefore a smaller government, so important trade-offs cannot be avoided.

45. False — sales taxes are unpopular for equity reasons; compared with income taxes, they raise the overall economic pie.

46. d

47. $8

48. True — what is revenue for the domestic government with a tariff becomes windfall profits for the importing companies with a quota.

49. False — if a country's comparative advantage lies in providing goods for which the production process is not labour intensive, then wages will fall relative to other factor returns. Thus, while the country as a whole benefits from free trade, without transfer payments, labour can lose.

50. False — by definition, a country cannot have a comparative advantage in producing everything.

51. d

52. The real after-tax yield with no inflation is 6(1 – 0.33) – 0 = 4. With 6 percent inflation, the nominal rate of interest would have to rise to the value given by i as determined in: i(1 – 0.33) – 6 = 4. That value of i is 15 percent. Since nominal interest rates tend only to rise about one for one with inflation, this example illustrates that the real after-tax return to saving is reduced significantly even by modest inflation. Lower saving means less investment in new capital. With less capital, workers are less productive, and the standard of living is lower.

53. True

54. c

55. c

56. 1500

57. a

58. b

59. a
60. $2.5 billion
61. b
62. True
63. False
64. 6 percent
65. True
66. d
67. The total currency in existence must be held in one of two places: in bank vaults as reserves or in public hands. Thus,

    currency = reserves + currency in public hands.

    We are given that reserves = 0.3(deposits), that currency in public hands = 0.1(deposits), and that currency = $1000. Thus,

    $1000 = (0.3 + 0.1)deposits,

    so deposits = $2500. The banks' balance sheets stipulate that liabilities (deposits) must be matched by assets (reserves plus loans). Thus, loans equal deposits minus reserves = (1 − 0.3) x $2500 = $1750.
68. True
69. a
70. c
71. a
72. d
73. b
74. a
75. c
76. c
77. b
78. d
79. Both involved the money supply curve intersecting the money demand curve on the flat portion of the latter — a situation that makes expansionary monetary policy of limited use for stimulating the economy.
80. Three examples are the personal income tax system, employment insurance, and deposit insurance. When a recession occurs, people's tax payments automatically fall if they lose income. Similarly, no recognition or implementation decisions are required to have total EI benefits paid out increase when unemployment rises. Both lower taxes and higher transfers stimulate demand just when it is needed. Deposit insurance forces the government to increase both transfer payments and the money supply automatically whenever a financial institution fails.

This automatic support keeps lack of confidence from spreading, so it stops runs against other financial institutions just when they would be most likely to occur otherwise.

81. d

82. b

83. a

84. b

85. True — in the long run, to maintain competitiveness, a Canadian inflation rate of 3 percent per year combined with an American inflation rate of 1 percent requires that the Canadian dollar depreciate at 2 percent per year. To avoid ongoing capital losses from holding wealth in Canadian dollar assets, bond holders demand an interest rate premium of 2 percent in Canada.

86. b

87. False — speculators who make money can stabilize markets and thus serve a positive social function.

88. b

89. False

90. The unemployment rate among skilled workers is not affected; those who already have jobs simply get higher wages. But if the minimum wage and welfare programs are indexed to the level of skilled workers' wages, then unemployment among the unskilled rises.

91. d

92. b

93. b

94. True

95. $242

96. Let n and r stand for the economy's growth rate and the interest rate. The present value of the flow of benefits coming from free trade equals

(initial GDP)$(0.03)[((1 + n)/(1 + r)) + ((1 + n)/(1 + r))^2 + ...]$.

As explained on page 259, the term in square brackets is equal to $(1 - n)/(r - n)$. In this example, with $r = 0.07$ and $n = 0.03$, the benefits of free trade equal 0.70 of a year's output.

97. $(1.005)^{30} = 1.283$; $(1.006)^{30} = 1.349$; $1.349/1.283 = 1.05$. Thus, the living standard would be 5 percent higher.

98. Rich and poor are given equal weight in adding up benefits and costs. A positive net benefit is interpreted as implying that winners could compensate losers, so the policy is supported — conditional on the understanding that an additional redistribution initiative is needed if this compensation is to be more than hypothetical. This is controversial since compensation often does not occur in practice.

99. Uncertainty is allowed for by raising the discount rate. This is controversial because it makes even potentially large items in the distant future have trivial present values.

100. While income inequality may be higher, average living standards will rise because national saving is higher. If the programs that are cut had been investments in either physical or human capital — not transfer payments — then the effect on average living standards could be reversed.

INDEX

READER REPLY CARD

We are interested in your reaction to *Economics*: *The Essentials*, Second Edition, by William M. Scarth. You can help us to improve this book in future editions by completing this questionnaire.

1. What was your reason for using this book?

    ☐ university course ☐ college course ☐ continuing education course
    ☐ professional ☐ personal ☐ other _____
       development interest _____

2. If you are a student, please identify your school and the course in which you used this book.

3. Which chapters or parts of this book did you use? Which did you omit?

4. What did you like best about this book? What did you like least?

5. Please identify any topics you think should be added to future editions.

6. Please add any comments or suggestions.

7. May we contact you for further information?

    Name:_____

    Address: _____

    _____

    Phone: _____

    E-mail: _____

(fold here and tape shut)

0116870399-M8Z4X6-BR01

Larry Gillevet
Director of Product Development
HARCOURT CANADA LTD.
55 HORNER AVENUE
TORONTO, ONTARIO
M8Z 9Z9